The Archaeology of th

The American Experience in Ar

UNIVERSITY PRESS OF FL

Florida A&M University, Tallah
Florida Atlantic University, Boca
Florida Gulf Coast University, Ft.
Florida International University, M
Florida State University, Tallahas
New College of Florida, Sarasot
University of Central Florida, Orla
University of Florida, Gainesvill
University of North Florida, Jackson
University of South Florida, Tamp
University of West Florida, Pensaco

THE ARCHAEOLOGY OF THE LOGGING INDUSTRY

John G. Franzen

Foreword by Michael S. Nassaney

University Press of Florida
Gainesville · Tallahassee · Tampa · Boca Raton
Pensacola · Orlando · Miami · Jacksonville · Ft. Myers · Sarasota

Printed in the United States of America

25 24 23 22 21 20 6 5 4 3 2 1

Library of Congress Cataloging-in-Publication Data
Names: Franzen, John G., author. | Nassaney, Michael S., author of foreword.
Title: The archaeology of the logging industry / John G. Franzen ; foreword by Michael S. Nassaney.
Other titles: American experience in archaeological perspective.
Description: Gainesville : University Press of Florida, 2020. | Series: The American experience in archaeological perspective | Includes bibliographical references and index.
Identifiers: LCCN 2020016452 (print) | LCCN 2020016453 (ebook) | ISBN 9780813066585 (hardback) | ISBN 9780813057583 (pdf)
Subjects: LCSH: Logging—United States—History. | Excavations (Archaeology)—United States. | Logging—United States—Antiquities. | Lumber camps—United States—History.
Classification: LCC HD9755 .F73 2020 (print) | LCC HD9755 (ebook) | DDC 338.1/74980973—dc23
LC record available at https://lccn.loc.gov/2020016452
LC ebook record available at https://lccn.loc.gov/2020016453

The University Press of Florida is the scholarly publishing agency for the State University System of Florida, comprising Florida A&M University, Florida Atlantic University, Florida Gulf Coast University, Florida International University, Florida State University, New College of Florida, University of Central Florida, University of Florida, University of North Florida, University of South Florida, and University of West Florida.

University Press of Florida
2046 NE Waldo Road
Suite 2100
Gainesville, FL 32609
http://upress.ufl.edu

Contents

Figures

Foreword

America's woodlands are deeply implicated in her natural and cultural history. The pine tree shilling, perhaps America's most famous colonial coin, symbolizes one of the Massachusetts Bay Colony's leading exports—pine trees for ships' masts. Yet Americans and their European predecessors have always maintained ambivalent attitudes about the woods and have failed to reconcile tensions among the commercial, environmental, and aesthetic values of our sylvan heritage. English colonists equated the wilderness with the unknown, fear, and savagery, providing ample justification for clearing the land along with the indigenous peoples who inhabited it. By the nineteenth century, Romantics like Emerson and Thoreau espoused the primeval comfort and solitude of America's remaining and rejuvenated forests, as they sought physical, spiritual, and metaphorical refuge from the growing urban centers of moral decay. All the while, our nation depended on the seemingly inexhaustible supply of exploitable lumber in the Eastern Woodlands for an endless variety of products that settlers and pioneers needed to establish a permanent and indelible footprint on the land. As choice tree species were cut and processed, the insatiable logging industry sought further opportunities in the South and then the West, employing new technologies, labor arrangements, and modes of transportation in accordance with local and global contingencies.

As boys growing up in suburbia outside Providence, my comrades and I often found solace (and mischief) in our own sylvan haven nestled along a mill pond connected to the Blackstone River. Away from the prying eyes of adults, we sought respite in the woods to explore, cut down (usually small) trees, erect shanties, and enjoy—if only briefly—dissociation from the concrete and asphalt jungle of our daily lives. The woods to us often seemed endless, much as they must have been seen by our colonial predecessors who built sawmills powered by rivers and streams in the New England countryside. When the settler-colonists weren't felling trees and sawing boards to construct homes and other forms of infrastructure, they were preparing fields and piling stones to form the iconic fences that testify to their success at emplacement and land appropriation. Clearing forests was essential in the colonial project to assert authority and identity, impose a new sense of order, and re-create the landscape to eradicate and reenvision places that could conceal unknown entities.

By the time logging became an industrial enterprise, Americans were well versed in the art of land clearance and had developed sophisticated techniques of cutting trees, sawing lumber, and moving the products of these activities to markets here and abroad. America's formidable forests required an industrial scale of activity to subdue these wooden beasts. While we may debate America's exceptionalism, there is little doubt about the quantity, quality, diversity, and accessibility of her woodlands. Whether viewed as fearsome, bounty for exploitation, or a source of spiritual renewal, all agreed that American forests were unequaled anywhere.

It is no coincidence that the time-transgressive nature of logging—from the Northeast and the Great Lakes to the South and West—was congruent with the ideology of Manifest Destiny that propelled Euro-American pioneers from sea to shining sea. The labor arrangements involved in logging required mobility that led to sites of varying function and size. As a result, most places were soon abandoned, leaving behind the detritus of the social and economic practices associated with corporate enterprises and their employees.

Because of the prevalence of logging and its centrality to the American experience, it has produced a larger-than-life mythos that paints loggers as cheerful, hearty, strong, male, and albeit somewhat simple folk who were content to wield a sharp ax and enjoy a warm meal at the end of the day. The logger is epitomized in the fabled figure of Paul Bunyan—"an icon of America's national character"—who never encountered a tree he couldn't cut or a log that he and his faithful blue ox, Babe, couldn't move. Yet, as with all allegories and even many historical accounts, the *his*tories surrounding our logging past contain elements in need of revision to represent contemporary concerns.

In *The Archaeology of the Logging Industry,* John Franzen surveys the existing literature on archaeological research conducted at logging sites to illuminate the archaeological residue created in the wake of the commercial cutting of trees predominantly in the nineteenth century, perhaps the heyday of the industry. As a retired USDA Forest Service archaeologist,

Franzen is well positioned to survey an enormous (often "gray") literature on logging and concisely characterize logging's dominant features. Unlike some aspects of the American experience, the archaeological investigations of logging sites were prompted by the passage of the National Historic Preservation Act in 1966. Despite the impetus for the work, logging parallels other industrial processes, yet exhibits its own distinctive attributes. Unlike other extractive industries, logging is a transitory activity due to the nature of its infrastructure, the extreme mobility of companies and workers, and the relatively rapid local and regional depletion of its resource base. The result is a wave-like movement stimulated by timber depletion in an area and knowledge of and access to exploitable timber elsewhere. Indeed, logging encapsulates many of the conditions and forces that were critical to the formation of the American experience, such as the abundance of natural resources, technological innovation, rapid industrialization, immigration, and the accumulation and unequal distribution of wealth that created and reinforced social inequalities.

The industrialization of logging was fueled by the increased demand for wood products associated with the growth in U.S. population, which more than tripled from 23 to 73 million in the second half of the nineteenth century (1850–1900). This explosion corresponded with the expansion of timbering. Documentary sources like census data and company records provide background for study, but archaeological research conducted at logging industry sites reveals information about people and places not mentioned in historical accounts and offers an alternative perspective on those that are. The scars upon the land detectable by archaeology include the lived experiences of workers and their families and the complexity of both environmental and social change, taking the study of logging beyond demographic and production statistics.

Historical archaeology, in its use of complementary sources—including material evidence, oral accounts, and documents—provides an alternative perspective to counter stereotypes perpetuated in popular literature over many decades and ameliorates some of the biases. For example, women worked in logging camps. While their work often went unremunerated, they cooked, raised children, laundered, and performed other tasks that underwrote the industry. Companies avoided labor costs when they did not need to hire cooks for communal dining, and men were fed by their wives and ate with their families in smaller living arrangements. Archaeological evidence also demonstrates that chronologies and technological developments are not always linear and lead to broad-scale changes. Rather, archaeologists have identified the coexistence of practices considered "old" or "new."

Archaeology can also inform the tensions between workers and management and differences in their living conditions. In the nineteenth century, the shift from axes to crosscut saws was advantageous to company owners because sawyers could be paid less than "choppers." Soon after, many companies implemented technologies associated with scientific management to deskill the labor force as a way to maximize profit, a trend which workers were generally unable to prevent. In other daily practices, however, workers obtained better camp conditions, as indicated by the presence of ceramics (as opposed to enamelware) and preferred food resources. One Northern Michigan company discontinued metal and adopted ceramic tableware during a period of worker shortages and labor unrest. As ceramics became more expensive relative to other alternatives, their presence suggests some acquiescence to workers' demands. During the nineteenth century, some highly independent owners/operators provided fresh beef and ceramic tableware, perhaps to ensure worker quality and retention. Despite these accommodations, American companies succeeded at lowering labor costs by employing the most recent immigrants whenever they could.

Comparative data are also informative. Patterns of kitchen refuse vary within sites, indicating that not all employees were consuming similar diets based on food remains. High rates of intoxicant use such as alcohol, tobacco, and patent medicines are known to characterize transient lifestyles. Loggers were no exception, even as certain practices came to identify specific social groups. Tobacco was widely used as snuff, chew, and in pipes, yet loggers were strongly prejudiced against cigarettes even into the twentieth century.

Loggers and their families came from diverse backgrounds, and archaeology provides clues about gender, age, race, class, and ethnicity. Archaeology illuminates the social and material ways ethnic minorities reacted to the challenges posed by discrimination, exploitation, and the generally difficult living and working conditions of industrial logging. A Native American logging camp in Northern Michigan exhibited evidence for sharing and consuming traditional foods and hiring family members. The contributions of women and children helped to maintain kinship bonds and facilitate social reproduction in the face of boarding schools, assimilation pressures, and economic hardship. Twentieth-century sawmills in Washington State employed Japanese workers who persisted in using traditional material culture and practices to adapt to living and working in a North American industrial setting. French Canadians introduced the camboose, a raised central hearth in a communal building that became the focus of cooking and sociability in the nineteenth century, long after iron stoves were introduced. This facility can only be understood in the context of the social relations that it engendered among loggers.

The archaeology of logging helps us not only to look back but also to the future; it brings the scale of clear-cutting and an increasingly denuded global landscape into acute focus. It is hard to deny that the lumber industry in North America contributed to the global environmental changes that define the Anthropocene. The industry has brought about both environmental and social costs, not all of which are readily apparent. Glocalization allows us to highlight local perspectives on global phenomena and exposes the connectivity of the American experience to people and places beyond our borders. Nevertheless, our analysis can and should start at home to reveal how landscapes degraded by industrial resource extraction and processing constitute the literal ruins of capitalism. Although many cut-over areas in North America have been reforested and continue to provide a variety of benefits to humans, they have still contributed to environmental degradation. Just over the past few years, particularly catastrophic wildfires fueled by global warming and woody debris left after logging are leaving conspicuous evidence in the stratigraphic record. Archaeology can address the denials, amnesia, and falsifications that limit our ability to perceive past and present problems and, thereby, play a role in moving forward.

It has been over a century since the Department of Interior transferred forest reserves to the Department of Agriculture for designation as National Forests. Within these and other protected lands are nonrenewable vestiges of the ways these tracts have been cut, managed, reforested, and preserved. Traces of logging life remind us that the American experience is marked by segregation, patriarchy, brutal competition, and economic inequality. Yet this same detritus can direct us to focus on how people responded to the challenges posed by industrial work settings. By doing so we may be able to gain some appreciation of our shared humanity even as we recognize, commemorate, and celebrate the diversity of logging activities and come to a new resolve of who we were as a people and who we hope to become.

Michael S. Nassaney
Series Editor

Acknowledgments

Many people played a role in the long-term process that eventually resulted in my completion of this book. For the last 18 years, I have benefited from the expertise and hard work of my colleague, friend, and successor as the Heritage Resource Program Leader at the Hiawatha National Forest, Eric Drake. His influence improved both the theoretical and practical aspects of my approach to archaeology. Eric and I collaborated on archaeological excavations at the First Nahma Sawmill and the two logging camps featured in chapter 8. Because food was so important to lumber industry workers, the contributions of zooarchaeologist Terry Martin were also critical to understanding these sites. In fact, his expertise and advice were essential to most of the archaeological projects I have been involved with in the Great Lakes region. Sean Dunham played a key role as our profession developed research questions about logging camps, as well as the appropriate methods and techniques for investigations. Other colleagues or mentors who have helped shape my thinking about archaeology and historic period sites in the north woods include Dean Anderson, Jan Brashler, Mark Bruhy, Marla Buckmaster, Rebecca Dinsmore, Jim Fitting, Jim Skibo, and Lyle Stone.

My interest in the archaeology of the logging industry developed in conjunction with research done in Northern Michigan's national forests under the auspices of the National Historic Preservation Act. The combined efforts of archaeologists, historians, and USDA Forest Service employees located numerous logging industry sites and provided the historical context necessary for research. This list includes various professions, including land managers, curators, and some of the most stalwart archaeological fieldworkers. Although many others contributed, I would especially like to recognize John Anderton, Elizabeth Benchley, Bill Bowman, Mark Branstner, Joe Carrick, Justin Carrick, Teresa Chase, Thor Conway, Missy Drake, Art Easterbrook, Jim Evers, Troy Ferone, Sandy Forney, Tony Godfrey, Eric Janulis,

Ted Karamanski, Deb LeBlanc, Pat Martin, Susan Martin, Judy Propper, Bill Rutter, and Don Weir.

Expanding my research on logging beyond Michigan and Wisconsin was challenging because much of the relevant archaeological literature remains unpublished. I very much appreciate the assistance of the following people for essential help in accessing reports and site information: Pat Emerson (Minnesota), Linn Gassaway (California), Thurston Hahn (Louisiana and Mississippi), Jonathan Horn (Oregon), Sharyl Kinnear-Ferris (California), Chris Lydick (Florida), John Richards (Wisconsin), Leith Smith (Maine), Annie Strader (Washington), Doug Wilson (Washington and Oregon), Rachel Watson (Louisiana), and regional coordinators for the California Historical Resources Information System (CHRIS).

This book could not have been completed without Michael Nassaney, Paul White, and LouAnn Wurst. Their comments on earlier drafts included a strategic mix of encouragement and criticism designed to improve the manuscript and keep me writing. I especially appreciate their generous donations of time to this undertaking.

Many small logging and milling operations, especially during the Great Depression, were organized as family enterprises, and both my paternal and maternal grandfathers worked in northern Wisconsin's lumber industry. I would like to acknowledge the influence and inspiration of my parents, George Franzen and Florence Cox, who passed down family stories and raised me to appreciate the natural and cultural legacy of Great Lakes forests. Last, but not least, I thank my spouse Kristine and my daughter Johanna, both of whom have shared, and perhaps sometimes endured, many experiences related to my archaeological explorations of logging sites and contributed in so many ways to the creation of this book.

1

Lumbering

The Most American Industry?

> The forests of America, however slighted by man, must have been a great delight to God; for they were the best he ever planted.
>
> John Muir, "American Forests" (1897)

Deforestation to make way for farming and provide lumber, fuel, and other commodities has been called the "single most important event in the evolution of the modern American landscape" (MacCleery 2011: 17). After developing slowly for two centuries along the East Coast during the colonial and early American periods, the logging industry expanded beyond potential agricultural areas and swept across North America. In many areas, logging represented the first large-scale alteration of the landscape by European immigrants and, as a frontier enterprise, it influenced patterns of later settlement. In fact, one former Forest Service chief wrote, "Lumbering is perhaps the most American of our manufacturing industries" (Greeley 1917: 60). The transitory nature of its infrastructure, the extreme mobility of companies and workers, and the relatively rapid local and regional depletion of its resource base differentiated logging from other extractive industries. Processes that broadly define the American historical experience characterize the logging industry: exploitation of abundant natural resources, technological innovation, rapid industrialization, immigration, and the accumulation but unequal distribution of great wealth. Logging is also one of the industries implicated in the ongoing period of global human-caused environmental deterioration that some are calling the Anthropocene.

Forests originally covered about half of the United States, but after colonization their extent decreased for about 250 years until reaching an early twentieth-century nadir. After nearly a century of fire suppression, reforestation efforts, and improved management, forests recovered to the extent

Figure 1.1. Lichens growing on leather boot at late nineteenth-century logging camp in northern Michigan, Bay de Noquet Lumber Company Camp 5, 20DE193. (Photo [1989] by author, courtesy USDA Forest Service, Hiawatha National Forest, Gladstone, Mich.)

that they now cover about a third of the nation. Some cutover areas that burned after logging remain treeless prairies, but reforestation occurred in most areas not farmed or otherwise developed either naturally or with the help of planting efforts like those of the Civilian Conservation Corps in the 1930s. Even where cutovers initially became farms, forests returned to some areas abandoned because of poor soils. However, in North America, most regrown forests look very different from those of precolonial times. Old growth timber remains scarce, with younger stands fragmented into smaller, more isolated, patches. In tree plantations, species composition is much less diverse. Because of the inherent interdependence of forest ecosystems, the removal of old growth timber affected a wide range of associated organisms.

From Maine to Oregon and from Lake Superior to the Gulf of Mexico, if one looks closely enough in the right places, many wooded areas contain evidence of earlier logging (Figure 1.1). Nature usually conceals these remains under a mantle of plants, fungi, lichens, and organic debris, but microtopography and vegetation differences hint at former building locations and transportation features. Even within reforested areas, small clearings remain where logging camps once stood. The relatively level and straight routes of abandoned railroad grades or wagon roads stand out from their surroundings. At former logging camp locations, earthen berms, pits, or leveled areas reveal where buildings once stood (Figure 1.2). Depending on the extent of existing vegetation and soil exposure, artifacts like axe heads, saw blades, food containers, bottles, and horseshoes remain visible on the surface. Artifacts and evidence of vanished structures offer information about living and working conditions. Harvesting operations moved frequently as timber was depleted, leaving behind numerous former camp and mill sites. For example, an estimated 10,000 logging-associated sites exist in Minnesota alone, with only about 700 of these currently recorded as archaeological sites (Minnesota State Archaeologist Office 2018). During the past 40 years, archaeologists have started to explore the logging industry and obtain information not available from written or oral history sources. This book surveys archaeological studies from across America to provide a new perspective on this part of our industrial heritage.

Figure 1.2. Earthen berms outlining barn or stable at early twentieth-century logging camp in northern Michigan (20DE27). (Photo [1991] by author, courtesy USDA Forest Service, Hiawatha National Forest, Gladstone, Mich.)

Logging, Forests, and the American Experience

The variety, abundance, and low cost of timber, combined with high demand, led to large harvests and diverse uses that "pervasively conditioned" American society (Hindle 1975). According to Lillard (1947: 138), forest products played a larger role in U.S. economic history than in the development of other nations. The logging industry accumulated impressive economic and demographic statistics, as well as widespread effects on landscapes and patterns of settlement. Between 1850 and 1909, annual lumber production in the United States rose from 5.4 billion board feet to an all-time peak of 45 billion board feet (MacCleery 2011: 22). Factors like the extreme individualism of both workers and company owners, intense competition, the presence of small-scale as well as large operations, and relatively isolated frontier settings, led historian Vernon Jensen (1945: 18) to declare: "nowhere in our broad diversified economy can an industry be found that has been any more American." In terms of economic value, lumber ranked among the nation's top five industries in every manufacturing census between 1850 and 1920 and placed second in 1850 and 1870 (Steer 1948). This industry employed a large labor force of recent immigrants and ethnic minorities who often lived in company-controlled residential areas. Folklore and cultural traditions support the argument that logging played a key role in defining modern America. The cowboy and the lumberjack became "symbolic stereotypes" associated with westward expansion in the second half of the nineteenth century (Williams 1989: 20). Although likely inspired by similar characters in earlier stories, the Paul Bunyan who became "an icon of America's national character" and a "symbol of strength and ingenuity" in the twentieth century was created by writers, artists, marketers, and advertisers for commercial and entertainment uses (Edmonds 2009: 110).

Rapid exploitation of forests by an industrializing nation was not unique to the United States, but the quantity, quality, diversity, and accessibility of the forests occupied by Native Americans at the dawn of the seventeenth century were in fact exceptional. Over thousands of years, high-density agricultural and pastoral societies eliminated or greatly diminished European forests. In general, timber resources in other parts of the world colonized by Europeans were commercially inferior to those of North America due to aridity, limited diversity, previous exploitation, or inaccessibility. Even after centuries of cutting, America's forests still include exceptional trees: world records in terms of wood volume (sequoia), height (coastal redwood), and age (bristlecone pine). Due to high precipitation, a long growing season, and low rates of natural disturbance, old-growth remnants of temperate rain forests like those along America's northwest coast support the greatest living biomass among the world's terrestrial ecosystems and include many long-lived and extremely large trees (Pan et al. 2013: 602).

Whether viewed as fearsome, bounty for exploitation, or a source of spiritual renewal, observers with different perspectives agreed that American forests were exceptional. Never had such a rapidly expanding industrial society encountered such an accessible timber-rich environment. John Muir (1918: 64) called forests in California's Sierra Mountains around Yosemite an "assemblage of conifers unrivaled on the globe." In the South, "vast forests of the long yellow pine (longleaf and slash pine), of matchless height and straightness" provided not only lumber, but tar, pitch, and turpentine (Troost 1846, cited in Hickman 2009: 3). Religious explanations for this abundance predominated, attributing our wealth of forest resources to the fact that Americans were a "chosen people" or fortunate recipients of natural grace. From early on, tension existed between commercial and environmental or aesthetic values (Figure 1.3). John Muir had it both ways for a while at Yosemite, operating a sawmill and enjoying long hikes through vast uncut old growth forests. Sawing sugar pine blown down by a wind storm, he admitted: "I like the piney fragrance of the fresh-sawn boards," demonstrating that an aesthetic appreciation of America's trees does not preclude transforming some of them into lumber (Muir and Badè 1924: 207–208, 211). In fact, conflict frequently characterized America's relationships with forests, ranging from the 1908–1913 Hetch Hetchy controversy, with John Muir unsuccessfully trying to prevent construction of a dam that flooded a scenic valley near Yosemite, to the 1970s Redwood Wars over protecting the last stands of America's tallest trees.

Logging provided raw material for many different purposes, but lumber stands out as the most significant product manufactured from wood. Variations in the suitability of different tree species for lumber played a key role in determining regional similarities and differences. Exploitation of the best species for lumber products, followed by their depletion, stimulated movement both within and between regions. As Holbrook (2016: 74) points out, "it wasn't a dearth of timber that drove the Maine men west. . . . It was a dearth of white pine timber." The initial focus on only the best white pine, and rising costs as it was depleted, resulted in multiple harvest episodes within some stands, as loggers returned for trees previously not worth

Figure 1.3. Chromolithograph (1884) by Joseph F. Kessler: "Preserve Your Forests from Destruction, and Protect Your Country from Floods and Drought." Note smoke rising from charcoal mounds in background. (Keppler and Schwarzmann, New York. Library of Congress, Washington, D.C.)

cutting. The best species for sawing into the lumber used to construct buildings are all conifers: lightweight, buoyant, and easy to float down rivers. Some, like white pine, possess an ideal combination of strength, decay resistance, straight grain, and workability. The proportion of trees commercially cut for products other than lumber remained relatively small during the time period encompassed by the archaeological studies included in this book, with several important exceptions. During the nineteenth and early twentieth centuries, charcoal production in the Northeast and Great Lakes consumed large amounts of wood from hardwood species like maple and oak. Other products eventually became important, most notably pulp for making paper. Compared to those preferred for sawing into lumber, smaller or otherwise less desirable logs could be used for paper making. In terms of volume (cubic feet of wood), between 1900 and 1940 the percentage of harvested timber used for pulp increased from 2 percent to 16 percent (USBC 1989). By 1970, pulp mills consumed 37 percent of the U.S. timber harvest volume. Much of this was (and is) obtained from reforested areas previously cut. However, numbers like these do not reflect the experiences of workers and their families or the complexity of changes in the landscape. Archaeology offers a relatively new way to explore this industry that goes beyond production statistics.

Historical Archaeology: An Alternative Source

Popular Oregon author and one-time logger Stewart Holbrook (1943: 151) stated, "Lumberjacks had no written records. . . . All reporting was done by word of mouth around the barrel stove." It is true that workers left few written accounts. Many were no doubt illiterate, and most written accounts came from bosses or visitors. But he is wrong that they only left behind oral traditions. Although usually anonymous, from coast to coast, north to south, a material record of their practices, accomplishments, and everyday life is reflected in the landscape or embedded in the earth. This record provides an alternative perspective to counter stereotypes perpetuated in popular literature over many decades. For example, Rollin Lynde Hartt (1900) described logging camp life using terms like "jovial hilarity" and "rough jocularity" and claimed that workers squandered all their earnings during a "solid week of reckless gaiety." Works by Holbrook (1936, 1943, 1948, 2016), Wells (1978), and Pike (1999) provide better known examples of this genre. Although talented writers, sympathetic toward loggers, and knowledgeable about logging, they emphasized the most sensationalized and entertaining aspects of this industry. Holbrook (2016: 42) describes loggers as "rough, tough, lusty, and thirsty," and only interested in "booze, bawds, and battle." Norwegians and Swedes, nationalities well known for involvement in temperance movements, were inexplicably characterized as "able drinkers all and whoremasters to a man" (Holbrook 1936: 194).

These descriptions could potentially be used to justify the exploitation of workers and the one-sided dominance of management within the industry. Holbrook (2016: 42, 99) indicates loggers "didn't give a tinkers dam for property" and that their main concern regarding working conditions was the "entertainment" available in nearby towns when logging terminated for the season. Wells (1978) says they were "satisfied . . . with low pay and difficult living conditions as long as they could get drunk periodically." Based on his many years as a timber cruiser for companies in northern Minnesota during the early twentieth century, Ryan (1980: 58) describes loggers as a "good natured hardworking group who complained or grumbled little about their job or living conditions," who just wanted "good food and a warm place to sleep." Supposedly, they were "willing to work as horses," and "it never occurred to them that things could, or even should, be otherwise" (Holbrook 2016: 47). Holbrook's tongue-in-cheek "The Lumberjacks Go Sissy" (1936) laments improvements in camp living conditions, especially the presence of married men and their families, and the resulting "disappearance of the old-time lumberjack." Even though deliberately exaggerated for comic effect, these distortions invite us to critique the "occupational mystique" of loggers, which is said to resemble that of sailors, cowboys, and fur traders (Lower 1968: 27). By emphasizing their "rugged independence" and other stereotypes, Prouty (1988: 5) thinks these accounts provided an excuse used by company owners to treat loggers as "expendable." The record of frequent injury and the physical stresses of working and living conditions supports this argument (Bernhardt 1979; Prouty 1988). As Prouty (1988: xviii) states, logging companies "used up people" as well as forests in pursuing profit.

Because it draws upon independent sources, archaeology provides an opportunity to explore the past without reproducing the biases found in popular literature. Besides occupational stereotypes, popular accounts of logging often include derisive characterizations based on gender, ethnicity, race, or class. These biases should be kept in mind when evaluating written sources. Given the early origins and wide dissemination of sensationalized accounts, we should consider alternative sources, as the scholarly efforts of historians have still not succeeded in displacing these narratives.

Reforested areas are just as misunderstood as the loggers who cut down the original old growth. Environmental stereotypes need to be dispelled, such as the categorization of contemporary forests as either pristine or totally compromised by past logging instead of more nuanced characterizations based on their actual history and current condition. Those who would continue to value forests only as commodities sometimes argue that once the original forest was cut, it ceased to be a "wild" place and is thus less worthy of concern regarding future human impacts. Often neglected as a source of environmental information, historical archaeology can help date cutting episodes and define their areal extent by locating camps, railroad grades, logging dams, and other physical remains of harvest activity (Whitney 1994: 10). Many of these features are not recorded in surviving historical documents. Archaeological sites also include the remains of native and non-native plant and animal species and evidence of events like forest fires and floods. They show how the remains of human activity are not simply obliterated over time, but rather incorporated into natural processes. This information permits a more holistic view of the past as it connects to the present and reveals mutually constituted relationships between society, technology, and ecology.

Using archaeology to learn about events and activities that took place in the not-so-distant past is a relatively new phenomenon. By definition, historical archaeology uses the historical record (including oral history) in conjunction with archaeological evidence. Founded in 1967, the Society for Historical Archaeology (SHA) specializes in the archaeology of the modern world (AD 1400–present). In North America this discipline focuses on the era since the beginning of European exploration. The Society for Industrial Archeology (SIA) represents individuals and institutions with similar interests. Inspired by work being done in Europe, especially Great Britain, it was founded in 1971 with a somewhat narrower focus: "historically significant industrial sites, structures, artifacts, and technology." Industrial archaeologists concentrate on the physical evidence of industry, technology, and industrial processes, including bridges, railroads, canals, landscapes, and communities. Considerable overlap exists between historical and industrial archaeology. In fact, some argue that it may not be necessary or wise to emphasize their differences and that industrial archaeology could be considered part of historical archaeology (Beaudry 2005). No precise date defines material culture that is too recent to be of archeological interest. In fact, writers like González-Ruibal (2019) recommend studying the recent or "contemporary" past through archaeology in order to address the environmental and social challenges of modernity. However, as a practical matter, many studies have been limited by the regulations implementing the National Historic Preservation Act, which state that a site or structure usually must be 50 years old to qualify for the National Register of Historic Places. Most of the studies mentioned in this book deal with sites occupied at some time during the century between circa 1840 and 1940. Historical archaeology has specific strengths, and studies of logging industry sites address some of these opportunities. As summarized by Little (2007: 29–38) these include using archaeology to critique the existing historical literature; reconstructing past lifeways; and understanding the concepts of modernity and globalization, including cultural interaction and change and the dynamics of economic connections at various scales. By dealing with these topics, archaeology counters some of the biases inherent in the historical record. Archaeology indirectly represents people often not mentioned in surviving documents and records, such as low status workers and racial or ethnic minorities, based on material evidence of their agency and identity.

A New Perspective: Logging, Archaeology, and the Anthropocene

In terms of theoretical orientation, this book responds to the social and environmental changes that define the modern world as shaped by industrial capitalism. In addition, it reflects optimism about the capacity of material objects to reveal social relations and forms of identity. These are not original or radical concepts: Wilkie and Bartoy (2000: 748) define historical archaeology as "synonymous with the archaeology of capitalism" and most archaeologists acknowledge "the social construction of time, space, and material culture" (Meskell and Preucel 2007: 16). Adding a "critical archaeology" viewpoint helps address ideological influences on the material remains of the lumber industry and how they are perceived (Leone and Potter 1999; Leone 1999, 2010). Popular histories of logging tend to naturalize and perpetuate existing social relations and consequently invite critique. As Leone (1999: 6) argues, "understanding the ideology of capitalism" is the "responsibility of all archaeology." In fact, Marx (1910: 278–282) specifically referenced logging, pointing out that harvest rates usually exceeded rates of new forest growth and that sustainable harvesting was "little adapted for private, and therefore, capitalist enterprise." Current issues like climate change, conflict over resources, forced migration, and inequality argue for the critical analysis of major industries like logging.

In recent years, some archaeologists have called for increased emphasis on the social aspects of industry, which were previously neglected by studies preoccupied with technology (Beaudry 2005; Casella 2006). An "explicitly social" approach to our industrial heritage emphasizes the lives and experience of workers (Casella 2006: 65). In essence, this social emphasis has expanded an "archaeology of industry" to include an "archaeology of labor," countering narratives that tended to reproduce past social relations (Shackel 2004, 2011). In order to address this issue, our literature survey emphasizes studies dealing with domestic areas and/or worker housing because they represent "the greatest personal impression a worker or a worker's family leaves in the material record of industry" (Fracchia et al. 2014: 54). Besides highlighting social organization, identity, agency, and resistance, the transregional literature survey in chapters 4–7 provides a starting point for assessing the possibility of industry-based ethnogenesis (Casella 2006: 70).

Just as researchers were accused of neglecting the social aspects of industrial sites, some analyses criticize historical archaeology for not paying enough attention to environmental issues (Deagan 1988; Hardesty 1999; Mrozowski 2006, 2010). In fact, it can be misleading (and ineffective) to separately critique the social and environmental effects of an industry. Given the current global state of affairs, all disciplines should consider how they could participate in the creation of more sustainable systems of living and nonliving things. Using the Anthropocene concept to frame this literature survey highlights the potential contributions of lumber industry archaeology to this effort. Earth scientists initially proposed the term Anthropocene for designating a geological epoch defined by human-caused changes in basic earth systems, such as climate (Crutzen and Stoermer 2000). Combining *anthropos* (human) with *kainos* (-cene, recent) follows the precedent of naming Cenozoic epochs based on the prevalence of fossil forms resembling "recent" species and thus refers to a time period defined by physical evidence of recent humans, rather than simply an "age of man" (Angus 2016). Most discussions of causal factors emphasize the industrial revolution, capitalism, and the effects of burning fossil fuels. To better target these concerns, González-Ruibal (2016a) recommends looking at the destructive effects of a "modernist ethos" common to multiple ideologies, not just those promoting capitalism. Some archaeologists advocate expanding the purview of Anthropocene studies to include earlier influences such as prehistoric agricultural clearing, but Solli et al. (2011: 63) recommend an "archaeology of the short term" as a better way to understand the present situation. In fact, focusing on more ancient periods risks naturalizing the current situation by following faint traces of Anthropocene roots too deeply rather than focusing on how and why human effects have so dramatically increased in the last several hundred years. After the term was first introduced by Crutzen and Stoermer (2000), it quickly took on a life of its own separate from the original geological proposal.

In recent years, researchers in a variety of disciplines, including archaeology, have contextualized a wide range of phenomena as "Anthropocene." During the early twenty-first century, hundreds of publications in numerous disciplines used this term in a variety of ways, and the concept continues to attract both popular and scholarly interest (Lidskog and Waterton

2016; Tsing et al. 2017). Two new interdisciplinary journals illustrate how the term is frequently used. The editors of *Anthropocene* indicate that its title "is intended as a metaphor to denote human interactions with Earth systems and does not imply endorsement for a new geologic epoch" (Chin et al. 2013: 2). Similarly, the self-described "transdisciplinary" *Anthropocene Review* focuses broadly on "the dramatic physical and biological changes caused by human activities" rather than on the formal geological proposal (Oldfield et al. 2013: 3). Some have criticized the term as "anthropocentric," but Morton (2016) points out how it could have an "anti-anthropocentric" effect: even though it highlights the global effects of humans, research usually shows how we have been unable to predict or control these changes.

Despite the term's geological roots, none of the Anthropocene's formal or informal definitions, or the associated artifacts ("index fossils" like plastics, concrete, aluminum, fly ash, and radionuclides) have been "set in stone" (Santana 2018). Some argue against its formal recognition by geologists (Baskin 2015; Santana 2018), but the term has been used so much in discussions about human-induced earth-system changes that it deserves attention, especially in the study of industries responsible for major environmental effects. It raises issues relative to many theoretical orientations, and the term's fluidity creates both pitfalls and opportunities. Whether or not geologists eventually adopt it as a formal epoch may now be a moot point: human domination of the so-called natural environment challenges the "philosophical, epistemological and ontological" assumptions of multiple disciplines, and this requires consideration and/or critique (Baskin 2015).

As a result, many scholars accept the "productive ambiguity" of the Anthropocene concept but also criticize the term (Baskin 2015; Barber 2018: 183). The most common complaint is that it implies that all humans share responsibility for effects like climate change when, in fact, a small subset of humanity controls decision-making and profits related to this process (Malm and Hornborg 2014). As part of various critiques, some less formal (and occasionally less serious) terms have been suggested by nongeologists as more precise in implicating causes and identifying effects: capitalocene, plantationocene, econocene, technocene, and several other -cenes (Malm and Hornborg 2014; Usher 2016). Rather than adopting what is essentially a geological term, González-Ruibal (2018: 10) suggests that archaeologists use "an archaeological counterpart" that emphasizes the effects of capitalism and modernity, such as "Age of Destruction." Regardless of how these terminological discussions evolve or which different disciplines and theoretical perspectives will become dominant, the historical archaeology of industrial enterprises like logging can benefit from addressing this concept more directly. Tsing et al. (2017), envisioning a "project" that scientifically, artistically, and politically addresses drastic human-caused alteration of global habitat with the involvement of people from different disciplines using different terminologies, suggest that one way to move forward amid debate is with "dialogue" among those who share goals but prefer different terms.

The lumber industry in North America contributed to global environmental changes that define the Anthropocene. Besides biotic effects (deforestation, species changes due to post-harvest succession, extinction, or the introduction of non-native or invasive species), industrial-scale logging is implicated in earth-system changes, such as increased erosion and sedimentation rates and the alteration of chemical cycles (carbon, nitrogen, phosphorous, etc.) (Chazdon 2017). In many areas, wildfire frequency increased after logging due to drier conditions resulting from overstory removal and the large amounts of dry woody debris left behind. Researchers are still documenting the wide range of changes caused by logging old-growth forests. Most cutover areas, even those promptly reforested, will remain different from previous forests for a very long time (Chazdon 2017). Construction of railroads and roads to access forests and haul logs also transformed the American landscape. Fill brought into flood plains to raise and level grades changed river meander patterns and cut off wetlands from their natural watersheds (Blanton and Marcus 2009, 2014; Bradley 2017). Although reforested areas in North America continue to provide a variety of benefits, they are nonetheless part of a long-term trend of global environmental degradation. New growth can efficiently sequester carbon, but it is estimated to take about 200 years to rebuild carbon storage capacity back to old-growth forest levels (Luyssaert et al. 2008). The use of various shifts and fixes to prolong unsustainable cutting of old-growth timber was perfected in North America during the nineteenth and twentieth centuries, and this approach now contributes to the destruction of tropical rain forests.

Anthropocene narratives usually focus on global effects, often neglecting specifics about localized activities that contribute to larger-scale social and ecological crises. In a case study of archaeological remains at a Danish coal mine, Vestergaard and Riede (2017: 12, 19–20) point out that global-scale studies tend to be "abstract and distant" while local studies provide more "concrete and tangible" evidence. Similar to Vestergaard and Riede's approach to a coal industry site, this book uses lumber industry sites to illustrate Anthropocene-related concepts. These sites provide local perspectives on global phenomena (glocalization) and thereby contribute to "bringing the Anthropocene home" (Vestergaard and Riede 2017: 12, 19–20). Given the urgency of current threats, Andreas Malm (2018: 15) provides a succinct question appropriate for a wide range of researchers addressing Anthropocene issues, such as social inequality and climate change: "How did we end up in this predicament?" This book is intended to help answer that question.

Scope of Research

This book surveys the existing literature on archaeological research conducted at logging industry sites. These studies provide information about people and places not mentioned in the historical record and offer an alternative perspective on those that are. As part of this survey, we reframe the archaeology of logging by using the interdisciplinary concept of the Anthropocene to highlight the social and environmental effects of this industry. While the fluidity and flexibility of this term may be problematic, it helps contextualize the archaeological remains of logging in ways that potentially connect with other efforts to understand the past and move forward amid the "ruins of capitalism" (Tsing 2015).

There is always a subjective aspect to drawing boundaries around a topic this broad. Archaeologists have studied charcoal making, so this is included, but the pulp and paper industry is not. It is more recent and has not been the specific focus of any archaeological studies. The naval stores industry is mentioned but not emphasized because it does not necessarily involve cutting down trees. Even though firewood cutting produced significant environmental effects, much of this activity was small scale and lacked the complex infrastructure associated with the lumber industry. Readers should note that the term "lumber" is sometimes used in a general sense that encompasses other products. Terms such as "lumber industry" or "lumber camp" are not always used restrictively to exclude operations that provided logs for manufacturing products other than lumber, such as charcoal, chemicals, paper, or plywood. Many so-called lumber camps that conducted clear-cutting during railroad logging operations provided logs for making a variety of products.

In chapter 2, nonarchaeological sources (documents and oral history) provide the basis for a brief history of the logging industry. Historical archaeologists agree on the importance of becoming familiar with the relevant

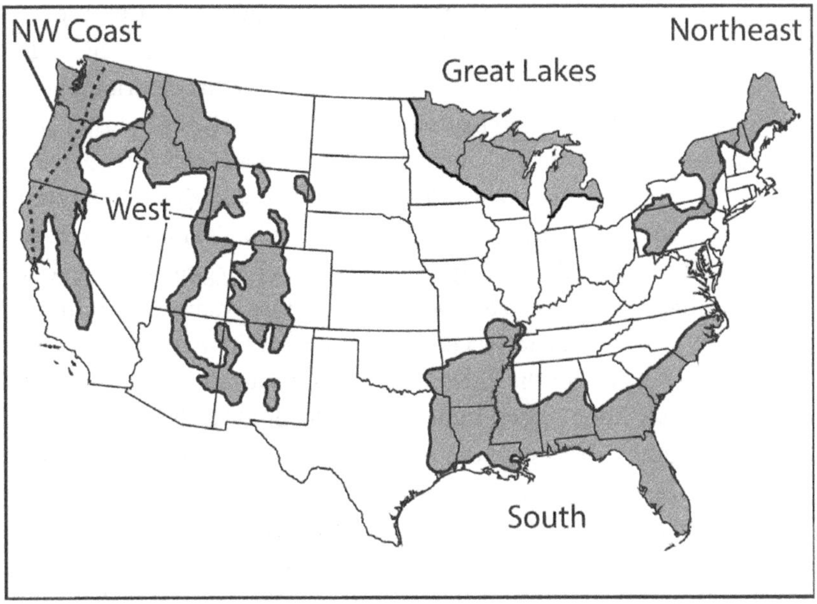

Figure 1.4. Core industrial logging regions of the United States, circa 1840–1940. (Drawing by Brady Ray Nelson, Genesis Graphics.)

historic literature prior to embarking on archaeological studies. In fact, archaeologists often use historical literature to develop hypotheses that they test using archaeological data. Following the precedent of historians and geographers, chapter 2 differentiates four major logging regions in the United States, largely on the basis of environmental, technological, and chronological differences (Figure 1.4). However, factors like immigration, consumer demand, business organization, and the movement of workers and capital transcended regional boundaries. On the basis of these connections, as well as increasing national influences during the twentieth century from trade associations, labor unions, and federal agencies, chapter 2 provides a framework for expanded comparisons of archaeological data from different regions.

Chapter 3 explains how federal legislation, as well as the recognition of historical archaeology as a separate discipline, led to increased archaeological interest in the logging industry during the 1970s. This chapter also reviews the methods and techniques used by the studies discussed in chapters 4–7 and identifies possible biases and gaps in this literature. A brief critique focuses on the limitations of research conducted under the auspices of the National Historic Preservation Act and a lack of adequate theoretical discussion in many previous studies. Chapter 3 concludes by describing some of the more productive research questions pursued at logging industry sites.

In chapters 4–7, a thematic approach summarizes and compares previous archaeological studies. The categories selected for organizing this literature survey have significant precedent. Archaeologists in California developed a document to guide the management of railroad logging sites, suggesting four broad interconnected "domains" for future studies: environment, technology, economics, and social/cultural factors (Tamez et al. 1988; Rock 1986). Archaeologists in the Great Lakes region suggested similar themes for guiding research at logging industry sites (Stiles 1994a, 1994b; Birk 1999; Moffat et al. 2011). These previous overviews, as well as the specific orientations of various studies encountered in the literature survey, led to the following topical organization: technology (chapter 4); spatial and environmental patterns (chapter 5); the daily lives of workers and their families (chapter 6); and social organization (chapter 7). The scope of each chapter is defined (and to some extent limited) by previous archaeological studies. Details counter the tendencies of some writers to overgeneralize about logging operations, showing that there is no such thing as a "typical" lumber camp or sawmill town and illustrating both shared patterns and individual variation. Analyses sensitive to such variation highlight the agency of both individuals and groups within settings often controlled by large companies or corporations. Because of the difficulty of locating unpublished literature, it is likely that some worthwhile studies were omitted, but all major logging regions are represented. Consolidating data that address similar research themes in multiple regions illustrates the importance of broader archaeological comparisons, especially in light of the national trends and interregional connections described in chapter 2.

Chapter 8 presents a case study that fills a gap in the existing archaeological literature on logging. Historical sources indicate that camps associated with the earliest commercial logging, which was concentrated in the Northeast and Great Lakes, consisted of two structures: an oxen hovel and a one-room log cabin referred to as a camboose shanty or State of Maine–style camp. We are unaware of any sites like these in the Northeastern or Great Lakes states previously excavated by archaeologists. Archaeological investigations at these two camboose shanties in Northern Michigan provide details on how traditions from the Northeast, Atlantic Canada, and the

Ottawa River Valley of Ontario and Quebec were carried west into the Great Lakes region by migrating loggers. As relatively early sites, they provide a valuable baseline for understanding the social-organizational and environmental changes that took place as the lumber industry expanded.

Chapter 9 highlights how archaeology provides a new perspective on forests, the logging industry, and the American experience. It recommends how future archaeologists might use logging industry sites and their associated settings to help in constructing an Anthropocene narrative that connects human and nonhuman entities in more sustainable ways. The chapter concludes with historical and literary references that suggest it is possible to reconcile both the utilitarian and aesthetic values of forests and to understand the historical effects of logging without reproducing a culture-nature dichotomy that contributes to further environmental and social alienation.

2

A Brief History of Industrial Logging in the United States

> The lumber industry throughout most of its life has been an aggressive, ingenious, unstable migrant.
>
> Vernon H. Jensen, *Lumber and Labor* (1945), 3

Prior to around 1820, the magnitude and organization of commercial lumber production in the United States remained essentially pre-industrial (Cox 2010: 47–48; Williams 1989: 161). However, starting from New England and Maritime Canada during the early nineteenth century, industrial-scale logging swept through American forests and reached the Pacific Ocean and the Gulf of Mexico before 1900. Geographer Evelyn Dinsdale (1965: 274) described this movement as a wave stimulated by the depletion of timber in one area and an awareness of abundant or less expensive timber elsewhere. Williams (1989: 193) points out that this wave increased in size as it moved west and south. Besides westward movement and expanded scale, characteristics distinguishing industrial logging from earlier cutting include increased labor specialization, capitalization, and technological developments, especially related to transportation. Demand for wood products increased as a growing population needed housing and other infrastructure. The development of other industries dependent on wood, especially mining and railroads, stimulated demand for products like support timbers, ties, and fuel. In many areas, logging represented the first major alteration of the landscape by European Americans. After it leaped ahead of agricultural settlement in the mid-nineteenth century, logging took place in frontier settings with little infrastructure beyond that which the industry created for itself. Due to its mobility and transience, Jensen (1945: 20) argues that as late as the 1940s, logging still resembled a frontier enterprise. The mobility required of "cut-out, get-out" logging retarded infrastructure development in logged areas without good agricultural soils or other resources that were in demand, and much of the infrastructure built specifically for logging was either portable or unsuitable for other uses. Many company towns abruptly ceased to exist. Returning for less valuable species, trees previously considered not worth cutting, or for the second growth that filled in original cutting areas usually required new infrastructure. As timber supplies decreased, both capital and labor abandoned previously logged areas, and similar practices and processes eventually characterized the four major timber producing regions: Northeast, Great Lakes, South, and West. Identifying regional similarities as well as highlighting and explaining differences provides an improved context for evaluating the significance of lumber industry archaeological sites and a potential framework for broader, more revealing comparative studies. Comparisons among sites and regions reveal the commonalities and contingencies of industrial logging in different social-ecological environments.

Native Americans utilized wood for many purposes during pre-European times, and wood resources played a key role in the colonial and the early American periods, but the onset of industrial-scale logging in the nineteenth century represented both quantitative and qualitative shifts, including landscape alteration at a continental scale with concomitant social and economic effects. Even though log procurement by Europeans in America had been ongoing for about 200 years, most of the logging-related archaeological sites discussed in this book were occupied during or after the rapid increase in industrial growth during the mid-nineteenth century. The "take-off" of American industries circa 1843–1860 cited by Rostow (1962: 38) coincides with the expansion of large-scale logging from Maine and the Northeast into the Great Lakes, the first of several regional movements of this industry as the nation's primary lumber sources shifted west and south. As described by Greeley (1951: 40), the industry became a "great nomad . . . driving from one virgin forest to another like a threshing machine from one ripe wheat field to the next." Four major migrations defined this process: from the Northeast to the Great Lakes, from the Great Lakes to both the West and the South, and from the South to the West. These took the form of various combinations of capital, owners, managers, and workers, but sometimes intact operations or entire companies moved long distances via rail. As Jem McKem (1921: 37) recounted, "Whole crews migrated bodily to the new lumbering regions." Early in the twentieth century, the Shevlin-Hixon Company transported 2,000 "lumberjacks" directly from

Minnesota to Oregon (Holbrook 2016: 144). A similar example, the Cady Lumber Company, moved nearly all its employees and their families (about 800 people), as well as equipment and supplies, from Louisiana to Arizona in 1924 (Lewis 2012). Most of their workers were African American, and even though the new location appeared more socially tolerant than the old, the company maintained segregated housing, with the black residential area referred to as "the Quarters," the same term used for areas where slaves were housed on plantations (Lewis 2012). On a smaller scale, the Tyoga Lumber Company moved not only employees but also "several carloads of horses and lumbering equipment" by railroad from Pennsylvania to the Upper Peninsula of Michigan in 1905 (*American Lumberman* 1905, cited in Parlin et al. 2011: 57). Like individual immigrants, it seems corporations sometimes followed their neighbors. For example, as midwestern forests were depleted, several Minnesota firms moved to the same area in central Oregon.

More commonly, individuals or family groups migrated in search of employment. Biographical accounts provide insight into this process, as many individuals worked in two or more regions of the country. Born in 1873, Jem McKem (1921: 37) started his career in the Great Lakes and later worked in Louisiana, Arizona, and Washington. While employed in the longleaf pine area of Louisiana at an isolated mill where most of the employees were "negroes," he witnessed a white supervisor murder a black employee. He described the event as a "shock" and "tragedy," and a few days later he quit and traveled by train to an Arizona mill where he joined a workforce of "cowboys, miners, and Mexicans" (McKem 1921: 47). Although capital and supervisors moved both west and south from the Great Lakes, most workers went west, because the South already had an abundance of relatively cheap labor (Jensen 1945: 75, 99–100). The following tongue-in-cheek account unintentionally provides an archaeological perspective on the movement of workers westward: "you could trace the receding timberline from Maine to Michigan by the discarded tobacco tags that came on Spearhead and Climax; but from Cloquet and Duluth to the West Coast the loggers' wake was to be strewn with the round tin covers of Copenhagen snuff, commonly known as Scandinavian Dynamite" (Holbrook 1936: 194). Small tin tags identifying brand names came pressed into compact plugs or twists of tobacco used primarily for pipes or chewing, while finely powdered snuff like the Copenhagen brand came in round cans and was usually placed between the gums and cheek. These artifacts reflect a change in tobacco preferences associated with the arrival of Scandinavian immigrants, who made up a large percentage of the workforce as cutting depleted the Great Lakes pine forests and the industry shifted to the west.

Regional Perspectives

Historians and geographers usually divide the United States into four major logging regions: Northeast, Great Lakes (Lakes States), South, and the West (Cox 2010; Jensen 1945; Williams 1989). Within the western United States, researchers often highlight a subregion consisting of the extremely productive temperate rainforests of coastal Washington, Oregon, and Northern California. Although many timber species were harvested and used for a wide variety of products, those most desirable for sawing into lumber dominated the spatial, temporal, and economic progression of the industry. Figure 1.4 is based on the extent of forest types that include the species most sought for lumber production, excluding areas in the Northeast and South that had been already been depleted prior to the mid-nineteenth-century expansion of industrial logging (Steyaert and Knox 2008; USDA Forest Service 1965; Waisanen and Bliss 2002).

Demand for building materials to construct housing increased as populations grew and settlement expanded into the Midwest and Plains. The following species were most responsible for determining regional movements, the development of new practices and technology, and the accumulation of capital: white pine in the Northeast and Great Lakes, southern pines (e.g., longleaf) in the South, and Douglas fir and western pines (e.g., ponderosa) in the West. White and longleaf pine eventually became depleted, but not before they had long runs of dominance. For example, white pine accounted for 60 percent to slightly more than 80 percent of the lumber produced in the Great Lakes area between 1869 and 1900 (Steer 1948). Industrial-scale cutting began with eastern white pine, preferred because of its strength, light weight, straight grain, decay resistance, and stability (Lockard 1959: 1; Peattie 2007: 26). Peattie (2007: 33–34) calls white pine "the most generally useful wood our country has ever possessed," and he celebrates nineteenth-century pine logging in the Northeast and Great Lakes as "the greatest chapter in the history of any nation's forests." As one forester reminisced, "We did not realize it at the time, but the white pine in the lake region was the clearest and most perfect timber that has ever been harvested in the United States" (Bardon 1934). Exhaustion of this resource propelled the logging industry across North America. The range of white pine extends from the

Atlantic coast of New England through Minnesota, within the mixed forest transition zone extending between the oak-dominated deciduous forests of the central heartland and the conifers of Ontario and Quebec. White pine habitat preferences help explain pre-1900 geographic patterns of logging. It generally grows best on soils rockier, sandier, or wetter than those most productive for agriculture. Other species remained abundant after white pine depletion, but although profitable, these were less suited for lumber production. Some firms remained active in the Northeast and Great Lakes and shifted to other species and products, but many companies and vast amounts of capital generated by white pine logging poured into the southern and western states, and many workers followed.

As the industry expanded, companies sometimes targeted other species based on comparisons with eastern white pine. Although not as abundant or widespread, Western white pine shares many characteristics with its eastern cousin. Peattie (2007: 61) describes ponderosa pine as "so light and soft textured that it sometimes passes for true white pine." Both ponderosa pine and sugar pine are "white pine–like" species (Lockard 1959: 2). Mature stands of sugar pine, actually the largest North American pine, can yield 100,000 to 200,000 board feet per acre (Peattie 2007: 52–53). In the southern United States, longleaf pine and other pine species collectively marketed as "southern yellow pine" filled a significant part of the niche once dominated by white pine because of their size, straight grain, strength, and decay resistance. Some also suggested bald cypress as a possible substitute for white pine. However, in terms of industry dominance and natural abundance, Douglas fir stands out as the species most worthy of comparison to eastern white pine. In the early twentieth century as logging took off in the Pacific Northwest, it became the "premier industrial tree of the world" (Peattie 2007: 109). It grows throughout the West but reaches enormous sizes in the coastal forests of Washington, Oregon, and British Columbia. Due to its rapid growth rate, some reforested areas have been commercially harvested one or more times after the initial cutting in the late nineteenth or early twentieth centuries.

According to industrial census records, between 1839 and 1940 only eleven states ever ranked among the top three lumber producers: California, Louisiana, Maine, Michigan, Minnesota, Mississippi, New York, Oregon, Pennsylvania, Washington, and Wisconsin (Steer 1948). However, states in the Appalachian and Rocky mountains also produced significant amounts of forest products. Industrial logging was concentrated in certain states because of climate and ecological conditions. Some states had relatively little commercially valuable timber because of aridity or agricultural clearing that took place prior to the mid-nineteenth century. In earlier years, logging coincided with the general progress of farming settlement, but in the mid-nineteenth century it expanded beyond the agricultural frontier. With the advent of industrial-scale logging, the commercial value of forest cover rather than the agricultural potential of soils determined land values in many parts of the country. As European American settlement expanded, the federal government sold large areas of American forests to private parties for much less than they soon would be worth (Lillard 1947: 148).

Starting in the Great Lakes and continuing through the southern and western United States, the lumber industry benefited from what Greeley (1917: 11) called an "unparalleled transfer of natural resources from public to private ownership." Accounts of this process sometimes fail to mention where all this public land came from. Between 1776 and 1887, the United States government obtained over 1.5 billion acres from Native Americans through treaty cessions or direct seizures under executive orders (Saunt 2015). In some areas, such as the Great Lakes, lumbermen acquired large blocks of this land soon after the signing of mid-nineteenth-century treaties. Once the General Land Office completed surveys, private timber cruisers identified the most valuable parcels. Company representatives then purchased their selections, often for a minimal cost of $1.25 per acre. Investors (or speculators) were also able to obtain forested tracts through various legal authorities intended to provide land for other purposes, such as homesteading. For example, the Timber and Stone Act of 1878 supposedly limited claims to 160 acres, but as Richard White (1992: 83) points out, this legislation contained "loopholes so large that entire crews of sailing ships walked through them and filed timber claims that they immediately sold." Lumber companies also purchased large tracts of forested land from railroad or canal companies that had obtained federal or state land grants as compensation for constructing infrastructure deemed necessary for economic expansion. This practice of government sales or grants of recently acquired Native American lands to favored European American groups or individuals actually began under colonial rule.

Northeast Region

The period of colonial and early American settlement by Europeans has been called a "Wooden Age" and an "Age of Wood" (Van Ravenswaay 1970;

Hindle 1975). Early cutting for lumber focused on white pine and was conducted by farmers who logged during the winter when transportation was easiest and farm chores less demanding. The majority of production was consumed locally, except for specialized products like masts and oak barrel staves. Limits imposed by demand and transportation costs restricted harvests to areas relatively close to settlements, major rivers, and harbors. Logging in the United States during the seventeenth and eighteenth centuries featured a combination of European traditions and American innovations: single-bit American-style felling axes, oxen dragging logs to waterways, water-powered sawmills, and rafts or sailing ships carrying lumber to markets.

Prior to the Revolution, British colonial policies restricted American lumber production. The Navigation Acts prevented free trade between the colonies and countries other than Britain, and areas of Maine and New Hampshire where logging was most important strongly supported independence (Lillard 1947: 122–127; Vietze 2018). Colonists also opposed the Crown's reservation of all large pines to supply mast timbers for the Royal Navy. Because white pine was the region's most sought-after wood for construction, restrictions on cutting and marketing for local use supposedly rivaled the tea tax in unpopularity. In fact, stylized images of white pine trees became symbols of resistance that appeared on Revolutionary War flags. Many colonists ignored royal restrictions, and the first lumber shortages occurred in the seventeenth century as timber was depleted near New England's early population centers. During the eighteenth century, areas in Maine and New Hampshire less desirable for farming began to focus on larger-scale logging in order to meet increased demand from areas previously cleared for agriculture and from developing urban areas, such as Boston. After the Revolution, demand increased and transportation infrastructure improved. Along with increased production, social divisions grew: owners of mills and timberlands gained wealth and status relative to those hired to cut, transport, and saw logs (Cox 2010: 323). In the early nineteenth century, areas in what was later to become the state of Maine began to emerge as America's first lumber industry frontier: a place where logging rather than agriculture motivated initial European American settlement and where timber resources, rather than the suitability of soils for farming, determined land values (Lillard 1947: 148).

After gaining statehood in 1820, Maine responded to increased timber demand with government policies supporting industrial expansion. In the 1830s, capital flowing into the state during a speculative binge consolidated timberland ownership into large blocks, and the scale and complexity of logging increased. Loggers modified rivers with dams and diversions. Instream structures called "booms" were used to sort and store floating logs belonging to different firms, which were identified by company marks. Conflict between firms occurred, but cooperative associations reduced tensions by coordinating river modifications and log drives (Cox 2010: 60). The Penobscot River system became the state's largest producer, with extensive boom construction in and around Bangor starting in 1825. By 1836, the Lower Penobscot became so crowded with mills and logs that a railroad was constructed to carry lumber from the uppermost mills to downstream docks (Cox 2010: 25). These mills, booms, and harbor facilities processed 3.36 billion board feet between 1832 and 1872, transforming Bangor into America's first "lumber capital," and they served as a model for the development of even larger and more complex water-based networks in other areas (Wilson 2005: 218).

These developments took place within a national context that extended far beyond Maine. During the first half of the nineteenth century, demand for lumber in the United States increased as a result of population growth (in part due to immigration), westward expansion of agricultural settlement beyond the original 13 colonies, and the growth of other industries. This era saw the United States changing from a rural society dominated by agriculture into an urban one dominated by industry (Williams 1982, 1989). A pattern established in Maine would define other lumbering frontiers: timber owners and lumber producers wielded political power that not only advanced their own interests but discouraged more sustainable and diversified development (Cox 2010: 54–61, 66). For example, regulations governing public waterways often gave priority to their use by lumbermen. Capital generated by lumber companies usually poured into expanding logging operations rather than funding other forms of development, and when pine ran short or became expensive, company owners sought greater profits in states farther west. Because seasonal logging and mill jobs had been available, settlements were established in interior areas with marginal soils, short growing seasons, and almost no other jobs. Hard times followed when the lumbering frontier moved elsewhere, and workers who wanted to continue logging had no choice but to follow. As a result, migrants from Maine influenced not only how logging was done in other states but their overall social and economic development as well, especially around the Great Lakes.

Maine remained an important lumber producer, but peak harvests moved west to other northern tier states where white pine grew well: New York and Pennsylvania. By the time systematic record-keeping began, Maine placed second behind New York (1839), and in 1849 the top three lumber producers were New York, Pennsylvania, and Maine (Steer 1948). By 1859, Pennsylvania led the nation, New York was second, and Michigan edged out Maine for third place. This illustrates the chronological and geographic progression of white pine depletion. Along with increased production, during this period the workforce became more specialized and much less reliant on part-time farmers. Other timber species remained abundant, but they could not satisfy customers wanting to construct buildings using the best quality lumber. Marketing and advertising no doubt contributed to these preferences. Hemlock often grew intermixed with white pine and was heavily cut to obtain bark (tan-bark) used by the leather industry as a source of tannic acid (Foster et al. 2014). As hemlock was inferior to white pine for sawing into lumber, loggers frequently left these logs behind after the bark was removed. Because peeling could only be done in the warmer months, tan-bark harvest took place as a separate, specialized operation. Tanneries were usually located close to bark sources because of transportation costs. Large numbers of hemlock trees were cut in Pennsylvania and New York, states consistently listed among the top leather producing states during the nineteenth century.

Canal construction starting in the 1820s aided lumbermen in adapting to the obstacles and opportunities of logging in New York, Pennsylvania, and beyond. In fact, the Erie Canal (completed 1825) not only helped access New York pine but eventually carried lumber from mills in Canada and Michigan to eastern population centers (Cox 2010: 89). Locations at either end of the Erie Canal became wholesale marketing and distribution centers. Albany, at the junction of the Mohawk River, Hudson River, and the east end of the Erie Canal, often ranked as the first or second largest lumber distribution center in America between about 1830 and 1890 (Howe 2018). At the other end of the Erie Canal near Buffalo and Tonawanda, New York, a six-mile stretch of docks and storage facilities located on the Niagara River, just downstream from Lake Erie, received lumber from mills around the Great Lakes (Williams 1989: 182–183).

Facilities constructed to systematically collect and sort floating logs illustrate the increased scale, complexity, and cost of logging as the industry moved west. Booms, dams, and other river modifications also reflect the industry's political power in obtaining nearly exclusive use of public waterways. A boom built in 1849 at the Great Falls of the Hudson River (Glens Falls, N.Y.) handled almost 5 billion board feet over 54 years (Defebaugh 1970 [1906–1907]: 316–317). In Pennsylvania, canals also extended the industry's reach, and one notable result was the Williamsport Log Boom built on the Susquehanna River in 1851. This 6-mile-long structure enclosed 450 acres of slack water and could hold nearly 1 million logs at a time (Taber 1995). Between 1868 and 1906, sawmills serviced by this boom produced 8 billion board feet of lumber. Like Bangor had before them, at various times Albany, Glens Falls, Williamsport, and Tonawanda laid claim to titles like "Lumber Capital of the World" (Slater 2013). Increases in the speed and scale of milling exacerbated tensions between labor and management, and in 1872 Williamsport was the scene of the first major lumber industry strike, which managers referred to as a "riot" because it was so disorganized (Jensen 1945: 41). Shorter hours apparently mattered more to these strikers than higher pay. Even though Pennsylvania had legislated an 8-hour day, this remained unenforced, and most mill workers worked 11 to 12 hours a day. The demand for 10-hour days without decreased pay was not met, and the strike ended without workers gaining collective bargaining rights. Management eventually made some concessions but remained firmly in control as the industry expanded into the Great Lakes region.

Great Lakes Region

Cox (2010: 149) describes late nineteenth- and early twentieth-century white pine logging in the Lake States as the "full flowering" of the industry. Many owners, managers, and workers followed the industrial frontier from Maine to the Great Lakes. In Canada, a parallel westward movement took place from the Maritime provinces and the Ottawa River Valley. In the Great Lakes states after the Civil War, "lumber manufacture took the form that molded its destinies" (Greeley 1951: 40). According to Jensen (1945: 45), "there has never been such a complete and rapid cutting of a forest of this size." Systems of vertical integration enabled some companies to control all aspects of production: cutting, transportation, milling, and marketing. Logging in Michigan, Wisconsin, and Minnesota supplied agricultural settlements in the southern portions of these states, but Ohio, Indiana, Illinois, and the Great Plains states provided an even larger market. Situated between three of the Great Lakes, Michigan shipped lumber both east and west and led the nation in lumber production for three decades from 1870 to 1900 (Steer 1948).

Michigan's Saginaw River system became the first major Great Lakes milling center, with numerous tributaries well distributed for moving pine logs. One-hundred twenty mills operated along the river by 1880, where schooners picked up lumber and carried it south and east to ports like Cleveland, Buffalo, and Tonawanda. A boom for collecting and sorting logs extended along 12 miles of river bank and employed 500 men (Kilar 1990: 25, 240). Annual production in Saginaw and nearby Bay City peaked in 1882 at over one billion board feet. Recent immigrants, mainly Germans, Poles, and French Canadians, made up a larger percentage of the workforce than at previous centers, and some blamed "foreigners" for increased labor unrest. With the involvement of the Knights of Labor, Saginaw's most significant strike occurred in 1885 (Jensen 1945: 61). Not surprisingly, the output of Saginaw mills peaked around this time. Workers demanded a reduction of the workday to 10 hours. Michigan's governor at the time was a wealthy lumber mill owner who called in troops to enforce bans on mass meetings and parades. Other countermeasures included arrests of strike leaders and bringing in replacement workers, but perhaps most discouraging were threats to permanently close mills, as most workers knew that log supplies in the Saginaw watershed were declining. The state enforced a 10-hour limit on the workday a few months after the strike ended, but most wages were proportionally reduced. This was a time of increased pressure on employees as companies used technological changes to force increases in the pace of work. They implemented these "speed-ups" by introducing new machinery; the pressure to work faster increased dramatically across the 1880s and 1890s with the installation of multiple band saws at many mills. This practice continued well into the twentieth century. According to the Industrial Workers of the World (IWW 1922: 57–58), "In large modern sawmills the efficiency or speed-up system is reduced to a fine science. The pace is set by machinery speeded up to the limit of human endurance."

The ease of shipping by water closely linked the Great Lakes region to lumbering in Canada. Lower (1968: 153–154) points out that the Great Lakes united rather than divided the lumber industry. Capital flowed from the United States to Canada, and in return came logs or lumber. Labor moved in both directions, but the United States enjoyed net gains because of greater opportunities (Lower 1968: 160). Tugboats towed rafts of pine logs across Lake Huron from Ontario to Michigan mills. This linkage was both commercial and social. American companies expanded into Canada and Canadians migrated "in droves" to work in Michigan lumber camps (Rickaby

1926: 20). However, as the turn of the century approached, the number of Scandinavian and Eastern European workers around the Great Lakes increased and proportions of Scotch, Irish, and French Canadians decreased (Engberg 1948).

While most of Saginaw's output went east, mills on the opposite (west) side of Michigan's Lower Peninsula shipped lumber across Lake Michigan to Chicago, which claimed the title of "world's greatest lumber market" in the mid-nineteenth century (Karamanski 2005). Mills in Michigan's Upper Peninsula and in eastern Wisconsin also shipped their lumber to Chicago. Besides the demand generated by its own rapid growth, connections by water, and later by rail, linked the city to tree-scarce areas of the Middle West and Great Plains (Cronon 1991). In the early twentieth century, Chicago's national significance within the lumber industry declined as Great Lakes pine became scarce. Expanded railroad networks eventually enabled mills in the South and West to ship directly to markets rather than going through centralized distributors.

As the industry extended into western Wisconsin and Minnesota, the Mississippi River and its tributaries served as major highways for moving logs to mills and lumber to markets. Rafting became especially important on the upper Mississippi; free-floating logs could be easily lost in shallows or backwater areas (Cox 2010: 152–154). To avoid this, shipments of floating logs enclosed by an end-to-end series of large logs chained together were guided downstream by tugs. Stacks of lumber could be bound together into rectangular rafts and transported in a similar manner. Problems arose, however, as various lumbermen tried to appropriate rivers for their exclusive use. Disputes occurred between different companies, between groups of upstream and downstream mills, and between the lumber industry and shippers that supported other industries or supplied settlements along the river. Logs on their way to downstream mills blocked lumber being shipped from upstream mills, but upstream mills delayed logs on their way downstream as they inspected them to secure those with their company mark.

The Chippewa River system in north central Wisconsin provided more lumber than any other Mississippi tributary, and events there illustrate the development of important organizational aspects of the industry (Williams 1989: 204). To ensure a steady supply for downstream mills in Wisconsin, Iowa, Illinois, and Missouri, a log storage area and sorting works were constructed at a location known as Beef Slough, near the Chippewa's junction with the Mississippi. After years of conflict over the use of this facility, one of the downstream mill owners, Frederick Weyerhaeuser, emerged as a leader and negotiated an agreement whereby mills as far downstream as St. Louis could systematically share Beef Slough (Ritter 2015). In 1880 he negotiated another agreement that included companies upstream into the heart of Chippewa River pineries and created a syndicate or "pool" to increase production. Eventually only one independent mill was left in the area. The rest were owned by or affiliated with Weyerhaeuser. These events marked the start of the Weyerhaeuser organization's transformation from regional to national domination. Frederick Weyerhaeuser clearly had practical knowledge of logging and milling, but what stood out was his ability to form business relationships to raise capital and coordinate or consolidate operations. Through such deft maneuvering, Weyerhaeuser avoided duplication of efforts and maximized the scale and efficiency of production. He used a "pool" of capital to expand land purchases, buy out other companies, and construct improvements. This did not eliminate all competition but significantly reduced its negative effects on profits. It also accelerated timber depletion and other environmental effects. Technological improvements increased production, but the primary driver was the increasingly effective deployment of capital. Some compare Weyerhaeuser's expansion to nineteenth-century monopolies in the steel and oil industries, while others point out that although some companies became dominant, the lumber industry always included a significant minority of smaller independent companies (Williams 1989: 221). Factors like the vast geographic dispersal of operations made it difficult for large companies to monopolize the industry.

With so much capital available, many lumbermen pursued higher rates of return by investing in other regions. Great Lakes pinelands had become harder to find and more expensive, and in 1900 Frederick Weyerhaeuser assembled investors to join him in purchasing 900,000 acres of timberland in Washington from James J. Hill's Northern Pacific Railroad for $5.4 million (Ritter 2015: 10). The deal included guaranteed discount shipping rates on Hill's railroad networks. Great Lakes firms faced a choice when the pine ran out: remain in the area and shift to other species or migrate. This dilemma resulted in a new phase of lumbering as some companies began using railroads to harvest the region's vast hardwood stands. As in the Northeast and South, the Great Lakes logging industry persisted in different forms after the best pine ran out. Hardwood species such as maple, beech, birch, and oak provided charcoal, chemicals, and a wide range of durable products, like flooring. Railroads also accessed inland stands of conifers that had survived the numerous fires that followed white pine logging. Species once harvested separately for nonlumber uses were included in clear-cutting strategies designed to maximize returns and offset the expense of railroad construction. Large companies found or developed markets for every species. They made cedar into shingles, shakes, railroad ties, and fence posts; spruce and balsam supplied the early pulp and paper industry; and tamarack provided mine timbers. However, companies seeking the best species for sawing into lumber moved south and west. In a sense, there wasn't enough room in the remaining Great Lakes forests for fully realizing the additional profit potential of the capital accumulated from cutting white pine.

As many lumbermen associated with the white pine era left the area, new enterprises focused on the remaining forests. In his quest for complete control of the manufacturing process, Henry Ford purchased 400,000 acres in Northern Michigan to provide hardwood lumber used in motor vehicle frames and trim, and he developed sawmills along with facilities to process logs for other products (Karamanski 1989: 161–166). During a time of increased labor unrest, the Ford Motor Company experimented with providing improved conditions for loggers. Ford camps in Northern Michigan included "freshly painted portable houses" with electric lights, steam heat, and laundry service (Butler 1922). Spitting on the floor was forbidden, a rule supposedly unpopular with older workers! Ford built relatively few of these improved camps because the logging camp era was coming to an end due to better road systems and affordable vehicles with internal combustion engines. Along with increased labor unrest, improved transportation systems led companies to get out of the business of running logging camps and to shift over to the jobber (independent contractor) system.

Southern Region

Walking through Florida in 1867, which he described as the "hot gardens of the sun, where the palm meets the pine," John Muir encountered a "shanty" occupied by loggers cutting "long pines for ship spars" (Muir 1916: 47–48). As in other regions, early logging in the South for local or specialized uses occurred in the most accessible stands close to water features. The southern lumbering region extended from East Texas to North Carolina, defined for our purposes by the mid-nineteenth-century extent of large stands of old-growth pine. Industrial-scale logging in the South took off after restrictions on purchasing land from the public domain ended with the repeal of the Southern Homestead Act in 1876 (Williams 1989: 240). Virtually all early capital came from northern investors, and depletion of white pine in the Lake States provided the impetus for rapid expansion in the South. In terms of large harvest volumes, the Gulf States stand out, especially Louisiana and Mississippi. Log drives occurred in some areas, but because of unpredictable flows, low swampy banks, and their uneven geographic distribution, river transport never dominated the region like it did in the Great Lakes states or Northeast. However, lumber company railroads spread quickly in the relatively flat coastal plains of the South, and their systematic (often dendritic) networks characterized industrial logging there (Williams 1989: 257–260). Railroad networks permitted more dispersed mill locations, and the South never developed mill clusters like Williamsport and Saginaw or centralized distribution centers as large as Tonawanda, Albany, or Chicago. Other differences included year-round logging and a labor force dominated by poor white farmers and freed slaves rather than recent European immigrants. Southern workers, often accompanied by their families, apparently were less mobile than workers in other regions. African Americans formed a majority of the lumber industry workforce in many areas, and racial divisions thwarted attempts to organize southern workers (Jensen 1945: 77).

Southern forests also supplied the naval stores industry, with longleaf and slash pine being the best sources. Although some colonial production derived from other pine species occurred in New England, the earliest large-scale naval stores manufacture took place in tar kilns concentrated in North and South Carolina. These were earth-covered mounds of stacked pine wood charred and baked so resin melted and drained into clay-lined pits (Southerlin 2013). As naval stores production spread throughout the South, gum (resin) was collected from deliberately scarred faces on living trees and transported to centrally located stills where it was boiled to produce turpentine and other by-products. Some lumber companies thought the resulting damage to the lower portions of trees and the consequent loss in value outweighed the extra income received. However, in the early twentieth century higher prices and less destructive gum collection techniques led many companies to schedule several years of turpentine production prior to cutting operations. The process of removing sections of bark, cutting grooves into the underlying wood, and periodically scraping off the resulting gum accumulations was labor intensive, and nearly all workers in this industry were African Americans. Well into the twentieth century, they endured "slave-like" conditions in remote turpentine camps, where armed guards prevented workers from leaving without permission and dogs were used to track down "run-aways" (Hickman 2009: 139–146).

Land ownership in the South eventually became concentrated in a relatively small number of companies with vast holdings. Southern yellow pine (a marketing term that included longleaf, slash, loblolly, and shortleaf pine) and cypress dominated lumber production, and Louisiana ranked either first or second among the nation's timber-producing states every year between 1906 and 1919 (Williams 1989: 272). The Great Southern Logging Company's Bogalusa, Louisiana, mill exemplified the large scale of the southern lumber industry, consuming 40–100 acres of forest per day and producing 250 million board feet of lumber in 1916 (Williams 1989: 262). Competition from large vertically integrated railroad logging companies nearly eliminated smaller independent operations (Williams 1989: 260–261). With railroad networks enabling the harvest of huge areas by a single operation, logging camps often resembled small villages, with stores, schools, churches, and single-family housing.

Company-provided housing in the South was segregated on the basis of racist ideology (Jones 2005: 1). Workers accused company stores (commissaries) of price-gouging, and their profitability helped offset logging costs. Wages paid in company scrip could only be redeemed at company stores. Employees in isolated lumber towns or camps lacked alternatives for shopping until road systems improved and car ownership became common. Unlike in other regions, southern lumber and naval stores companies reduced labor costs through convict leasing and debt peonage (Shofner 1981; Donegan 2013). These racially based forced-labor practices continued into the mid-twentieth century with some of the worst abuses taking place in Florida. Southern lumber companies formed trade associations that facilitated cooperation to an extent not seen in the Northeast or Great Lakes. They focused on instituting "factory-style" management of labor to prevent unions from gaining power. Williams (1989: 263) called the resulting system "the epitome of industrial capitalism." Compared to other regions, lumber workers in the South endured longer hours for less pay, although they earned more than tenant farmers or laborers in the turpentine and sugar industries (Green 1973: 169). Political and economic structures described as "feudal" forced southern lumber industry workers to "choose between submissive servitude and starvation" (Creel 1915: 76–77).

Sawmill towns in the South grew rapidly but usually declined as soon as the surrounding forests disappeared. Jensen (1945: 79) points out that the length of time timber supplies lasted determined the character of company towns. Large-scale cutting decreased during the 1930s as timber became scarce, and the industry entered the so-called peckerwood mill phase, characterized by internal combustion engines powering small, often portable mills and hauling logs and lumber with trucks. One mid-sized steam mill operated by the Crowell Lumber Company at Longleaf, Louisiana, did not close permanently until 1969 and remains preserved in a museum setting as a reminder of the "golden age" of lumbering in the South (HABS/HAER 1984). The southern "pine belt" produced one-third of the timber harvested in the United States between 1900 and 1949 (Jones 2005: 17). One author concluded, "Never in American economic history was an industry more prodigal in handling precious raw materials than were the southern lumber mills" (Clark 2004: 2). With the nearly complete disappearance of old-growth longleaf pine forests, the only direction left to go for prime timber was west.

Western Region

North America was exceptional in terms of forest resources and the volume of industrial logging during the nineteenth and twentieth centuries, and the Pacific Northwest stood out within North America. Temperate rain forests like those in coastal areas of Washington and Oregon contain the greatest living biomass per unit area found in any of the world's terrestrial ecosystems (Pan et al. 2013). Sometimes called the Douglas fir region, these forests included commercially valuable Sitka spruce, western hemlock, and western red cedar, as well as coast redwoods in Northern California. In drier inland areas throughout the West, different conifer species assumed importance, with ponderosa pine the most abundant and widespread. In both wetter and dryer western forests, cutting and hauling in lower elevations took place during most of the year. Although lumber remained the most important western product, some operations focused on shingles, railroad ties, utility poles, and timbers for constructing bridges, docks, and other large structures. Eastern capital funded early western operations. For example, 10 out of 21 companies acquiring redwoods between 1880 and 1902 originated in the Great Lakes states (Williams 1989: 303).

Companies and jobs migrated westward as cutting depleted southern timber. Many southern firms moved to Oregon, but in 1923 the Long-Bell Company shifted operations from Louisiana to Washington, where they built what, at the time, was the largest sawmill in the world (McClary 2014: 1). Because the region's climate led to prolific tree growth, equipment had to be adapted for cutting, transporting, and milling logs much larger than those from eastern or southern pines. Steeper terrain required longer and higher railroad trestle bridges, and flumes, chutes, or rail inclines transported logs down the steepest slopes. Abrupt gradients made many western rivers unsuitable for log driving. The earliest logging in the West consisted of "tidewater" operations in coastal areas with lumber being transported by ship. The first transcontinental railroads reached Washington and Oregon in 1883–1884, and after the Great Northern Railroad arrived in 1893, shipping costs decreased and large quantities of lumber started moving east (Williams 1989: 297–298). All this, along with increases in capacity based on advancements in steam-powered yarding and milling, set the stage for the "greatest harvest of timber the world has ever known" (Adams 1961: 16). Mechanized techniques like high-lead and skyline yarding added speed and capacity in the early twentieth century (Williams 1989: 301, 316–317). Mechanization also increased accident rates, but workers earned higher wages in the West compared to other regions (Jensen 1945: 110). Increased production required companies to focus on land acquisition. Increases in capital investment and production were mutually reinforcing. Western states, especially Washington and Oregon, took over as the leading lumber producers in the 1920s, eventually producing half of the nation's supply. Some companies became large enough to trigger accusations of monopoly. For example, Weyerhaeuser eventually owned 50 million acres nationwide, with major holdings in the Lake States, South, and Pacific Northwest (Rutkow 2012: 193).

Besides increasing production, technological changes occurring in the West had important social implications. Holbrook (2016: 175) argues that because of differing conditions, loggers moving from other regions faced more challenges than migrating sawmill workers did. Attempts to organize workers developed slowly in the Great Lakes and were suppressed, sometimes with ruthless violence, in the South. Lillard (1947: 284) posits that because they "lived and worked beyond the sight and sympathy of the general public," lumber industry workers failed to attract support for advancing their interests. The tensions between management and labor reached a climax in the Northwest during the early twentieth century. As managers pushed for lower costs and faster production, increased visibility and public awareness, as well as better communication among workers, contributed to successful collective action and threats of legislative attention. Social reformers and journalists also targeted the industry: "As a community, a lumber camp is a sad travesty at best" (Tugwell 1920: 472). Jensen (1945: 6) offered a concise, if somewhat oversimplified, analysis: the industry's problems came from treating forests as a "mine" and not a "crop." Voices for change even emerged from within the forestry profession:

> Housing, sanitary arrangements, and hours of labor too often have been outrageous, and living conditions intolerable, and this because the lumber camp and the lumber town exist only long enough to skin the timber from the land. . . . Under such circumstances the woods worker easily becomes voteless, landless, womanless, homeless, and hopeless, and therefore discontented, restless, and sympathetic with destructively radical doctrines.
>
> (Society of American Foresters 1919: 932–933)

Statements like this illustrate the growing awareness of connections between the environmental and social costs of this industry. Locally and regionally, unsustainable timber harvest practices inhibited workers from organizing and gaining political power by forcing many of them to frequently move in search of work.

Some of the much-feared "radical ideas" mentioned by the Society of American Foresters (1919) were spread by the Industrial Workers of the World (IWW or "Wobblies"). A militant socialist union founded in 1905, they organized workers by industry rather than craft. Conflict between labor and management increased in the Northwest as this region became the center of American lumber production. This was the only lumbering region where large-scale union organization eventually succeeded, but early efforts proved costly to all sides. In 1916, a gun battle in Everett, Washington, between deputies and IWW protesters killed at least seven (Lins and Johnson 2019). Organized by the IWW in 1917, the most significant lumber industry strike in U.S. history shut down 85 percent of the camps and mills in the Northwest and demanded an eight-hour workday and better camp conditions (Holbrook 2016: 127, 134). The union later credited the 1917 strike for improvements: "Bunk-houses are smaller and less crowded. Sheets and pillows are furnished, and there are bath-houses and drying rooms" (IWW 1922). In a sense, the IWW won a battle in 1917 but lost the broader struggle to establish themselves in the region. Labor conflict continued and, combined with "war hysteria," led to the 1919 Centralia Massacre, a deadly gun battle between IWW members and vigilantes (Jensen 1945: 137–142). Union leaders were imprisoned, and internal disagreements further weakened the organization. Perceived by many as anti-American anarchists, the IWW never again attained the level of influence they enjoyed in 1917.

During this pivotal time period, world affairs played an important role in relations between labor and management within the logging industry. In order to ensure an adequate supply of Sitka spruce lumber for building military aircraft, the federal government took control of a large segment of the industry in Washington and Oregon during World War I (Tonsfeldt 2013; Williams 2013, 2016). This unprecedented intervention occurred because labor shortages and conflict between workers and management prevented companies from meeting the demand for lumber. As a consequence, strikes were forbidden, but the government essentially forced companies to improve working conditions. As Holbrook (2016: 208) put it, "war and the Wobblies" finally forced an eight-hour day and other concessions. One outcome was the presence of more women and children in the camps as more family housing became available. The army constructed 130 miles of railroad and a large mill complex for sawing spruce at Vancouver, Washington, and deployed troops in logging camps to assist in production and discourage union activity. This large-scale initiative ceased abruptly when the war ended, however. The government auctioned off equipment and buildings to private companies and released surplus lumber for sale slowly so as not to flood the market and depress prices. By the late 1920s, relations between labor and management in central Oregon, as well as working conditions, were considered far superior to those in the Great Lakes and the South (Tonsfeldt and Claeyssens 2004). Large companies sawing pine in south-central Oregon and Northern California employed innovative technology and national marketing that became a standard imitated in other areas.

The abundant timber resources of the Northwest enabled the region to dominate the industry as the twentieth century progressed. Developments there influenced other regions, but at reduced scales. The depleted forests of the Northeast, Great Lakes, and South still produced forest products, with a high percentage derived from smaller trees, including many growing in previously cutover areas. Holbrook (1943: 164) described logging in the Northwest as it existed in 1941. Steam-powered machinery remained in use but was being replaced by gas-powered tractors, which were better suited for selective logging because they didn't cause as much damage to nearby unharvested trees. Most camps were accessible by roads and included hot showers and electric lights. Larger companies employed professional foresters and engineers, and some also pursued measures to prevent forest fires and ensure reforestation. Holbrook (1943: 164) mentions one tradition that continued after the war: "No workers eat better food than west coast loggers." By the 1940s to the 1950s, railroad logging, with its extreme capital requirements, had ended, and in many areas, employees commuted to work from their homes.

National Perspectives

National-scale influences on the lumber industry that began in the late nineteenth century increased in importance during the early twentieth century. Better transportation and communication networks, as well as the development of nationwide marketing contributed to this trend. In 1902, a number of regional associations, including the Southern Lumber Manufacturers Association and the Mississippi Valley Lumbermen's Association, merged to form the National Lumber Manufacturers Association (Fickle 1970: 149). Some labor organizations, like the IWW, remained active in multiple regions. In 1911–1912, the Brotherhood of Timber Workers (BTW) organized strikes against companies in Louisiana and Texas. After affiliating with the IWW in 1912, theirs became an interracial effort. Besides lockouts, companies joined forces with state and local law enforcement in a violent military-style response to unions that took advantage of the Jim Crow legal system (Green 1973: 161–163). Companies exploited racial issues to fight organized labor. If unions were "white only," companies used African American strike breakers, but they also employed "race-baiting" to discourage white membership in biracial organizations. The BTW eventually included African Americans, and although their efforts fell short of objectives, they demonstrated the power of organizing by class rather than race. Besides their efforts in the West, in 1916–1917 the IWW organized a strike by workers at the Virginia and Rainy Lake Lumber Company in northern Minnesota (Haynes 1971). Although law enforcement and company-funded deputies effectively eliminated union activity, modest improvements in wages and working conditions followed. During the World War I era, companies and the press vilified IWW strikers for socialist or communist associations and argued for government assistance in breaking strikes and eliminating the organization for the sake of "national security."

Conditions during the Great Depression also stimulated episodes of labor unrest, and several organizations less radical than the IWW proved effective. The 1935 Sawmill and Timber Workers' Union (STWU) strike in Northern California, Oregon, and Washington was one of the largest, most successful lumber industry job actions due, in part, to prolabor New Deal policies and the region's ample supplies of high-value timber (Jensen 1945: 164). This achievement resulted in a permanent union presence and collective bargaining. Another relatively successful action took place in 1937 under the leadership of the Minnesota Timber Workers Union, with strong support from populist farmer organizations and the state's governor (Mitchell 1999). Union leadership in Minnesota included loggers with American Indian and Finnish backgrounds. In contrast, an unsuccessful 1937 strike in Michigan's Upper Peninsula faced an unsympathetic governor and violent assaults from local vigilantes (Bernhardt 1979). Likewise, union efforts in the South remained largely unsuccessful. Even so, collective resistance had increased public and legislative awareness, and improvements in other regions eventually came about in conjunction with New Deal policies. In terms of the overall well-being of workers, however, gains were probably offset by reductions in the workforce due to resource depletion and technological innovations. Companies used both mobility and technology to keep production high and labor costs low. As a result, even with fewer workers, the rapid rate of forest consumption continued.

Extensive deforestation was not simply the result of a growing nation's need for lumber. Episodes of overproduction occurred throughout the history of this industry, often due to speculation in timberlands that failed to appreciate at the expected rate and added to cash flow problems. Many firms remained undercapitalized relative to the amount of debt carried and other expenses (Jensen 1945; Cronon 1991: 191). Cutting continued even when prices were low, and companies sold lumber below cost to stay in business and try to recoup losses later. This problem became especially severe in the early twentieth century. As a former Forest Service chief recalled, "Magnificent virgin timber was too often forced upon sluggish customers at less than the cost of production. . . . It was less costly to manufacture at a loss than not to manufacture at all" (Greeley 1951: 42). The Great Depression exacerbated this situation. In a memorandum submitted to President Hoover in 1930, lumber industry representatives described the results of chronic overproduction: "It is threatening the forest industries with economic chaos. It is contributing to destructive lumbering, unnecessary waste of wood, and the premature cutting of timber needed in the future" (Galloway 1931: 11). Besides these practical considerations, for several decades critics of the industry had raised noneconomic concerns: "Clearing has surely now gone far enough; soon timber will be scarce, and not a grove will be left to rest in or pray in" (Muir 1897: 147). Muir may have been overly optimistic, however, when he wrote: "God has cared for these trees, saved them from drought, disease, and avalanches; but he cannot save them from fools—only Uncle Sam can do that" (1897: 157).

As awareness of these problems grew, federal and state government policies increasingly influenced the nation's timber industry. The general public and elected representatives became more aware of devastating "cut out and get out" practices, and concerns mounted about future supplies and erosion damage. In 1891 Congress authorized the creation of forest reserves through the withdrawal of large areas of public domain lands. The Organic Act of 1897 affirmed that these reserves were intended to ensure a "continuous supply of timber." In 1905 the Department of Interior transferred these areas to the Department of Agriculture for designation as national forests. Initially managed primarily for watershed protection and fire prevention, timber sales were allowed but regulated. Because some national forests lacked any nearby infrastructure, harvesting required large investments, including the construction of new sawmills, so the Forest Service awarded large, long-term, and lucrative timber sale contracts. Logging operations on national forests resembled those occurring on private lands but began to include conservation measures. Locations of camps, railroads, chutes, and other buildings and structures constructed in national forests had to be approved by Forest Service officials (USDA Forest Service 1911). The Forest Service mandated certain harvest practices to reduce fire risk, encourage reforestation in cutover areas, and avoid damage to watersheds.

The Weeks Act of 1911 permitted federal acquisition of lands already denuded by cutting or burning, enabling the creation of additional national forests in eastern and southern regions that needed reforestation, erosion control, and fire prevention. The Knutson-Vandenberg (K-V) Act of 1930 authorized Forest Service tree nurseries and required deposits from timber sale purchasers to cover reforestation costs. During the New Deal era, debates between laissez-faire and regulation advocates played out relative to timber harvest on public lands. The National Industrial Recovery Act

(NIRA) was used in an attempt to ensure sustainable timber harvest levels on private lands, but the Supreme Court declared this act unconstitutional (Rajala 1999: 132–137). Government and industry tried unsuccessfully to limit lumber production and stabilize prices (Jensen 1945: 157). One of the most popular New Deal programs, the Civilian Conservation Corps (CCC) played a role in expanding management activities in public forests, including firefighting, reforestation, timber stand improvement, and the construction of infrastructure such as roads that would make future timber harvests more efficient and allow access for other uses. Although USDA Forest Service policies have affected the timber industry since the early twentieth century, the agency's influence increased between World War II and the 1960s, when the amount of timber cut on national forest lands rose from around two billion board feet to nearly twelve billion board feet per year (Clawson 1983: 75). Much of this volume came from the more or less systematic liquidation of many old growth stands in the Pacific Northwest and northern Rocky Mountains. This trend was tempered by dwindling supplies of large trees and legislation like the Multiple-Use Sustained-Yield Act of 1960. Additional influences on federal forest management later in the twentieth century included the designation of certain areas where logging was not allowed or strictly limited: Wilderness Areas, Research Natural Areas (RNAs), designated old growth stands, and areas such as wetlands that were not suited for timber harvest because of likely resource damage or the lack of assured regeneration.

In parallel with government policies contributing toward standardization, as the twentieth century progressed, many companies implemented scientific management principles. This approach, sometimes referred to as Taylorism, emphasized centralized decision-making and maximum control over production (Rajala 1999: 51–53). Technical experts, mainly engineers and foresters, planned harvests. Based on detailed mapping of timber stands and topography, they determined the best placement of cutting units, railroads, roads, yarding areas, and logging camps. Many decisions once handled by foremen or individual workers were now made by centralized management. Silvicultural practices to encourage reforestation began in public forests and on some private forest lands. It had been common for companies to essentially abandon cutover areas, which would then revert to public ownership for nonpayment of property taxes. Companies were enthusiastic sellers of both cutover and forested land to federal and state governments during the Great Depression. Lumber companies once owned many areas now included in national and state forests, and these lands contain abundant traces of past logging operations.

For over a century, logging in the United States followed a pattern of capital accumulation, expanded scale, and resource depletion, with particular adaptations used to secure "cheap" timber and labor, including strategic mobility and technology development. This progression over time and space resulted in "metabolic rifts": social and environmental costs not borne by timber producers that reduced the stability and sustainability of forest ecosystems and surrounding communities (Foster 2013; Auerbach and Clark 2018). Even though progress toward sustainability has occurred, the particular ecosystems or resources now being sustained are often very different than those of the original forests. The archaeology of this industry can provide a new perspective on this situation, in contrast to documents that emphasize the concerns of management, such as technology and transportation. Geographic and temporal gaps in the written historical record also become apparent when the focus shifts from broad trends to more local phenomena. In the following chapter, we discuss the approaches used by archaeologists to provide new insights into the nature and effects of this industry.

3

Archaeological Approaches to the Logging Industry

> The greatest single defect in most historical scholarship is the greater preoccupation with written records than with other kinds of evidence. We shall continue to have a badly distorted view of the last sixteen centuries until this myopia is corrected.
>
> Lynn White, *Scientific Methods in Medieval Archaeology* (1970), 3

One of the first investigations of an American logging industry site by professional archaeologists took place at the 1847–1853 location of Sutter's Sawmill, best known for its coincidental association with thc California Gold Rush (Fenenga 1947; Heizer 1947). Heavy equipment and hand excavation uncovered portions of the mill's original foundation of sugar pine timbers. Dimensions of 60 × 20 feet matched the recollections of mill operator (and gold discoverer) James Marshall. The mill's relationship to mining no doubt motivated researchers, who conducted fieldwork on the centennial of the Gold Rush, and White (2017) includes this project in his book on the archaeology of the American mining industry. However, not until the 1970s did large numbers of logging industry–related sites receive attention, and this chapter summarizes how and why this took place. The results of archaeological projects very much depended on the goals and methods of researchers. Broad trends within archaeology during the last 50 years affected what has been learned, and a critical assessment of past work provides useful lessons for the future.

National Historic Preservation Act and Section 106

In the vast majority of cases, the pursuit of archaeology at logging industry sites resulted from the passage of the National Historic Preservation Act (NHPA) in 1966 and the late twentieth-century emergence of historical archaeology as a specialized discipline. During this period, archaeologists ventured into more recent time periods and began exploring sites besides those associated with famous people or dramatic historical events. Growing alarm over the loss of nonrenewable resources, such as historic buildings and archaeological sites, as well as the public benefits that accrue from their stewardship provided the impetus for passing the NHPA. This act established the National Register of Historic Places and the following criteria used to determine whether sites are eligible for listing (Electronic Code of Federal Regulations 2019, https://gov.ecfr.io/):

> The quality of significance in American history, architecture, archeology, engineering, and culture is present in districts, sites, buildings, structures, and objects that possess integrity of location, design, setting, materials, workmanship, feeling, and association, and:
>
> A. That are associated with events that have made a significant contribution to the broad patterns of our history; or
>
> B. That are associated with the lives of significant persons in our past; or
>
> C. That embody the distinctive characteristics of a type, period, or method of construction, or that represent the work of a master, or that possess high artistic values, or that represent a significant and distinguishable entity whose components may lack individual distinction; or
>
> D. That have yielded or may be likely to yield, information important in history or prehistory.

Archaeological research values pertain to eligibility under criterion D, but archaeological sites can be eligible for the National Register for reasons other than their information value. For example, archaeological surveys combined with historical research can demonstrate site significance under criterion A based on little or no subsurface archaeological investigation. Criteria A–C are primarily associative or commemorative: archaeological sites can be eligible under these criteria independent of their value as sources of information about the past.

A key provision of the regulations implementing the NHPA is called Section 106, which requires decision-makers to take into account the potential effects federally funded or licensed projects might have on historic resources eligible for the National Register of Historic Places. As the section 106 process was applied to projects throughout the United States (mainly those occurring on public lands), researchers discovered many archaeological sites related to the logging industry. For some sites threatened by earth disturbing projects or processes like erosion and illegal relic collecting, additional studies, including archaeological excavation, were conducted under the auspices of the NHPA. These were usually funded by federal agencies planning activities like timber sales and road building or by private companies constructing projects that utilize public lands, like pipelines or electrical transmission lines. Dixon and Smith (2017) describe an example of the Section 106 process as it played out regarding sites once occupied by Chinese workers who supplied wood to mining-related settlements in Nevada.

Historical archaeology seeks to expand, provide alternative perspectives, or, if necessary, contradict interpretations of the past based on historical documents. Because this requires detailed familiarity with the documentary record, some historical narratives were prepared specifically to provide a framework for the archaeological evaluation of lumber industry sites. Some of this work appears in thematic studies for listing multiple properties on the National Register of Historic Places (Beidle 1992; Birk 1999; Elliott 1992; Merritt and Ayres 2014; Moffatt et al. 2011; Sherman 1999; Stein 1993, 2006; Stiles 1994b). In fact, these references are actually National Register of Historic Places Multiple Property Documentation Forms (National Park Service Form 10-900-b). Other historical studies of logging done to support decision-making required by the NHPA were issued in formats less specific to the National Register program (Baker and Shoup 1979; Brown and Elling 1981; Conners 1997; Gregory 2001; Isaacs 1989; Karamanski et al. 1983, 1984; Maniery and Baker 1997; Sawyer 1988; Shoup and Baker 1981; Wyatt 1999). Using documents and oral history, some of these provide detailed descriptions of specific logging operations. Most were prepared by historic preservation staff employed by state or federal agencies or historical consultants under contracts with these agencies. These studies contributed to the identification and protection of archaeological sites and provide historical background for future archaeology. Although these historical studies were important, this book focuses on literature reporting the results of archaeological fieldwork.

Typologies and Chronologies

In order to organize research and conduct comparisons, archaeologists and historians devised typologies of lumber industry sites based on functional and chronological differences. Karamanski (1989) divided activities associated with the procurement and processing of timber into five phases: awareness, acquisition, forest operations, transportation, and milling. Both logging companies and historians have emphasized transportation as the "key problem of the lumberman. . . . He must move a heavy, bulky, cheap raw material from a wilderness area to the centers of civilization" (Rector 1953: 13). Bryant (1923) estimated that transportation costs represented 75 percent or more of the total cost of logs delivered to mills. The energy sources used for log transportation and milling define geographer Evelyn Dinsdale's (1965) three-phase framework for analyzing chronological and spatial change in the American lumber industry. Archaeologists and historians adapted this approach for categorizing lumber industry sites in the Great Lakes states (Franzen 1984; Karamanski 1989; Moffatt et al. 2011; Overstreet et al. 1983; Stiles 1994a, 1994b). During the earliest stage, industrial activity relied on wind and water power, followed by a period dominated by steam power. The sequence concludes with a final stage powered by electricity and internal combustion engines. Even though technologies overlapped during transitions, each phase is associated with the region that dominated the logging industry when a particular technology was introduced. On this basis, the following technological "core areas" were defined: wind and water in the Northeast, steam in the Great Lakes and South, and internal combustion in the Pacific Northwest (Dinsdale 1965: 273). Besides generalizing about the origins of dominant technologies, chronologies of the logging industry sometimes take into account the tree species being harvested or products being produced. In providing an overview of the Great Lakes region, Karamanski et al. (1983) defined three major phases: river drive/pine, railroad/hardwoods, and gasoline/pulp. This scheme is obviously broad and was not meant to be rigidly imposed: considerable overlap existed between phases.

Unfortunately, emphasizing technology as an independent variable that defines typologies and chronologies can limit our ability to explain cultural dynamics. Technology-based narratives often fail to adequately consider the importance of other variables. One of the most negative results of this ideological bias is the attribution of sociocultural change to seemingly independent and inevitable technological change. Rigid typologies and chronologies may perpetuate deterministic notions and inhibit better understanding of the contingent and socially constructed aspects of technology. Historical archaeology provides a critique of so-called typical or composite descriptions that are often part of technology-dominated models. In fact, explaining occurrences of technology that are different than would be expected on the basis of broad industry trends can serve as a worthwhile research objective. In such instances, exceptions may either "prove" or "improve" chronologies by explaining divergent cases.

The typologies defined in thematic studies illustrate regional variations in the industry as well as differences in archaeological approaches. There is widespread agreement that residential sites like logging camps, townsites, and sawmill settlements have archaeological research potential. Archaeological remains of other features, especially those related to transporting logs, may also have information value but are more likely to be valued for the associative or commemorative reasons described under National Register of Historic Places criteria A or C. Some typologies are deliberately general to accommodate future discoveries of unanticipated variation. In Minnesota, for example, Birk (1997, 1999) used two basic categories: habitation or complex properties and transportation properties. Similarly, in Utah, Merritt and Ayres (2014) break down railroad tie production sites into domestic, transport, and processing functions. Like Birk, Moffatt et al. (2011) used the categories "habitation" and "transportation." Habitation subtypes used in Wisconsin refer to more specific logging functions and architectural features: State of Maine–style (camboose) camps (see chapter 8), dingle-style camps, transitional camps, railroad logging camps, railroad car camps, log driving camps, timber cruiser camps, and farms operated by lumber companies. Typologies of transportation properties also reflect chronological differences: the Pine Stage defined by Moffatt et al. (2011) includes dams, booms, log landings and rollways, sled roads, and supply (tote) roads while the later Railroad Stage includes grades, bridges and trestles, and maintenance facilities. Some typologies reflect regional differences, especially in log transportation. Western examples include chutes, flumes, and inclines required because of steep terrain (Beidle 1992; Stein 1993), while turpentine camps and tent camps are included in the South (Sherman 2001). Most of these thematic studies discuss potential research topics that might make sites eligible under criterion D.

Other Sources: Historical Documents and Oral History

Historical archaeology is defined in part by its use of multiple sources: material evidence, written documents, and oral history. Some researchers encounter a wealth of nonarchaeological information about the specific sites they are studying, while others are faced with making interpretations without any site-specific information beyond what is recovered archaeologically.

However, even when sites are not mentioned specifically in historic documents like maps, diaries, or company records, land ownership and property tax records sometimes reveal the likely operators and periods of logging activity. For example, no written sources specifically mentioned the Triangle Lake site (20ST123) in Northern Michigan, but land records for the area surrounding this logging camp included three contracts for timber cutting rights, with two of these specifically for hemlock and dated 1895 and 1898. Artifacts found at the site indicated an occupation during the 1890s, confirming that it likely supplied bark to a nearby tannery for tannic acid extraction (Gilbert/Commonwealth 1985). Census records enumerating occupants of specific logging camps are rare, but, when available, they provide a wealth of demographic information. Lumbermen from LaCrosse, Wisconsin, started the Wind River Lumber Company in Washington, and archaeologists studying their Camp No. 3 discovered the occupants were listed in the 1910 census (Mack 2005). Few had local ties and more were born in Wisconsin (seven), where the company originated, than in Washington (one), showing the tendency of companies to bring experienced employees from previous areas of operation. Listed occupations reflect the camp's organization and the use of steam-powered logging equipment. The presence of a single teamster indicates the presence of horses, but six employees had jobs related to steam-powered machinery. The only women present were a cook and waitress.

Seldom is there a documentary record for a logging camp as complete as that of the Underhill camp on Grand Island, Michigan, operated by the Timber Department of Cleveland-Cliffs Iron Company (Hardwick 2008). This included a wealth of corporate records as well as oral history and photographs. The camp operated from 1916 to 1920, and documents mention details like the influenza epidemic of 1918, which spread to the camp and affected production. An archaeological study utilized only a small fraction of this exceedingly rich documentary record but included (as an appendix) a detailed inventory of all tools, equipment, and supplies present just before the camp ceased operation (Hardwick 2008). The 1920 U.S. Census also listed the site's occupants. Contracts and inspection reports detail work scheduling and the quantities and species of timber cut.

Many historic photos of logging and milling operations exist in repositories across the United States, but they often lack documentation adequate for research use. The temporary or portable nature of architecture limited the survival of structures at many sites, but New Deal photographers documented 1930s logging camps in Wisconsin and Minnesota (HABS/HAER 1936; Lee 1937). When available for vanished structures, well-documented historic photos enhance the interpretation of their material remains. Vaughan (1990) used archival sources, including photographs, to analyze the remains of buildings that had been burned or demolished at two logging camps in California's Stanislaus National Forest. Archaeological inventory at the sawmill town of Millwood, located in California's Giant Sequoia region, relied on historic photos to help identify the mill location and related company structures, such as the horse barn and warehouse (Gassaway and Kline 2011).

Documents, including photographs, usually reflect the perspectives of those in positions of power, but oral history is similar to archaeology in that they both tend to counter this bias. Unfortunately, potential interviewees with firsthand knowledge of nineteenth-century operations were already scarce when archaeologists began studying logging sites in the 1970s and 1980s, and earlier recordings or transcripts are rare. However, oral history has played an important role in archaeological studies of daily life at early twentieth-century logging camps. In some cases, researchers formulated specific interview questions to enhance the recovery and interpretation of archaeological data. Stencel (2000) conducted archaeologically informed oral history interviews with former employees of the Goodman Lumber Company Camp E in northern Wisconsin, which cut maple, hemlock, and basswood circa 1919–1922. In conjunction with fieldwork, these interviews identified locations of structures and activity areas. Boswell et al. (1990) admit that the majority of information in their archaeological report on the Pratt River Logging Camp in western Washington came from oral and documentary sources, but archaeological findings often prompted their informants to recall information and thus "grounded" the study. Oral history and archaeology agreed on the railroad-related storage and maintenance function of the site but disagreed regarding specific construction techniques and the types of equipment present (Boswell et al. 1990). Gregory (2001) also pointed out the importance of oral informants for identifying and interpreting archaeological remains. He gives an example of a relatively inconspicuous area of soils impregnated with petroleum residues that was identified by an interviewee as the former location of a railroad roundhouse. Hills et al. (1996) carried out an ambitious and productive oral history program in conjunction with archaeology at the site of the 1928–1940 Weyerhaeuser Camp 2 site in Oregon. Along with documents and archaeology, 14 interviews with former residents shed light on many aspects of life at this large camp. Archaeology and oral history identified and described an employee "tent town" not mentioned in written records.

Field Characteristics and Data Collection

The field characteristics of lumber industry sites vary in accordance with factors like original construction materials, age, duration of occupation, vegetation cover, amount of postabandonment disturbance, and soil formation rates. In general, camps were more transitory than mill settlements and their remains less conspicuous. Large quantities of surface refuse remain at some later or disturbed sites, while all artifacts are concealed under vegetation and soil at others. However, artifacts commonly occur near the surface within organic soil horizons. To deal with very shallow cultural material, researchers in California and Wisconsin developed excavation techniques using metal detectors and minimal clearing with rakes or trowels (Bruhy et al. 1993; Elliott 1990; Overstreet et al. 1983; Vaughan 1990) (Figure 3.1). However, relatively deep feature deposits with complex stratification also exist at some sites, including privy pits, cellars, and wells or water holes (Cramer 2003; Drake 2003; Dunham and Branstner 1995; Hahn et al. 2005; Hardwick 2008). In certain settings, significant amounts of organic deposition occurred after abandonment. At a California mill settlement called Falk, more than 30 centimeters of redwood duff accumulated on top of structures that had collapsed sometime after 1937 (Rich and Roscoe 2009). The remains of water-powered mills are often located in flood plains: four meters of sediment covered the timber base of the Gallatin Mill in Pennsylvania (Frye et al. 1995). Archaeologists used pumps during excavation around the wooden foundation of the Robinson-Herrling Sawmill in Wisconsin (McQueen 1995; Pletka 1993). In some cases, short-term priorities led to the construction of mill settlements in poorly drained or flood prone areas. At the Good Land Mill in Louisiana, the water table extended to within

Figure 3.1. Archaeologists mapping the remains of a late nineteenth-century logging camp (47FR142) in northern Wisconsin, investigated by Great Lakes Archaeological Research Center (Overstreet 1982; Overstreet et al. 1983. Photo [1981] by author, courtesy USDA Forest Service, Hiawatha National Forest, Gladstone, Mich.)

20 centimeters of the ground surface (Whelan and Pearson 1999). Another Louisiana cypress mill included 175 structures built inside a "ring levee" kept dry by pumps (Hahn and Schwab 1998).

Researchers investigating logging sites commonly encounter evidence of unauthorized artifact collecting (looting), an illegal activity on federally managed public lands and in most state-managed areas (Franzen 1992; Gassaway and Kline 2011; Gilbert/Commonwealth 1988; Richner 1986). Before the advent of metal detectors, relic hunters targeted glass bottles, and their digging damaged many logging industry sites. Ryan (1976: 48) describes most camp sites in northern Minnesota as "pretty well dug up" by artifact collectors. As a result, the presence of unbroken bottles on the surface may indicate that sites remain undisturbed (Gilbert/Commonwealth 1985, 1988). In order to prevent their future loss, in certain situations archaeologists have systematically collected intact bottles and other at-risk items found on the surface (Franzen 1995).

Many studies of logging industry sites have been limited to surface evidence of artifacts and structural features. Some researchers supplemented surface observations with small-scale subsurface exploratory techniques like shovel tests, soil coring, and metal detecting. Among studies that conducted actual excavation, most involved areas less than 15 m^2, often in the form of test units rather than larger blocks. In some settings, artifacts could be exposed by simply clearing vegetation and organic surface debris. Elliott's (1990) study of the circa 1919–1922 Tate Creek railroad logging camp in Northern California included controlled surface collection and excavation, but because cultural material was very close to the surface, researchers simply raked away forest litter and duff to expose shallow material lying above the mineral soil horizon. Samples and diagnostic artifacts were collected, but most items were analyzed in the field and left on site.

Compared to some other types of sites, relatively few archaeological studies of the lumber industry have collected data through advanced remote sensing or geophysical survey techniques. A study underway at a nineteenth-century logging camp in Northern Michigan employed magnetic susceptibility readings indicative of iron-rich or organic "hot spots" in order to identify areas for test excavation (Surface-Evans 2017). In recent years, several projects have used LiDAR (light detection and ranging) technology to identify archaeological traces of previous logging in America's forests. In conjunction with geographic information system (GIS) software, these studies document distributional patterns that are not always obvious at ground level. For example, LiDAR identified literally thousands of charcoal-burning platforms (hearths) in the forests of Connecticut and Pennsylvania (Johnson et al. 2015; Sams et al. 2012). This technology has also located other types of logging-related sites, such as tar kilns in South Carolina (Southerlin 2013) and logging dams in Minnesota (Arnott et al. 2013). Some of these Minnesota dams as well as two 1915 splash dams in Northern Idaho were mapped in more detail using ground-based three-dimensional (3D) laser scanning (Arnott et al. 2013; USDA Forest Service 2012).

Artifact Analysis

When analyzing artifacts from logging industry sites, archaeologists have used classification systems that group different types of objects into categories intended to reflect their original functions or contexts. To varying degrees, these approaches either follow or were inspired by South's (1977) system that includes the following categories: kitchen, architecture, furniture, arms, clothing, personal, tobacco pipes, and activities. For tracking functional variability of structures and activity areas within sites, Overstreet et al. (1983) divided artifacts into kitchen, architecture, personal, and activities categories, as well as various subcategories. They also demonstrated the importance of trade catalogs as a key source for identifying artifact functions. In particular, the Marshall-Wells Hardware Company catalog (1912) included not only tools and hardware, but even cookhouse supplies specifically for logging camps. At another Wisconsin camp, Richner (1986) used the following categories to identify the function of different structures: domestic, work and transportation, personal, and architectural. Some researchers devised artifact classification systems by modifying categories from one or more previously developed systems. Aspects of three different classification systems were used to define a system for analyzing material from worker housing at two sawmill settlements in Louisiana (Adams 1980; South 1977; Sprague 1981). The dominant categories were domestic (household or kitchen), personal (clothing/adornment or indulgences, including alcohol), health/hygiene, and architecture (Hahn and Schwab 1998; Whelan and Pearson 1999). Historical archaeologists in the western states have preferred a system developed by Sprague (1981): personal, domestic, architectural, industrial/commerce, and transportation related. Sprague's system was often modified for different sites. For example, Elliott (1990) adapted it to classify artifacts into subcategories within four broad categories: architectural, kitchen, personal, and industrial. Varying approaches may have helped accommodate particular site characteristics, but variation between classification systems makes it difficult to compare assemblages from different studies.

A Brief Critique

One criticism of logging industry archaeology is simply that not enough of it has been done. Dependence on federal Section 106 funding has limited the size and scope of many projects. Progress has also been slow because of the "preserve and avoid" strategies implemented by many land management agencies in response to Section 106. These identify and protect sites but generate relatively small amounts of data compared to more intensive studies. As a result, huge areas have been inventoried and numerous sites located, but information on these sites is often restricted to that derived from surface remains or very limited exploratory excavation. Far fewer projects included large excavations and detailed site-specific historical research. The resulting pool of known sites is thus large and geographically broad, but shallow in terms of detailed information. This approach produces an interesting example of research bias. Because the relevant data are more accessible, archaeologists can end up emphasizing the same topics stressed by company owners and managers: the technologies used to transport logs and transform them into lumber. Workers, of course, focused on their jobs, but they remained concerned with food, working and living conditions, and ultimately their physical and social reproduction. Material remains relating to domestic topics are often less obvious and more difficult to recover than those related to the cutting, transportation, and processing of logs. Dominant political and economic forces silenced or obscured certain groups, camouflaged certain processes, and tended to discount both the realities and rights of the poor and disenfranchised.

Many studies discussed in this book consist of unpublished manuscripts, technical reports, theses, or dissertations on file with various federal and state agencies or universities but not readily available to researchers. These sources comprise what is sometimes called the "gray literature" of archaeology. In recent years, universities and agencies posted some of these documents online, but many are still very difficult to locate and obtain. Access to some state and federal documents has been deliberately restricted because they contain locational information that relic collectors could use to illegally remove artifacts from public lands. Some of these restrictions make it difficult even for professional archaeologists to access reports. Most unpublished reports are produced in small quantities for very limited distribution. Recommended solutions to these problems usually involve calls for allocating increased funding for preparing and disseminating professional reports as well as generating written (or other media) summaries or popular accounts for the public. This is certainly a worthwhile goal, but most of the funding for this work comes from variable and unpredictable federal budget appropriations. Some recommendations might be easier to implement than obtaining budget increases, however. Many early reports are not available in digital format, and photocopies can be costly. The expense of travel and the potential difficulty of getting paper copies or remote access to digital media complicates comparative research using data from different states and regions. Increased emphasis on making unpublished reports available online is recommended.

There are several reasons the lumber industry sites studied thus far may not represent the full spectrum of sites that potentially exist. First and foremost, nearly all studies result from activities on public lands. This introduces bias favoring certain geographic or environmental zones. Public lands in the East are often "lands nobody wanted," resulting from property tax defaults that occurred after forests were cut and/or burned. In the West, public lands tend to be more arid, more rugged, at higher elevations, or less accessible than areas where private development has occurred. In both the East and the West, early lumber industry sites located on what later became productive agricultural land are unlikely to have been studied, whereas sites in cutover areas, with poorer soils and harsher climates unsuitable for agriculture, are more likely now to be on public land and available for study. Certain types of sites are also less likely to have been studied: compared to logging camps, mill sites frequently coincide with locations where towns or cities developed and are not well preserved or accessible.

Given its importance to the American economy, logging seems underrepresented in the archaeological literature compared to other extractive industries, especially mining. Using Jstor (http://www.jstor.org 2017), a search for the words *mine*, *mining*, *smelter*, *furnace*, *logging*, *lumber*, *sawmill*, or *pulp* in the titles of articles, comments, and reviews found that titles with mining-related terms far outnumbered those with logging-related terms in the journals *IA, The Journal of the Society for Industrial Archeology* and *Historical Archaeology*. A cursory examination of the HABS/HAER database reveals the same underrepresentation of logging and the lumber industry. The advanced search tool for the Library of Congress HABS/HAER/HALS prints and photographs online catalog (2017) located four times as many survey titles with mining-related terms as those with logging-related terms. In some areas, mining preceded other extractive industries, and the earliest sites in a given area attract interest. Researchers may be less interested in the logging industry because its remnants are less visible. Logging sites, especially camps, were widely dispersed while mining activity was often concentrated. Logging camp sites often lack visible surface remains, while mining often creates conspicuous and long-lasting landscape features. The ready availability of building stone in many mining areas resulted in more persistent structural remains. Logging was also more transient than most American industries. Even sawmill towns had relatively short life expectancies, with both machinery and portable buildings easily moved by rail to the next large block of forest scheduled for cutting or sold if the company's timber supply was exhausted. Labor union organizers enjoyed more success among miners than loggers, and noteworthy strikes and violence occurred at mining sites. This affected the frequency of written documentation and commemorative activities. Perhaps as a result of one or more of these factors, the logging industry lacks coordinated, long-term, and regionally focused archaeological research projects, like those of mining in Nevada and Michigan (Hardesty 2010; White 2017).

The sample of logging sites studied by archaeologists also includes geographic gaps. Although Maine and the Northeast played a key role in the industry's development, far more lumber industry sites have been investigated in more recently developed regions (Figure 3.2). In fact, this literature survey failed to locate any publications or reports on archaeological excavation specifically focused on nineteenth-century logging in Maine. To better understand this situation, copies of all archaeological site forms for logging camps were obtained courtesy of the Maine Historical Commission. Only one of these sites appears to date to Maine's early to mid-nineteenth-century logging boom, and it was reported by a relic collector and apparently never field verified. Based on a decision made by the Maine Historical Commission in 1976, the state gave priority to the identification, evaluation, and protection of colonial period sites dating from the early seventeenth to the mid-eighteenth centuries. They recognized later sites such as those relating to the nineteenth-century logging industry as deserving attention, but at a "secondary level." This explains the lack of archaeological interest in sites linked to the earliest industrial-scale logging in America.

Decisions in other states, such as Texas and Mississippi, also limited the likelihood of investigations at lumber industry sites. Guidelines promulgated in 1999 by the Texas Historical Commission declared that most late nineteenth- and early twentieth-century sites in Texas "do not warrant extensive excavations because the data recovered will not make a substantive contribution to our understanding of the human activities that occurred at these sites" (Denton 1999: 13). Barile (2004) and Young (2004) document how this bias against more recent sites representing poor people and lacking standing architectural features resulted in African Americans being underrepresented in historical and archaeological research. The state listed surviving mansions of lumber company owners on the National Register of Historic Places but considered the archaeological remains of worker housing to lack "integrity" because standing structures had deteriorated or been demolished. This effectively excluded many lumber industry sites once occupied by African Americans from being studied and recognized

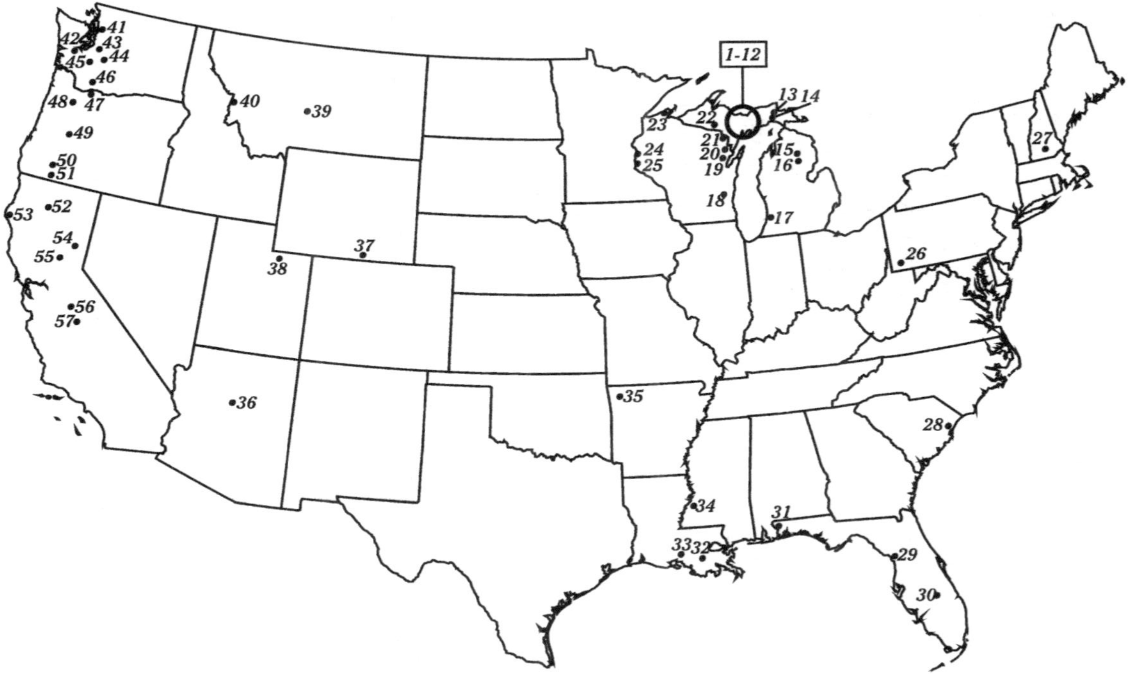

Figure 3.2. Locations of selected sites mentioned in text: 1. Trespass Camboose; 2. Mason's Purchase; 3. Vanwinkle and Montague camp, 20DE272; 4. Bay De Noquet camp 6; 5. Bay De Noquet camp 5; 6. 20DE234; 7. Moses Camp; 8. First Nahma Sawmill; 9. Triangle Lake; 10. Coalwood; 11. Underhill camp; 12. South Manistique; 13. Pendill's Mill; 14. Dick Townsite; 15. Kneeland and Bigelow camp; 16. Big Creek Dam; 17. Blendon's Landing; 18. Robinson-Herrling Mill; 19. Sherry and Gerry camp; 20. Goodman Lumber Company Camp E; 21. Menominee–Bayshore Company camp; 22. Elmwood; 23. Trout Point; 24. Marine Mill; 25. Hersey and Bean Mill; 26. Gallatin Mill; 27. Nichols–Colby Mill; 28. Singleton Mill; 29. Rosewood; 30. Nalaka; 31. Molino Mills; 32. Goodland Cypress Company; 33. Donner; 34. Brown-Cozzens Mill; 35. Van Winkle's Mill; 36. Saginaw and Manistee Company Camps 3 and 18; 37. Wyoming Tie Hack camps; 38. Standard Timber Company camps; 39. Bunkhouse Creek camp; 40. Sheep Creek; 41. Japanese Gulch; 42. Yama; 43. Barneston; 44. Pratt River; 45. Manley–Moore Company; 46. Wind River Company Camp 3; 47. Bingham's camp; 48. Porter-Castens/Ladee camp; 49. Shevlin-Hixon Lava Caves camp; 50. Pelican Bay Company (Hub) camp; 51. Weyerhaeuser Camp 2; 52. Tate Creek camp; 53. Falk; 54. TY-3687; 55. Cole and Nelson Mill; 56. West Side Lumber Company Camps; 57. Enterprise Mill. (Drawing by Brady Ray Nelson, Genesis Graphics.)

through the Section 106 process. In 2013, archaeologists specializing in African American sites and the Texas Historical Commission cooperated on a planning document that finally recognized the potential significance of late nineteenth- and early twentieth-century sites, including sawmill settlements and logging camps (McDavid et al. 2013). Dixon and Smith (2017) addressed similar issues regarding circa 1860s–1880s sites occupied by Chinese timber workers in Nevada. Some considered these sites too small, ephemeral, or disturbed for meaningful research, but when studied as a group, they provided a valuable record of a marginalized group of workers (Dixon and Smith 2017).

Although this book discusses published and unpublished literature from all geographic regions, to some extent it emphasizes the Great Lakes states of Michigan, Wisconsin, and Minnesota. In part, this is due to the fact that the author conducted research in this region and had better access to its unpublished ("gray") literature. However, this emphasis also makes sense in terms of geography and chronology. One author described the pine era in the Great Lakes region between 1870 and 1900 as the industry's "Golden Age" (Rickaby 1926: 18) and another calls it the "full flowering" (Cox 2010: 149) of American lumbering. The Great Lakes area represents an intermediate position in the chronological and geographic progression of the industry, which started in Maine in the early nineteenth century and extended throughout the West and South by the early twentieth century. The white pine–logging era in the Great Lakes included both early small-scale operations that might be considered "pre-industrial" and the start of the modern industrial era when lumbermen adopted scientific management, expanded vertical integration, and maximized economies of scale. Workers and capital migrated from Maine and other parts of the Northeast to the Great Lakes, and the Great Lakes later supplied these same resources for developing the industry in the West and South. For all these reasons, Great Lakes archaeology warrants attention from logging industry researchers in other regions.

Research Questions

Many studies of lumber industry sites share a deficiency that is common within historical archaeology: a lack of explicit questions or problem statements to guide research. Work at logging sites reflects the lack of attention to theoretical issues that characterized all of historical archaeology in the late

1980s (Honerkamp 1988: 5; Cleland 1988). As of the late 1990s, similar concerns persisted regarding the lack of adequate theoretical discussion (Lees 1999; Schuyler 1999), and this problem has continued into the twenty-first century. According to Delle (2008: 123), "much of American historical archaeology is atheoretical (if not antitheoretical)." These critics point out that theory can steer research toward "questions that count" (Cleland 1988) and "big questions of anthropological interest" (Lees 1999: 63). Another related recommendation that applies to logging industry research is for "broader comparison" (Schuyler 1999: 68), and transregional patterns emphasized in this book highlight this potential. Another recommendation is for using system-wide rather than single-site perspectives to focus on "extractive networks" (Cleland 1988: 16). Lipe (2009) suggests that one step to improve both theoretical shortcomings and dissemination of research results would be for federal agencies to involve larger numbers of archaeologists during Section 106 consultation in the hope that better research designs can be formulated.

The extension of context development and research questions beyond the logging industry to include other types of rural work camps offers a promising approach (HARD 2013). In developing a nationwide NRHP context for labor, Fracchia et al. (2014) identify key site types for understanding how labor contributed to Euro-American settlement of rural areas: logging camps, railroad camps, temporary mining communities, and migrant agricultural camps. Maniery (2002) compared aspects of sanitation, health, and diet at a twentieth-century dam construction camp in California with similar features in other western labor camps, including some associated with logging.

Besides the general problem of inadequate research designs, some studies of lumber industry sites may rely too heavily on historical documents relative to archaeology. An interdisciplinary approach makes historical archaeology a powerful tool for exploring the past, but when sources disagree or when the results of field investigations are sparse, some researchers put more faith in documents than in the archaeological record (Deagan 1988: 10; Feinman 1997). Historical archaeologists study complex systems and settings by working across arbitrary disciplinary boundaries, but obstacles such as small sample sizes, poor preservation of sites and artifacts, and the expense of fieldwork, especially excavation, create an inherent risk of relying too heavily on documents for expediency's sake rather than because a site truly lacks archaeological potential.

The following paragraphs summarize some approaches that explicitly mention research questions or discuss theoretical perspectives. In a pioneering study to provide baseline data for future work at logging camps, Overstreet (1982: 70) recommended that researchers pursue "humanistic, historical, and local interest questions," as well as topics informed by social science, such as technological change, ethnicity, status differences, and human impacts on the environment. In general, later studies in the Great Lakes pursued similar topics and questions (Richner 1986; Bruhy et al. 1993; Dunham and Franzen 1997; Franzen 1992, 1995, 1999; Dunham and Branstner 1995). For example, test excavation at four Michigan camps examined "foodways, ethnicity, and living conditions" (Dunham and Branstner 1995: 29). Branstner and Dunham (1997) summarized the development of lumbering-related research questions in the Great Lakes region by comparing two symposia. In 1984, Theodore Karamanski of Loyola University organized a session called "Cultural Resources of the Logging Frontier" at the annual meeting of the Society for Historical Archaeology (SHA) in Williamsburg, Virginia. Four papers were presented on spatial analysis, the use of historical documents dealing with the lumber industry, and the evaluation of specific features like logging dams. Twelve years later, another session entitled "The Upper Great Lakes Lumber Industry: An Interdisciplinary Perspective" was held at the 1996 SHA annual meeting in Cincinnati, Ohio, with 11 papers presented. These papers illustrate expanded interest in a variety of lumber industry topics. The session's published abstract cites an interdisciplinary interest by archaeologists and historians in "social and economic processes" through studies emphasizing technology, social history, labor history, and settlement patterns (Branstner and Dunham 1997). Seven of the papers given were later revised and published in the *Michigan Archaeologist* (Branstner and Dunham 1997).

A number of studies have explored the role of ethnicity and race at logging industry sites in different regions (Bastian 1999; Bastian and Rutter 1987; Campbell 2017; Carlson 2017; Douglass 2000, 2002; Drake 2003, 2018; Hahn and Schwab 1998; Hartse 2017; Lee 2008; Solury 2004; Whelan and Pearson 1999). To varying degrees and with different emphases, they deal with the social and material ways ethnic minorities reacted to the challenges posed by discrimination, exploitation, and the generally difficult living and working conditions of industrial logging. Several of these studies demonstrate the synergistic value of using three distinct sources: archaeology, oral history, and written documents, especially when they portray the same people, places, or events in very different ways (Bastian and Rutter 1987; Bastian 1999; Drake 2003, 2018).

Along with those from the Great Lakes, some early California studies of the lumber industry stand out in the effort to define archaeological research questions. Based on historical research and oral history, as well as archaeological surveys, James Rock (1986) suggested research topics related to railroad logging. He later joined a group of other California archaeologists and historians who outlined four interrelated domains for research at logging industry sites: environmental, technological, economic, and social/cultural (Tamez et al. 1988). Although these efforts were limited to advice on how future archaeological research might be done, several later studies developed site-specific archaeological research designs based on their recommendations. Elliott's (1990) data recovery project at the circa 1919–1922 Tate Creek railroad logging camp in Northern California focused on spatial patterning potentially related to social status. No evidence of ethnicity was discovered, and patterns identified appeared to correlate with occupational status. The recommendations of Tamez et al. (1988) also influenced studies in adjacent states.

In Oregon, Hills et al. (1996) formulated an ambitious research agenda for archaeological study at Weyerhaeuser Camp 2, examining variability within this large railroad logging settlement in terms of food, health care, housing, consumer choice, and the role of women. This was intended to determine whether the spatial arrangement of the site reflected socioeconomic or demographic variation, and archaeology identified clear differences among four separate living areas (see chapter 7). Similarly, researchers at the Lava Caves camp in Oregon targeted a wide range of questions related to commodity markets, consumer choice, subsistence patterns, and material cultural variability among different social groups (Bowyer et al. 1995). Most noteworthy relative to the site's function within the lumber industry were artifacts indicating the presence of numerous women and children. Married workers lived with their families in separate housing units, and their wives took care of shopping, cooking, and laundry. Many companies preferred hiring married men during this period, and the savings from eliminating or reducing communal bunkhouse and mess hall costs may have compensated for the expense of providing portable family dwellings. Howe (2015) addresses this issue directly in his dialectical/relational study of daily life at the Coalwood logging settlement in Michigan, where artifacts related to work that took place within the home, usually done by women, are interpreted as evidence of the "free labor" that often contributed to commodity production.

The following four chapters summarize the results of previous archaeological studies in a way that builds on these more problem-oriented or theoretically explicit studies. Each chapter is organized around a central theme: technology, spatial patterning and the environment, daily life, and social organization. Loosely based on previous efforts to organize archaeological research efforts at lumber industry sites in California and the Great Lakes states, these chapters broadly categorize the different kinds of information that might be recovered through archaeology. However, a more specific focus is necessary to guide research at any given site, and researchers should expect to encounter many connections between variables that appear to relate to different themes.

4

Driving Forces?

The Technology of Cutting, Moving, and Processing Logs

> Tools and technologies are not inherently good or bad, inevitable or autonomous, progressive or regressive; . . . they are merely vehicles and applications of human beings.
>
> Joel Dinerstein, "Technology and Its Discontents," (2006), 591

Before describing specific archaeological studies of logging technology, this chapter presents an overview of major technological changes that spread relatively quickly across different regions. These changes define a functional and chronological context for research at logging industry sites. During the second half of the nineteenth century, improved transportation, marketing, and communication between regions enabled new ideas and products to diffuse rapidly. Articles and advertisements in widely circulated trade journals like *American Lumberman* spread the word on new equipment and machinery. Loggers adapted new technologies for use in different regions. For example, a Michigan lumberman invented the first portable steam engines for moving logs with steel cables, but these machines had greater impacts in other regions. In the Northwest, steep topography made this equipment essential, and steam engines placed on barges pulled logs out of vast southern cypress swamps. Large diameter trees made the chainsaw especially useful in the Northwest, but it soon spread nationwide, even for cutting small diameter trees for pulpwood. Broad chronological and geographic variations in technology are known from documentary sources, but archaeology can discern smaller-scale differences. Logging-site archaeology requires an understanding of technological context in order to discover possible correlations with nontechnical phenomena. In a sense, we need to know about technology in order to get beyond technology. The following section is based on documents rather than archaeology and summarizes the technology used in different stages of the logging process. Descriptions of archaeological studies that focus on technology follow this historical overview.

Historical Background—Logging Technology

Felling and Bucking

Axes and crosscut saws played key roles during the first century of industrial logging in North America. The single-bit American felling axe was developed during the eighteenth century as local blacksmiths manufactured tools for American loggers. It was heavier, with a shorter and wider blade, than axes made in Europe. The peavy joined the logger's essential tool kit during the mid-nineteenth century. It had an approximately five-foot wooden handle, tipped with an iron spike and a hinged hook, greatly enhancing the ability to manipulate logs by hand (Figure 4.1). Early loggers used single-bit American felling axes to cut (fell) trees, but once logs were on the ground, they employed crosscut saws to cut (buck) trunks into shorter sections. However, the cutting edge of these saws lacked a mechanism to carry sawdust out from the cut, and they would bind if used in a horizontal position to cut standing trees. Two significant changes in these basic logging tools took place during the second half of the nineteenth century. Crosscut saws with sawdust-expelling teeth called rakers became available in the 1870s and could be used for felling as well as bucking. Loggers adopted this tool quickly, as felling with a saw was faster and easier than with an axe (Figure 4.2). Rector (1953: 206) cites an 1874 letter indicating that a Wisconsin company made the change to the modified crosscut in the mid-1870s, and an 1876 article notes that this shift taking place throughout the industry was advantageous to company owners because sawyers could be paid less than "choppers."

Even after loggers adopted saws for felling, they still used axes for some tasks, including notching trees on the side facing the desired direction of fall prior to completing felling cuts with a saw from the opposite side, delimbing after trees were on the ground, and clearing roads and trails. First developed around 1850, double-bit axes eventually replaced single-bits. The advantages of double over single bits included better balance and aerodynamics. Having two separate blades that could be sharpened for different tasks also provided versatility: one could be finely honed for felling, while

Figure 4.1. Lumberjacks using peaveys to remove logs from the banks of Little Fork River, Koochiching County, Minnesota. (Photo [1937] by Russell Lee. Library of Congress, Prints and Photographs Division, FSA/OWI Collection, LC-USF34-030035-E.)

Figure 4.2. Loggers and their tools after cutting Douglas fir, Washington, circa 1905. (National Archives and Records Administration, USDA Forest Service Photograph Collection, Negative No. 16191, Washington, D.C.)

the other could be kept at a more obtuse and less fragile angle for more abrasive tasks (Jager 1999; Weisgerber 1999). Double-bits became widespread in the northeastern states between 1860 and 1870 (Mercer 1929: 11) and by the early 1880s in the Pacific Northwest (Cox 1974: 228). Jager (1999) refers to this change as a "small revolution" in harvest technology. Felling and bucking resisted mechanization because they required a unique strategy based on the characteristics of individual trees and their surroundings, and the tools used for this work remained essentially unchanged from the 1880s until the post–World War II advent of chainsaws (Lucia 1981).

Yarding, Skidding, Decking, Loading

Once they were on the ground, delimbed, and cut into manageable lengths, scattered logs were usually dragged (skidded) from cutting areas to centralized collection points and temporarily piled in stacks (decks) until the next leg of their journey, although some were immediately loaded onto sleighs, wagons, railroad cars, or trucks. If cutting areas were close enough, some logs could immediately be stacked adjacent to the rivers, lakes, railroads, or roads that would carry them to mills. The bulk and weight of logs made transportation a major logging expense. Oxen supplied the power for skidding, decking (stacking), and loading at early operations in all regions, but horses soon replaced them. Each animal had advantages and disadvantages, with the hardier but slower-moving oxen having one peculiar advantage: loggers preferred them as an emergency food source if supplies ran low. The most efficient skidding with draft animals required frozen ground, and sleigh hauling required snow and below-freezing temperatures. So-called Big Wheels pulled by draft animals were a Michigan innovation for moving logs that did not require winter conditions (Figure 4.3). One end of a log would be suspended above the ground from an axle that connected two large (about 10-foot diameter) iron-rimmed wooden wheels. Supposedly developed by Cyrus Overpack in the 1870s, Big Wheels were limited to relatively level areas without too much undergrowth (Quinlan 1975). In warmer parts of the country, loggers used Big Wheels and wagons instead of sleighs.

Horace Butters of Ludington, Michigan, obtained the first patent for steam-powered skidding machinery using wire rope or steel cables in 1883. The history of this innovation provides another example of transregional connections within the logging industry. Born in Maine, Butters worked as logger on the Penobscot River, moved to Michigan in 1851 where he established his own successful mill, and finally migrated to North Carolina

Figure 4.3. Hauling logs with big wheels pulled by mule team, Irwin County, Georgia. (Photo [1903] by E. Block. National Archives and Records Administration, USDA Forest Service Photograph Collection, Negative No. 40094. Washington, D.C.)

in 1888 where he produced cypress lumber. He licensed his patent to the Lidgerwood Manufacturing Company of New York, which refined his concept, obtained additional patents, and marketed nationally (Butters 1896: 256–258). With cables that could extend 2,000 feet, this machine was sometimes placed on "pull boats," which enabled logging in previously inaccessible southern swamps.

Depending on their geographic setting and available technology, some operations reduced the steps in the transportation process by skidding logs directly from cutting areas to landings along rivers or railroads that would carry them to mills. For example, certain operations maximized the penetration of railroad spurs into stands being harvested to the extent that all logs were within the reach of cables pulled by portable steam engines called donkeys. In later years, gas-powered tractors replaced both draft animals and steam engines.

In certain areas, a delay took place between the adoption of steam power for sawmills and railroads and the widespread use of steam machinery for initial transport during forest operations. Although steam-powered skidding and loading equipment was invented in the Great Lakes, it was during

Figure 4.4. Steam-powered machinery moving logs in the Cascade Mountains near Seattle, Washington. (Photo [ca. 1918] by Darius Kinsey, labeled "steel spar skidder with swinging loading boom." Library of Congress Prints and Photographs Division, Washington, D.C.)

the late nineteenth and early twentieth centuries in the Pacific Northwest and South where this technology became most dominant for yarding and loading (Figure 4.4). At first, cables powered by steam engines pulled logs along the surface in "ground lead" logging (Rajala 1993). This method was soon improved by running cables through pulleys mounted on top of specially trimmed spar trees so that only one end of a log dragged on the ground. This was called "high lead" logging, and it doubled production but also increased accidents. This process of technological evolution culminated in "skyline" logging, where multiple cables mounted on spar trees or portable steel towers lifted logs completely off the ground as they were carried. Internal combustion engines replaced steam engines for cable skidding in the 1930s to 1940s. Where topography allowed, tractors provided another internal combustion option for moving logs. Many early crawler tractors used for logging were produced by the Caterpillar Company and called "Cats." These vehicles could be modified for earth moving and road construction (as bulldozers).

Hauling Logs to Mills

The final step in the transportation of logs to mills relied on water (river drives or towed rafts), railroads (steam or diesel), or internal combustion engines (trucks). Many variations and combinations of transportation methods occurred. Only coniferous species like pine, cedar, spruce, and fir were buoyant enough to float down rivers or tow across lakes in booms. One company in Michigan drove logs partway down a river and then transferred them to railroad cars for the rest of their journey to avoid a wide and shallow channel segment where logs were often lost (Benchley et al. 1993). Where lakes provided convenient connections between cutting areas and mills or where rivers widened to the extent that current became inadequate, large numbers of logs assembled into rafts could be towed, held together in a "boom"—a perimeter of large logs connected by chains. Geographic scale and power sources for towing varied over time and space. Short trips across slack-water stretches of rivers used winches or turnbuckles powered by men or animals. Longer trips, including some on the Great Lakes or Pacific Ocean, relied on tugs powered by steam or internal combustion engines, but storms could produce huge losses. As with other expenses, companies considered transportation costs in relation to anticipated lumber prices. Climate and weather dictated the rhythm of early logging because it depended on river drives and sleigh hauling. Snowless or unusually warm winters prevented sleigh hauling, and droughts reduced river flows to levels inadequate for carrying logs (or for generating power to operate saws). Besides speeding up transportation and sawing, steam power offered two other advantages: locational flexibility and freedom from seasonal limitations.

The advent of steam power increased the amount of capital needed to pursue logging, and this led to increased operational scale, consolidation, and monopoly. Railroads were the quintessential steam technology. Researchers studying multiple logging operations or sites sometimes begin by sorting them into two categories based on whether or not they utilized railroads. Nonbuoyant hardwood species like maple, beech, and oak couldn't be easily transported to mills until railroad networks developed. Steam engines were used to power locomotives and sawmills long before they became common in the woods for dragging logs to centralized collection points. In a sense, harvesting had to speed up and match the increasing capacity of steam-powered railroads and mills.

Steam power revolutionized log transportation, and Bajema (1991) calls railroads the single most important technological development in the industry's history. Logging companies constructed both narrow- and standard-gauge systems in accordance with the locations of their timber stands and mills. Because using railroads for logging was such an important innovation, controversy exists regarding who first employed it. Although not the earliest example, Rector (1953: 196) credits the 1877 construction of the Lake George and Muskegon logging railroad in Michigan, highly successful in a low snow year and widely publicized, for the rapid spread of railroad logging. During the mid-nineteenth century, loggers depleted pine timber within several miles of water features, but additional pine remained in areas farther away from water.

Sawing Logs into Lumber

National lumber production grew rapidly as sawmill technology improved, despite local and regional variations in the scale and pace of change. Improved mill technology stimulated changes in harvesting: increased sawing capacity required more logs. Steam replaced water power for mills, but it took longer to penetrate into the woods beyond railroad grades. As a result, for many years the industry straddled different technological eras by obtaining power from steam as well as from older sources like wind, water, and the muscles of animals and men. For a while, technological enhancements like the perfection of river drives through watershed modifications and cooperation between companies helped water transport systems keep pace with mill improvements. However, technical and organizational changes periodically forced "speed-ups" in worker productivity. The installation of multiple steam-powered band saws at large mills stands out among these changes. Although the first experiments with band saws date to the early nineteenth century, it wasn't until the 1880s that band saw designs finally met the production and reliability goals of large mill owners (Prescott 1910). Various other changes chronicle the evolution of sawing technology from water power through various types of steam-powered systems. However, the salvage or resale of obsolete or unwanted equipment makes it difficult for archaeologists to discern the exact nature of sawing technology at many abandoned mill sites.

Patterns of Technological Change

The 1870s and 1880s represent a transitional period for both technology and living conditions: the shift from single-bit axes to crosscut saws and double-bit axes for felling trees; the replacement of oxen with horses for transporting logs; the provision of better food for loggers; and the introduction of architectural changes reflecting larger operations with increased specialization and separation of activities (Rector 1953; Larson 1949: 78, 176–178; MacKay 1978: 80, 89; Karamanski 1989: 67–69). Rector (1953: 208) calls the 1870s a "period of trial and experimentation in logging methods," which included larger sleighs and sprinklers to maintain ice roads. By the 1880s, steam railroads and stand-alone steam donkey engines for skidding became well established. Steam engines also powered cranes used for stacking and loading logs. By circa 1910–1920 a variety of steam-powered machines were available, including the Clyde Skidder, the American Log Loader, and the McGiffert Self-Propelling Log Loader (Rector 1953: 244–247). The McLean Loader was basically a steam-powered crane mounted on a railroad car (Rector 1953: 123). Some machinery moved by rail could be placed on heavy timber runners and then dragged into position using its own power and cables attached to trees or stumps.

Capital-intensive advances in mechanization, such as railroads and other steam-powered equipment, greatly favored large companies to the disadvantage of smaller ones. The trend toward bigger camps, bigger loads, and bigger sawmills continued (Rector 1953: 214). To the extent that they remained in business, some smaller companies maintained older technology. Later, as cutting depleted the best timber for lumber production everywhere except the Northwest, overall production declined and pulpwood dominated the harvest in many areas. During the 1930s, trucks, tractors, and portable mills became more available. Even though large companies remained in control, internal combustion engines facilitated smaller-scale, independent operators for harvesting and initial transport. Because they retained ownership of most timberlands, large companies didn't fear competition from landless loggers, and from the 1930s through the 1950s most large lumber producers got out of logging operations and instead contracted with independent loggers (jobbers) to supply their mills with logs.

Technological changes that occurred later in the first half of the twentieth century include the shift from steam to electricity for powering mills, the replacement of railroads by truck logging, and the circa 1940s adoption of the chainsaw (Lucia 1981; Williams 1989: 315–320). These developments continued to reduce the number of workers necessary for harvest operations, and mid-twentieth-century development of road systems and other infrastructure (often constructed with public funds) eventually made logging camps unnecessary. The development of gas engine technology along with improved roads made truck logging less capital intensive than railroad logging and facilitated an increase in smaller individual harvesting operations from the 1930s forward, the so-called Gyppo loggers (Williams 1989: 319). They operated as independent contractors, freeing large companies from the expense and risks of operating camps.

Explaining why some operations used combinations of technologies or why some used obsolete technology can be potentially informative. Examples include the persistence of river drives after railroads became dominant and the continuation of railroad logging after most firms adopted truck hauling. The last log drive on the Clearwater River in Idaho took place in 1971; the last Weyerhaeuser Company railroad hauling logs in Oregon closed in 1990; and the last steam sawmill in Oregon operated until 1969 (Wisner 1995). Large, highly capitalized corporations as well as small "haywire" operators sometimes worked in adjacent areas. Early adopters of new technology and anachronistic holdovers of old technology highlight the dynamics of various economic and social processes.

Archaeology of Lumber Industry Technology

Researchers who identify themselves as "Industrial Archaeologists" have been criticized for being overly concerned about technology and not paying enough attention to the social aspects of industrialization, while others identifying as "Historical Archaeologists" have been accused of not giving industrial sites attention commensurate with the historical importance of the industrial revolution. Martin (2009: 294) calls some of these critiques "unfortunate" and "unnecessary" distractions that divide researchers without advancing knowledge about the past. There is a growing consensus that both the technical and social aspects of industrialization are important, and that there is room for everyone regardless of whether one pursues industrial or historical archaeology. In fact, some have suggested that less attention be paid to these labels, as their purported specialties are far from being mutually exclusive (Beaudry 2005).

While some technology studies tend to be more descriptive than explanatory, they provide data potentially usable for problem-oriented research in the future. Some of this information would have been lost forever were it not for this work. Constructed to withstand heavy weights, intense pressure, vibration, impacts, and weathering, structures related to transportation and

Figure 4.5. Foundation for steam-powered machinery at Faber Sawmill, destroyed by 1896 hurricane. Atsena Otie, Cedar Key National Wildlife Refuge, Florida. (Photo [2017] by author.)

processing technology often persist as aboveground ruins. Remains of masonry foundations or platforms with embedded iron bolts or rods that once anchored massive boilers and engines frequently occur at former steam-powered sawmill sites (Figure 4.5). Large metal components were occasionally abandoned (Figure 4.6). Throughout many forests, men, horses, and machines moved massive amounts of soil as they cut and filled to create level railroad grades. Logging crews constructed long earthen embankments across flood plains adjacent to logging dams. Records do not survive for many operations, and material remains help resolve conflicting accounts based on multiple archival and oral history sources, identifying specific technologies used at particular places and times (Rock 1986).

Although one historian opined that "All sawmills were fundamentally alike in basic structure" (Maybee 1960: 30), archaeological remains of machinery and tools exhibit significant variation. However, preservation issues exist. As a result of the transitory nature of this industry (caused by rapid timber depletion), mill operators usually removed technological infrastructure to sell or reuse elsewhere rather than abandoning it. If machinery became unserviceable or obsolete, it could be recycled as scrap metal.

Figure 4.6. Abandoned boiler from circa 1876–1896 Eagle Pencil Company Mill, Cedar Key, Florida. Boiler is about 12 feet long, upside down, with fire box on the left. Note covering of oysters and other mollusks. (Photo [2017] by author.)

Features in or close to waterways, like dams, booms, docks, and mills were often destroyed by floods or clearing of channels for navigation. Storms frequently demolished mills built very close to lake or ocean shores in an attempt to minimize transportation costs. Because of this, the archaeological remains of residential or domestic areas are sometimes better preserved than the industrial remains at mill settlements. After rails were removed, more recent forest users converted logging railroad grades into roadways. Written records provide details on technology, but these sources can be biased. Accenting the concerns of management, they provide information on technology but tend to neglect the impacts of technology on workers. Historical photographs often lack adequate information about when and where they were taken. In part, because of these limitations, some archaeological studies focus on describing or explaining technology in a way that overlooks social factors.

The Historic American Engineering Record (HAER) includes information about logging industry technology (both extant structures and ruins) useful for archaeological studies of less well-preserved features. Photography and measured drawings form the bulk of HAER documentation.

Written documentation varies greatly, ranging from one-page forms with minimal information to comprehensive and detailed histories that place sites in well-developed contexts. Examples include a circa 1880 logging dam in northern Wisconsin (HABS/HAER 1980; Vogel 1980), a water-powered sawmill (HABS/HAER 1984), and early twentieth-century charcoal-making pits in New Jersey (HABS/HAER 1937). Wisner (1995) prepared both a narrative report and HABS/HAER documentation (1997) about a "last-of-its-kind" steam-powered 1938–1939 Oregon sawmill that was still operating commercially in the 1960s. Besides marshaling physical evidence, Wisner conducted interviews and utilized historic documents and photographs to make a comparative record available for archaeologists to use when analyzing sawmill sites where much of the machinery has been removed.

Water Power for Transport and Sawing

Walter and Merritt (2008) estimated that over 65,000 water-powered mills had been constructed in the eastern United States by 1840, with especially high densities in the mid-Atlantic Piedmont. This estimate includes grist mills, but many also sawed lumber or powered saws along with other machinery. Single families with minimal hired help operated most of these small mills, many of which predated the industrial "take-off" that defines the focus of this book. However, the cumulative impacts of small but numerous dams significantly affected waterways. Deep deposits of fine sediments built up behind dams and buried stream-side wetlands. Most aboveground remnants of late eighteenth- through mid-nineteenth-century water-powered sawmills in the Northeast are not well preserved. One exception was the Nichols–Colby Mill in New Hampshire, recorded by the Historic American Buildings Survey in the 1930s (Penn and Parks 1975; HABS/HAER 1984). Built in the early nineteenth century, the mill had circular-saw machinery, installed between 1839 and 1840. Reaction-type water wheels were added around 1850. Measured drawings prepared before this relatively intact mill was destroyed provide a baseline for archaeologists studying the remains of water-powered sawmills at other locations.

In all regions, the earliest water-powered mills supplied lumber for local needs at fur trade or mining settlements, forts, and other relatively isolated communities. Water-wheel and sawing technology improved, and as industrial logging spread from the Northeast to the Great Lakes during the mid-1800s, water-powered mills still produced most of the lumber being sawn. The water-powered mill sites discussed here operated for varying periods of time between about 1807 and 1885. Wet sediments often preserve wooden timber or log foundations of mills built in or adjacent to stream channels (Borden 1995; Blair 2001; Branstner 1999; Frye et al. 1995; Heizer 1947; McQueen 1995; Pletka 1993). Timbers identified include white oak in Pennsylvania and Wisconsin (Frye et al. 1995; McQueen 1995) and sugar pine in California (Heizer 1947). Other wood remains encountered include headraces and tailraces. Adjacent dams are sometimes better preserved than mill remains, and some consist of timber cribs filled with earth and stone. Determining the types of saws and water wheels once used is challenging in the absence of historic accounts but is sometimes possible based on the configuration of other features or fragments of broken machinery found in excavation units within or adjacent to mill foundations. Examples include fragments of turbines (Pletka 1993; McQueen 1995; Frye et al. 1995), flutter wheels (Branstner 1999; Frye et al. 1995), and a tub wheel (Borden 1995). Because of their locations in or adjacent to stream channels, mill sites face many preservation issues. Besides exposure to floods and erosion, machinery salvage and the clearing of channels for navigation after abandonment damaged many sites. For example, at the Mill Creek site in Michigan, dam segments were well preserved, but researchers found no traces of the sluice, spillway, or other mill components. However, the adjacent settlement provided a wealth of information about the residents and activities besides lumber production (Martin 1985).

Only a few features related to the transportation of logs using river drives have been studied in detail. Fortunately, documentation of a well-preserved logging dam in Wisconsin provides a comparative record to use when analyzing less well-preserved sites (HABS/HAER 1980; Vogel 1980). An interdisciplinary study on the influence of logging on the main stem of the Indian River in Michigan's Upper Peninsula established a large-scale context for studying these features (Benchley et al. 1993; Benchley 1997). No excavations took place, but this study included detailed recording of logging dam remains as well as fluvial geomorphology investigations. Remnants of 10 dams show that they were constructed of logs (both hewn and round), spikes, bolts, brush, and sand. Large rocks and clay were generally not available in these areas. The Chicago Lumber Company used these dams to transport pine logs from the 1880s through the early 1900s. Benchley et al. (1993) identified how logging dams could have slightly different functions. Although they all held back water that could be systematically released to flush logs downstream, some backed water up into existing lake basins to

Figure 4.7. Timber sluiceway of circa 1905 logging dam in Oscoda County, Michigan (20OD25). (Photo by John Halsey, courtesy State of Michigan Archaeological Site File, Lansing.)

store for later release, some helped push logs through shallow downstream areas, and one pooled water into an area where logs were collected and put on railroad cars. After the company constructed this railroad to avoid the lower portion of the river where logs frequently became jammed or lost in side channels, river drives only occurred on the upper portion.

Good in-stream preservation of logging dams is relatively rare due to floods, erosion, and the deliberate removal of structures to facilitate navigation. However, Halsey et al. (1997) describe an unusually well-preserved logging dam in Michigan's Oscoda County consisting of extensive earthen embankments and a wooden sluiceway (Figure 4.7). Based on land ownership and tax records, it was probably built between 1901 and 1905 and is the best preserved feature of its kind in Michigan. There must have been hundreds or even thousands of such logging dams built, and the authors remark that its "survival is providential, its condition exceptional" (Halsey et al. 1997: 124). The Louisiana Division of Archaeology (2015) documented a 758-foot-long logging-style dam in an unusual context. It was built across the Red River in 1864 by the Union Army under the supervision of Lieutenant Colonel Joseph Bailey, an experienced Wisconsin lumberman. As a result, a fleet of Union gunboats stranded by low water and facing certain capture or destruction escaped downstream when the water level rose. This unusual dam was built without formal engineering input using materials "at-hand" in the same "folk technology" tradition as Great Lakes logging dams (Vogel 1980). Archaeological excavation during a low-water episode exposed well-preserved remains and previously unknown construction details.

If rivers were too far away from cutting areas or otherwise unsuited for log transportation, loggers sometimes diverted water from streams or springs into trough-like structures called flumes, especially in the mountains of western North America. Smith (1992) described archaeological remains of the Blue Ridge flume in California's Shasta and Tehama Counties. This circa 1872–1878 V-shaped flume carried rough-sawn pine lumber 42 miles from the Cascade Mountains to the Sacramento Valley and gained attention as an "architectural spectacle." Structural remains consisted of rock piers, scattered lumber, and hardware (braces, bolts, galvanized sheet metal). Refuse associated with cabin sites used by flume tenders included Chinese ceramics and opium tins.

Similar to flumes, but relying primarily on gravity and lubricants instead of water, chutes carried logs down steep slopes to collection points where other forms of conveyance, usually rail or river, took over. Cort Sims (1983) provides an overview of logging chute technology and describes examples of these features remaining in northern Idaho. Cables or ropes pulled by men, horses, oxen, or steam engines sometimes assisted gravity in moving logs down chutes. Grease, oil, and, when possible, water or ice reduced friction, but in some cases measures were required to keep logs from traveling too fast! Sims (1983) suggests chutes varied in terms of function and style and could be studied to reveal the dynamics of technological change. Archaeological remains of three log chutes in Idaho ranged from 2,400 to 9,300 feet in length and dropped between 800 and 1,100 vertical feet. Logs used in their construction were identified as western larch or Douglas fir. Associated artifacts included containers for the oil and grease used to reduce friction.

Maniery (1991) documented surface remains at an early twentieth-century chute system in the Plumas National Forest in northeastern California consisting of a main chute two miles long, five branches, the ruins of six trestles, and three logging camps. Artifacts all predated 1915 and included hoops and slats from 40-gallon barrels that once held grease used to reduce friction in less steep sections. Segments of wire rope and cable indicate a steam donkey pulled "trains" of logs down the chute. Refuse deposits define the main camp area, which probably consisted of portable structures. Using log chutes to take advantage of gravity as a free energy source had to be weighed against the expense of their construction, operation, and the reduced value of logs damaged during transport. Frequent injuries and fatalities among workers and bystanders may have also been considered. Logs sliding down chutes reached high speeds, and accidents occurred when massive logs jumped the chutes and became airborne. Between 1930 and 1940, chutes were replaced by the construction of additional railroad spurs as well as by tractors and trucks powered by internal combustion engines.

Charcoal Production Technology

Although sawmills processed the majority of logs commercially harvested between the mid-nineteenth and early twentieth centuries, from colonial times until after World War I, kilns converted large quantities of wood into charcoal, which provided fuel for smelting iron, copper, and silver. Straka (2014) notes the geographic correlation of charcoal production sites with mining areas. For example, all suitable wood within 50 miles of Eureka, Nevada, disappeared after less than a decade of silver production (Straka 2014: 111). Iron production similarly impacted forests. Of Northern Michigan, Rominger (1881) observed that by the late 1870s all forests had been cut around the area's iron mines and blast furnaces. Charcoal production was the most time consuming and expensive part of iron-making, requiring over 50 percent of the workers employed by furnaces or forges (Frye and Frye 1989: 53, citing Paskoff 1983: 29). Colliers made charcoal in permanent brick or stone kilns and in more easily constructed temporary charcoal "pits," where stacked mounds of wood were covered with layers of soil and carefully tended by "burners" to avoid complete combustion (Figure 4.8). To maintain the coverings and allow proper air flow, workers climbed onto these mounds during combustion and occasionally fell through. These features are sometimes called platforms, ovens, earthen kilns, or hearths instead of "pits," a term which is a holdover from an ancient method of charcoal production. Prior to the Civil War, temporary structures produced almost all charcoal. Although eventually replaced by coal, charcoal production peaked in 1890 and remained important until after World War I. HABS/

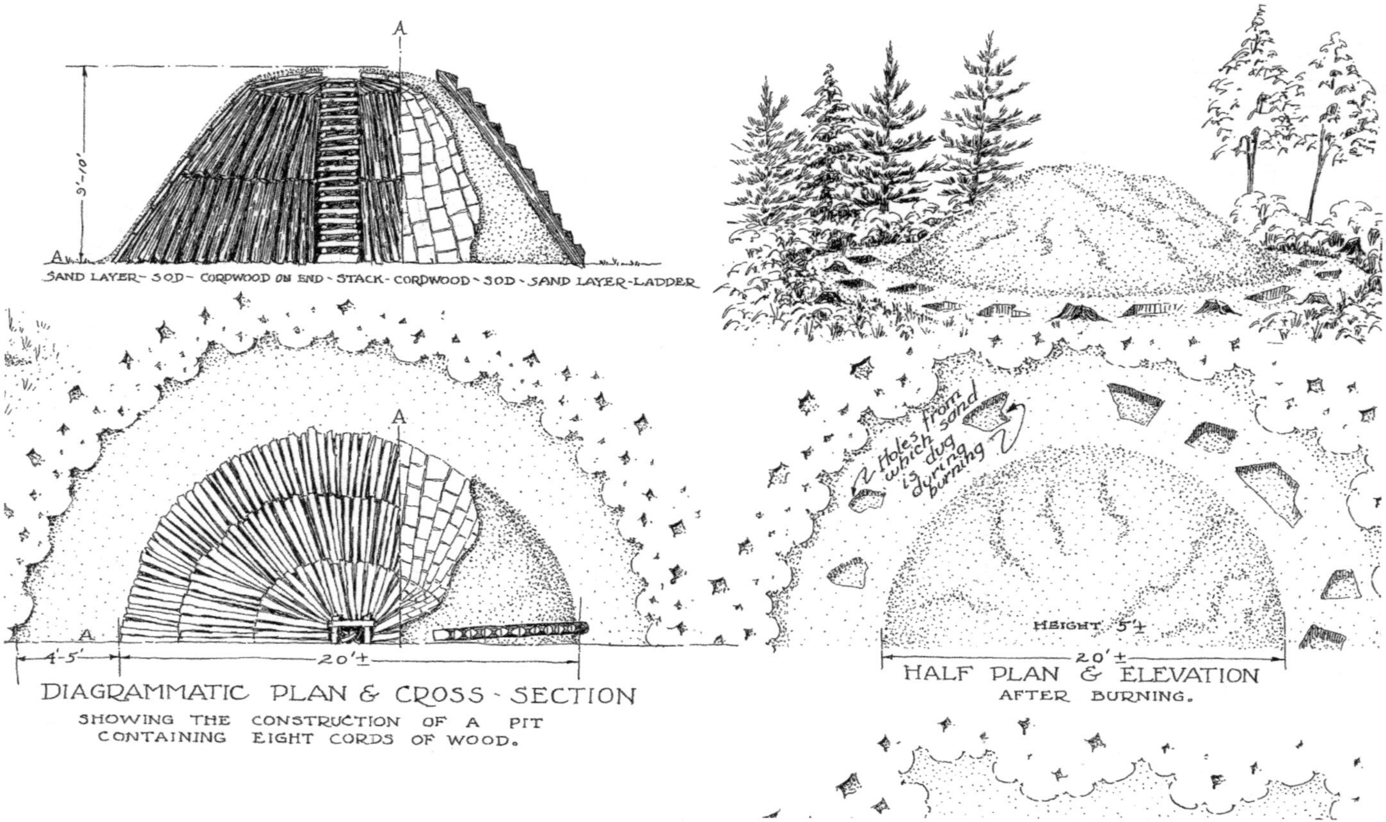

Figure 4.8. Charcoal pits, Lakehurst, Ocean County, New Jersey. (Drawings [1936] by Frederick A. Eckhart. Library of Congress, Prints and Photographs Division, HABS, Reproduction No. HABS NJ, 15-LAK.V, 1.)

HAER (2012) documented intact or partially standing masonry kilns, and O'Rourke (1997) analyzed different construction methods based on archaeological excavation at masonry kilns in Northern Michigan.

Corporate records provide few details about making charcoal in temporary earth-covered platforms or mounds, but archaeology sheds some light on this little-known activity (Figure 4.9). Based on excavation and surface evidence, researchers in Missouri, Maryland, and Nevada identified the size, shape, and environmental setting of temporary kiln sites along with associated features, such as roads and worker habitations (Frye and Frye 1989; Reno 1996; Straka 2014; Wettstaed 2003; Zeier 1987). Relatively consistent test trench profiles across three features excavated by Zeier (1987) included, from top to bottom, a charcoal and soil layer representing post-abandonment deposition and remains of a covering that controlled combustion; large chunks of charcoal mixed with smaller fragments and dust; and a thin layer of burned soil. Reno (1996) explained archaeological characteristics of pit kilns as a result of both global context and a "localized

Figure 4.9. Cross section of borrow trench along edge of circular feature where charcoal was produced in an earth-covered mound, 20AR8, 09-10-03-1039. The mound was located to the left of the trench shown in photo. Exposed by Lake Superior shoreline erosion, Alger County, Michigan. (Photo [2002] by Eric Drake, courtesy USDA Forest Service, Hiawatha National Forest, Gladstone, Mich.)

mode of production" that was not directly controlled by the companies who used the charcoal. In fact, some evidence suggested that charcoal makers resisted management's dominant ideology and the latest technology. This study could serve as the basis for comparison with charcoal production in other regions (Reno 1996). The social effects of the charcoal industry may have been as dramatic as the environmental impacts: "at its best, the job of making charcoal was not for any normal human being" (Sloane 1965: 57–58). Besides being dirty and dangerous, the work was not well paid.

Steam for Sawing and Transportation

A wealth of written documentation on logging railroads is available. Some of this information appears in historical studies specifically prepared to facilitate archaeology. For example, Glover's (1984) detailed study of former logging railroads in New Mexico's Lincoln National Forest provides the historical information necessary for archaeological studies of this system. Bajema and Brashler (1997) briefly describe the railroad, sawmill, shipyard, and village at Blendon Landing along the Grand River in southwestern Lower Michigan. An adjacent seven-mile-long railroad grade built in 1857 may represent one of the first times a railroad was constructed and used specifically to haul logs, although most of the authors' evidence came from historical rather than archaeological sources. They did locate an excavated cut for the grade and numerous fragments of strap iron rails (Bajema and Brashler 1997: 106). The authors see the railroad as key to what they call a "very early, if not the earliest, example of extensive clear-cutting." Records indicate that besides pine, this mill shipped black walnut, cherry, oak, and hickory to the East Coast and England. Rock (1986) points out what is perhaps the most important aspect of railroad logging: it required large amounts of capital. Railroads not only facilitated clear-cutting. In a sense, they almost required it to offset increased capital investment costs.

The steep terrain found in the western United States required specialized adaptations for transporting logs by rail. Besides harvesting timber, the Pratt River Logging Camp in western Washington, operated from 1936 to 1941 by the North Bend Lumber Company, served as a maintenance facility for the company's railroad network. Investigations there revealed a firebrick concentration from a steam engine boiler and a partially standing structure where sand was dried to use for increasing traction on steep or sharply curved railroad segments (Boswell et al. 1990). The site also included the remains of a small bunkhouse and four sections of railroad grade. At another railroad logging camp only 35 miles from Portland, Oregon, Paullin (2007) studied surface evidence and conducted detailed mapping supplemented by historical research. Originally Camp 1 of the Porter-Carstens Lumber Company, the Ladee Logging Company later used this camp. It operated from 1923 until 1931 and includes remains of what the author describes as "a spectacular engineering feat": a 3,500-foot inclined logging railroad segment (incline), where steam-powered cables raised and lowered rail cars on a steep (65%) grade. Based on detailed investigation of an early twentieth-century operation in Oregon, Tonsfeldt and Gray (2008) show how archaeological fieldwork can reveal the configuration of logging railroad networks and their relationship to environmental, economic, and technical variables.

Field investigations at steam sawmills often encounter well-preserved boiler and engine foundations that once held machinery in place. Construction materials varied, including logs and earth (Praetzellis and Praetzellis 1993), stone masonry (Brandon and Davidson 2005; Clouse and Steiner 2000; Kloss 2002; Terrell 2005), stone and brick (Day et al. 1997; Grinnan 2013), and brick and concrete (Southerlin 2008). Based on fragments of broken blades, researchers determined that circular saws had been used at two mills (Day et al. 1997; Praetzellis and Praetzellis 1993) and gang saws at another (Terrell 2005). Archaeologists have also recorded fly wheel locations (Brandon and Davidson 2005; Terrell 2005) as well as the presence of cisterns for supplying water to boilers or accommodating overflows (Brandon and Davidson 2005; Cramer 2003). One site included evidence of a previous water-powered mill and a second boiler location for a planing mill (Clouse and Steiner 2000). Remains of a sluiceway that carried logs to the mill from a nearby river survived at a site in Florida (Grinnan 2013). Even though steam engines enabled lumbermen to build mills without having to rely on moving water to power saws, they still constructed many steam mills along waterways because these locations remained advantageous for moving logs and lumber.

Archaeology that investigated both technological questions and social aspects of workers' daily life took place at a small 1880s sawmill settlement in California, operated by a resident owner-manager (Praetzellis and Praetzellis 1993). Field research identified the boiler and engine location, blacksmith area, and a cabin area where workers lived, including an associated refuse deposit. Double circular saws with replaceable teeth sawed lumber at this site. Based on its remote location and the owner's limited capital, researchers predicted simple, easy-to-maintain, and relatively inexpensive technology, local building materials, and limited landscape modifications. Evidence of a plain cylindrical wood-burning steam boiler rather than a more complex and fuel-efficient tubular boiler confirmed these expectations. Solid foundations for the boiler and steam engine were constructed with local stone, massive cedar logs, and soil. Finally, the site was laid out relative to local topography so that gravity assisted the movement of water and logs to the mill and of lumber away from the mill. Regarding social aspects of the settlement, researchers hypothesized that perhaps management exerted less social control because of the operation's small scale (12–16 employees), a lack of bureaucracy, and a relatively flat hierarchy (the owner was probably also the on-site manager). Numerous alcohol containers show accommodation of worker desires, but they only occur in nonindustrial areas of the site. This suggests that the owner controlled drinking only to ensure production, in contrast to patriarchal prohibition attempts by large companies supposedly intended to morally improve employees.

Hand Tools and Blacksmithing

Archaeological studies provide a way to test ideas about specific tool types. Information derived from written sources (historical documents) may lack the details or sample sizes to support generalization. Findings from archaeology in the Great Lakes region provide specific details on changes in hand tools that are consistent with the generalized chronology obtained from historical sources. Excavations recovered only single-bit axe heads from two Michigan logging camps dating to the late 1860s (chapter 8). Consistent with an 1870s operation, 32 single-bit axe heads, but no double-bits, were also recovered at the Sherry and Gerry site in Wisconsin (Bruhy et al. 1993). Perhaps representing the end of a transitional period, an 1880s Menominee–Bayshore Company camp in Wisconsin yielded 10 double-bit and one single-bit (Overstreet et al. 1983). Although saw sharpening was a specialized task, files used to sharpen axes and other tools are also common finds. The frequency of files (and fragments) found in domestic areas at some sites shows workers were responsible for sharpening tools on their own time (Elliott 1990; Durocher 2018).

At the Menominee–Bayshore camp in Wisconsin, one of the first logging camps investigated by archaeologists, the largest amount of material recovered came from the blacksmith shop, where artifact concentrations revealed the forge location and an adjacent scrap area. In fact, one researcher concluded that the blacksmith area had great potential for future study because it was essentially a "microcosm of logging camp life" (Overstreet 1982: 70). Besides the salvage, repair, fabrication, and modification of iron objects, the duties of some blacksmiths included horse-shoeing and saw-filing. Blacksmiths sometimes lived in structures attached to their work areas. Blacksmith areas can document technological variation: the Menominee–Bayshore camp excavated by Overstreet et al. (1983) included iron shoes for oxen, horses, and mules.

The current literature survey includes five archaeological projects with samples from blacksmithing areas: two mill settlements (Rich and Roscoe 2009; Valentino and Brandon 2005) and three logging camps (Gilbert/Commonwealth 1985; Overstreet et al. 1983; Vaughan 1990). All five studies encountered high artifact densities and concentrations of metal scrap. Coal, clinkers, or slag were noted at four. Horse-related items like shoes, calks, or shoe nails occurred at three (Overstreet et al. 1983; Gilbert/Commonwealth 1985; Vaughan 1990). Three studies identified specific anvil or forge locations, with Valentino and Brandon (2005) employing magnetic fractioning at Van Winkle's Mill to pinpoint the forge based on the differential distribution of hammer scale and iron shavings. The Van Winkle site also illustrated the post–Civil War transition from charcoal to coal as fuel for heating forges. At the California mill settlement of Falk, where the blacksmith shop was adjacent to the locomotive engine house, valves, pipe fragments, and other steam-related items were found (Rich and Roscoe 2009). The adjacent "break room" at Falk contained personal and domestic items resulting from changing clothes, eating meals, or taking rest breaks. Food-related items suggest that the company cookhouse delivered meals to the workers in this structure. Both rooms contained buttons and rivets from brand-name suppliers of work clothes, including two San Francisco firms: Levi Strauss and the Elosser Heynemann Company that produced the "Can't Bust 'Em" line.

Conclusions and Recommendations—Technology

Archaeological evidence showing concurrent use of both older and more recent technologies belies oversimplified typologies and chronologies. Although generalizations about regional movement and technological change provide a framework for comparative research, throughout the temporal and spatial progression of the industry, rates of change varied. Practices considered "old" or "new" sometimes coexisted, and archaeology can identify and explain some of these contrasts. Researchers should be attuned to unexpected variations in technology. Small firms might have to rely on older equipment. Variations can also be informative about technological innovation, idiosyncratic diversity, or even ill-advised operations that may not have been successful. For example, one twentieth-century camp foreman in Michigan, concerned that his operation's round-trip hauling distance could injure his horses, purchased two trucks. After the horses delivered each load of logs, the trucks carried them back to the cutting area. This logger later recalled, "We could not think of hauling the timber in the truck, all we could think of was the horses" (Karamanski et al. 1983: 104). Introducing new technology was not always successful. At the First Nahma Sawmill in Michigan, steam replaced water power in the 1850s, but the operators couldn't pay back loans that financed upgrades and had difficulty in maintaining machinery (Franzen and Drake 2010). Smaller operations found steam especially problematic: the relative benefits are much greater at higher levels of production (Atack et al. 2007). In a sense, the First Nahma Sawmill operation was too small for the most advantageous use of steam.

Both steam and internal combustion engines required capital investments that some loggers could not afford. As a result, they delayed acquisition of new machinery or purchased it gradually while continuing to use older technology. Even large companies combined older and newer types of equipment as they weighed the costs and benefits of technological changes. Instead of steam donkeys, Weyerhauser Camp 2 (ca. 1928–1940) in Oregon used nine gas-powered tractors (tracked vehicles or "cats") for yarding logs. However, the company retained two McGiffert loaders (steam-powered cranes mounted on railroad cars) for loading logs. Another example of mixed technology comes from Kneeland-Bigelow Company's Camp 8 in Northern Lower Peninsula Michigan, which operated between 1920 and 1927, just before the transition to mechanized logging in this area (Riordan 1980). It appears investment at this site started with camp amenities. The camp had a generator for electricity and could be reached by road, with several cars usually parked there. However, logging was still done with horses, crosscut saws, and axes.

In general, archaeological studies of lumber industry technology have described or explained the causes of technological change in terms of obstacles like remoteness and steep topography. Based on the high levels of mechanization eventually achieved, Holbrook (2016: 170) describes early to mid-twentieth-century logging in the Pacific Northwest as "a gigantic factory without a roof." Technological adaptations are usually interpreted simply as part of the quest for more timber and greater profits, but mechanization based on steam or internal combustion engines reduced corporate dependence on the skills and experience of labor, amounting to an overall "deskilling" of the workforce (Rajala 1989, 1993, 1999). Even though mechanization created some new roles for skilled workers, the total numbers of workers needed decreased. New technologies also transferred control over the pace of work from workers to machines. Rajala (1999) cites evidence, often in the words of owners and managers, that they initiated technological changes to establish a standardized "factory regime" less reliant on skilled workers. In contrast to the eventual success of workers in obtaining better camp conditions and shorter work hours, their resistance to the imposition of "dangerous and oppressive technologies" was far less vigorous and apparently failed to enhance safety or job security (Rajala 1999: 6).

5

More Than Artifacts

Spatial and Environmental Aspects of Logging

> The description, definition and identification of a place is thus always inevitably an intervention not only into geography but also, at least implicitly, into the (re)telling of the historical constitution of the present. It is another move in the continuing struggle over the delineation and characterization of space-time.
>
> Doreen Massey, "Places and Their Pasts" (1995), 190

There is a long and pervasive tradition in archaeology of studying the spatial dimensions of human behavior. This often involves a search for environmental variables that influence the distribution of archaeological evidence as well as spatial patterns reflecting different forms of economic and social organization. To some extent, archaeological studies dealing with spatial aspects of the logging industry vary depending on the scale of investigations. Landscape-level research involving multiple sites usually focuses on environmental and technological variables, while smaller-scale studies of intrasite patterns (including architecture) often consider social factors. For example, timber stand distribution, topography, and transportation technology may explain the locations of logging camps and sawmill settlements, but when analyzing the internal organization of sites, some researchers consider ideologies that supported social division and separation. Rather than discussing only studies that "borrow" environmental information from other disciplines in order to conduct spatial analysis, this chapter also presents archaeological research that generated new environmental data, often in ways that facilitate bridging the so-called nature-culture divide and understanding the creation of landscapes by combinations of industrial logging activities and natural processes beyond human control.

Some of the studies in this chapter show that archaeologists don't always "dig" when structural and artifactual evidence is visible on the surface.

Some researchers use analytic approaches similar to those of historical geography, with archaeology simply providing the location of sites or features and limited information on their age and function. Archaeology expands research opportunities beyond restrictions imposed by gaps in historic records and oral history. For example, historic maps and other records identifying railroad grades, roads, camps, and river modifications for a given area and time period may or may not exist, but surface remains often reveal the location, configuration, function, and approximate age of these features. They facilitate spatial studies based on data from archaeological surveys that did not include excavation. Even so, topics like intrasite organization and architecture usually require more intensive work, including subsurface investigation of residential/domestic areas.

Intrasite Spatial Organization and Architecture

In the absence of evidence like maps or photographs, studying the layout and internal variation of logging industry sites must rely on archaeology to determine the function of different structures and activity areas. Even though most logging camp structures were built for short-term use, wooden elements of some collapsed or decayed structures remain visible. In the Northeast and Great Lakes, distinctive earthen berms often outline former structure locations. Formed by piling soil against the outside bases of walls to insulate floors from winter drafts, these berms accurately depict the footprint of former buildings. In other regions, "flats" or leveled areas sometimes reveal where buildings once stood, especially in steep or more rugged areas. Determining the function of different structures usually depends on artifact analysis, although cases occur where the configuration of structural remains is distinctive enough to indicate their function, as in the case of root cellars, for example.

Identifying the function of different structures and activity areas requires familiarity with historical literature about logging. The lack of prior settlement and the distance of logging operations from population centers required the construction of isolated task-specific sites, which served both residential and industrial functions and ranged in size from one or two buildings to small towns. Space was needed for sleeping, cooking and dining, record-keeping, sheltering draft animals, bathing, storage, waste disposal, and industrial or craft activities, such as blacksmithing, carpentry, and tool maintenance. The extent of different activities and their arrangement varied. For example, detailed timber cruise reports (field estimates of forest product values) note the sizes of structures used for various functions at 18 circa 1916–1941 sites operated by the logging division of Cleveland-Cliffs Iron Company in Northern Michigan (Franzen 1984). Bunkhouses, mess halls, stables, barns, and hay sheds were always the largest structures, and based on size, there is little chance that they would be confused with offices, blacksmith shops, single-family residences, or other kinds of buildings found at camps. Depending on their design and materials, structures could be disassembled, moved, or abandoned and allowed to deteriorate. Some reuse by hunters, trappers, or squatters occurred after abandonment.

At most logging camp sites where the function of different structures has been reliably identified, excavation supplemented surface evidence. At the heart of every logging camp, most activity centered around the bunkhouse (men's camp) and a cookhouse (cook camp) that included space for dining. Former cookhouse locations are relatively conspicuous, given the large quantities of refuse produced. Middens including animal bones, food containers, and tableware often occur adjacent to these structures, although refuse disposal in later years took place farther from living areas. Refuse associated with bunkhouses is smaller in scale and usually consists of items associated with clothing, footwear, and smoking. An assemblage associated with a circa 1910 bunkhouse in Washington included a mix of architectural (such as nails and pane glass) and personal items (Mack 2005). Numerous buttons, suspender clips, rivets, buckles, snaps, eyelets, grommets, shoe tacks or nails, and shoe lace hooks showed that bunkhouse residents literally "threw" unwanted clothing and footwear "out the door." The author attributes the high frequency of these objects to the "wear and tear" of logging and the efforts of loggers to repair damaged items. This pattern appears in other regions as well: Richner (1986) recovered an assemblage dominated by personal items adjacent to a feature interpreted as a bunkhouse in northern Wisconsin.

Barns or stables for workhorses, as well as "hovels" for oxen, exhibit distinctive artifact associations (horse, mule, and oxen shoes; curry combs; haywire) and occasionally include surface characteristics indicating their function. At the Triangle Lake logging camp site in Michigan, the surface of a large rectangular structure location exhibited shallow drainage trenches and depressions that suggest two rows of stalls separated by a central aisle (Gilbert/Commonwealth 1985). Besides ox shoes and other transportation-related items, excavation in the former oxen hovel at the Sherry and Gerry camp in northern Wisconsin encountered organic deposits derived from animal waste and/or fodder (Bruhy et al. 1993). Camp builders often placed blacksmith shops near barns or stables. Artifacts associated with blacksmith shops include high densities of metal objects and distinctive remains from heating and using the forge (see chapter 4).

The remains of structures used for offices, equipment storage, saw-filing, or separate housing for higher status individuals have proved more difficult to identify. At several sites, based in part on a process of elimination, researchers identified camp office locations or the foreman's cabin, which often shared the same space (Bruhy et al. 1993; Horn 1987; Richner 1986; Stencel 2000). In Wisconsin, a 6 × 8-meter structure with a mix of personal, domestic, industrial, and architectural items, including a padlock, was identified as a camp office (Richner 1986). Likewise, along with tobacco and firearms items, a homemade alarm system led Horn (1987) to designate a structure location at Bingham's camp in Oregon as the foreman's cabin. Through a process of elimination, including its location on a knoll with a "commanding" view of the Goodman Lumber Company Camp E in Wisconsin, Stencel (2000) identified a 7 × 9-meter structure as a camp office. An example of a storage building comes from a 14 × 10.5-meter structure at a Wisconsin camp that apparently burned between logging seasons with supplies and equipment in place. Artifacts included "nested" stacks of enamelware plates and 10 double-bit axe heads (Overstreet 1982; Overstreet et al. 1983). At a Schroeder Lumber Company camp in northern Wisconsin, evidence of tool storage (a cache of 18 crosscut saw blades) led Richner (1986: 92) to identify a 5 × 10-meter feature as a "saw filer's shack."

The spatial arrangement of structures often reflects their functional relationships. Detailed sketches of early twentieth-century Michigan camps made by timber cruisers show that bunkhouses (men's camps) were always next to the cookhouse (Franzen 1984). Archaeology has confirmed this relationship and several other spatial associations between different buildings. For example, at a Menominee–Bayshore Company camp in Wisconsin, the root cellar was next to the cookhouse, the blacksmith's next to the stable, and storage for tools and kitchenware was adjacent to the cookhouse and bunkhouse (Overstreet 1982; Overstreet et al. 1983). At another Wisconsin camp, no structures were more than five meters from another structure, with the exception of the oxen hovel which was 25 meters away from all other structures (Bruhy et al. 1993). Relatively few privy locations have been confirmed through excavation, but they appear to be closely associated with bunkhouse locations (Hardwick 2008).

The location of refuse deposits in relation to structures is an important aspect of intrasite settlement plans. Hills et al. (1996) address this topic, describing "sheet trash" concentrations with varying content that identified building functions and activity areas. For example, rather than being hauled away, tobacco tins at Weyerhaeuser Camp 2 occur where tobacco use took place near the bunkhouse, dining car, and maintenance facilities. Whether located nearby or at a distance, the largest refuse deposits at Weyerhaeuser Camp 2 relate to the preparation and consumption of food. Even though this camp included some amenities and improvements desired by workers and reformers, refuse was often deposited immediately outside structures. Hauling to more distant locations apparently only occurred when areas close to structures appeared to be "full" (Hills et al. 1996). In general, both archaeology and documents suggest that, over time, food and kitchen waste disposal took place farther from camp structures. At four nineteenth-century camps in Michigan, kitchen refuse deposits occurred near cookhouse door openings (Dunham and Branstner 1995). Some twentieth-century camps exhibited kitchen refuse dumps along the edges of sites, but less refuse in central areas (Elliott 1990). At a 1923–1931 camp in Oregon, Paullin (2007) recorded a kitchen refuse dump "several hundred feet" from the cookshack. This reflects increased concerns about work camp sanitation in the twentieth century.

The number of structures in camps relates to the scale of logging operations and the extent to which activities became more specialized and separated over time. Using both historical site plans and sketch maps of well-preserved archaeological features at sites in Northern Michigan, Franzen (1984) compared eight pre-1910 logging camps to 13 post-1910 camps to see if trends inferred from documents would be reflected archaeologically in the overall number of separate structures. Earlier sites included three to five structures, while the more recent group ranged from six to twelve. Dinsmore (1985) tested a similar idea, but she sampled a different part of the state and divided her sample based on technology rather than chronology. The nine railroad logging camps in her sample averaged 3.8 structures, while the four non-railroad camps averaged two structures. Both of these studies confirmed a trend toward increased numbers of structures as operational scale increased along with occupational specialization and social differentiation. These changes took place in conjunction with technological developments, such as increased mechanization of forest operations and better railroad connections between camps, mills, and markets. This tendency toward increasing size culminated in the West where provisions for single-family housing and three- or four-man cabins for single men, rather than barracks, resulted in logging camps that could include hundreds of structures (Clark 2002; Hills et al. 1996).

Functional and social differentiation as well as topographic constraints and the modes of transportation servicing camps resulted in different layouts. Once early camps expanded to include more than two or three structures, they tended to form loose clusters surrounding an open central area (Dunham and Branstner 1995; Franzen 1984; Gilbert/Commonwealth 1985; Hardwick 2008; Horn 1987). The advent of railroad logging resulted in camps with distinctly linear arrangements. Records for large twentieth-century companies in the Great Lakes, including site plans and photographs, frequently document rectangular buildings arranged in rows with narrow (gable) ends facing transportation features (Franzen 1984). Archaeological examples of linear camp arrangements include sites in Michigan and West Virginia (Brashler 1991; Gilbert/Commonwealth 1988). When large companies began offering improved housing for workers during the early twentieth century, some logging camps became so large that they resembled small towns. The largest logging settlements included structures like schools, community halls, and substantial camp stores or commissaries. Companies arranged structures at these camps into separate functionally or socially similar zones, rather than simple linear alignments.

Weyerhaeuser Camp 2 in Oregon provides a good example of a large logging camp, with an archaeologically and historically documented layout consisting of sectors defined by functional and social differences, including four separate living areas, a food preparation and dining area, an industrial area for equipment maintenance, and an administrative area that included a store (Hills et al. 1996). The size and permanence of structures and the relative costs of discarded consumer goods identified the occupational, economic, and social status of different residential areas. These areas included family cabins, small portable bunkhouses for single men, residences for managers and higher paid workers ("brass row"), and "tent town" (canvas tents and homemade wooden structures occupied by necessity when company housing was not available or by choice to avoid rental costs). Another archaeological example of a large camp with a sectored layout is the Hub camp, operated in Oregon by the Pelican Bay Lumber Company in the mid- to late 1920s and investigated by Winema National Forest through detailed GPS (Global Positioning System) mapping of abundant surface remains (Clark 2002). At this camp, bachelor workers slept in railroad cars with bunks. This area also included an institutional kitchen and dining facilities in railroad cars. Workers with families resided separately in portable structures associated with abundant personal and domestic artifacts, including items representing women and children. The industrial portion of the site included blacksmithing debris, a grindstone, machine and engine parts, tobacco tins, and buttons and rivets from men's work clothes.

Archaeological studies of mill settlements designed, owned, and operated by lumber companies also documented evidence of spatial organization defined by a combination of functional and social differences. For example, a circa 1904–1916 sawmill settlement called Dick, located along a major railroad in Northern Michigan's Chippewa County, had a maximum population of about 400. Detailed mapping documented 150 surface features and defined industrial, commercial, and residential sectors of the site (Anderton et al. 1996). Another mill town in Northern Michigan, South Manistique, produced nearly one billion board feet of pine lumber between 1883 and 1899. An archaeological survey and test excavation project found evidence of at least 100 structures where 300–400 people lived and worked (Riordan and Barton 1982). Researchers easily distinguished industrial and residential sections. Sectored arrangements contrast with "preindustrial" layouts that lacked clear separation between domestic and industrial areas. At the circa 1822–1870 Wernwag Mill in West Virginia, the owner-manager lived close to the mill amid a cluster of industrial structures, an arrangement more characteristic of a craftsman than a capitalist (Shackel and Paulus 2010).

The expansion of railroad networks in the late nineteenth and early twentieth centuries enabled the establishment of mill settlements in interior areas away from large bodies of water. One example is Minertown (1899–1933) in northern Wisconsin, where Demeter et al. (2010) conducted detailed recording of surface features. Significant numbers of Kentuckians arrived in the Upper Great Lakes during the 1920s, and there is evidence of ethnic segregation in housing at Minertown. Researchers determined the function of many structural features by comparing archaeological evidence with historic photos and oral history accounts. The most prominent features included stone foundations, earthen berm outlines, and pits. These occurred in four sectors: industrial, early residential, late residential, and the barn area. Specific structures included the company store, a boarding house, and single-family residences. The researchers concluded that the site had potential for research on life in a company town and the community's economic and social organization (Demeter et al. 2010).

Depending on the type of structures originally present, as well as preservation and sampling issues, archaeological investigations can reveal specific architectural characteristics of former logging site structures. Because these buildings were intended for short-term use, few remain intact. Even though many historic photos of logging camps exist, very few are accompanied by information on dates, locations, and occupants, which severely limits their value for research. In some cases, inferences can be made about structures on the basis of the size and outline of berms or foundation remains. Variables like size, shape, floor plans, and internal segmentation are more accessible through archaeology than details of perishable features. Depending on climate conditions, length of time elapsed since abandonment, and the species of wood utilized, decayed cabin logs or sections of collapsed frame structures occasionally survive. Remains of minimal foundations for structures occur, usually brick piers or aligned rocks (Clark 2002; Morris et al. 1994; Whelan and Pearson 1999). Harder to detect, locations where small portable wood-frame shacks or cabins on wooden skids once stood have been identified by the surrounding refuse left behind and traces from leveling the ground surface prior to their placement (Brashler 1991; Vaughan 1990).

Archaeologists recording remnants of logging camp buildings often begin by trying to determine whether they used log or frame construction. At the risk of overgeneralizing, earlier, more remote, or less well-financed camps were usually constructed with logs, while frame buildings characterized later, more accessible camps associated with larger companies. One archaeological study looked at two camps in Arizona that illustrate a transition from log to frame construction: the Saginaw and Manistee Lumber Company's Camp 3 (ca. 1906–1910) and Camp 18 (ca. 1920–1922) (Morris et al. 1994). Camp 18 was a denser settlement with more frame and fewer log structures than Camp 3, and foundation stones were present at Camp 18 but absent at Camp 3 (Morris et al. 1994). This company only used portable frame structures at operations established after Camp 18.

Inferences about log structures (all of those discussed here utilized horizontal log construction) are sometimes based on remnants well enough preserved to identify wood species and notching techniques (Ayres 1983, 1996; Horn 1987). For example, at Bingham's camp in Oregon, aboveground structural remains were abundant, although none of the buildings were intact. Partially standing walls consisted of pine logs joined by saddle or V-notching (Horn 1987). Even when walls have deteriorated to the point where no surface evidence remains, fragments of logs embedded in earthen berms have been recovered (Richner 1986; Overstreet 1982; Overstreet et al. 1983; also see chapter 8). In an archaeological study focusing on partially standing log structures, Ayres (1983, 1996) looked at circa 1867–1930 sites in the Uinta Mountains of Utah. Workers living in these cabins produced railroad ties, bridge timbers, and fuel wood for the transcontinental railroad. Well-preserved log cabin remains fell into groups: pre-1912 and 1912–1930. Cabins built after 1912 used wire nails, frequently included lumber, were heated by stoves, and often included more than one door and window. They also utilized larger logs than earlier structures and exhibited more complex notching, sawn log ends, gable roofs, and wall coverings, such as newspapers. Earlier structures used cut nails, and included smaller logs, fireplaces, axe-cut log ends, hewn framing, shed roofs, saddle notching, and uncovered interior walls. They usually had just one door and not more than one window. Based on names carved or written on structure walls, site-specific documents mentioning occupants, and remains of Swedish-language newspapers used for chinking, Ayres attributed the circa 1912 changes to an influx of Swedish and other Scandinavian workers.

In more humid climates, fewer log or lumber components remain visible on the surface, especially at older sites. The earliest industrial-scale loggers in the Northeast and Great Lakes lived in square or rectangular horizontal log structures known as camboose shanties, notable for the presence of an open, indoor fire hearth (the camboose) used for both cooking and heating. In the Great Lakes region, these are also called "State of Maine–style" camps. All indoor activities, whether domestic or industrial, took place in this single room; the only other structure at these camps was the oxen hovel. Chapter 8 analyzes two archaeological examples of camboose shanties. Another distinctive type of log building revealed by earthen berm outlines (embankments) at Great Lakes logging camps is a long double structure where cooking/dining and bunkhouse sections connect end to end into a breezeway-like space called the "dingle" (Figure 5.1). In the Great Lakes region, several of these structures have been the subject of archaeological test excavation (Bruhy et al. 1993; Dunham and Branstner 1995; Dunham and

Figure 5.1. Dingle-style logging camp near Lincoln Pond, Maine. Cookhouse and bunkhouse are connected. (Photo [1902] by H. E. Tiemann. National Archives and Records Administration, USDA Forest Service Photograph Collection, Negative No. 29407. Washington, D.C.)

Franzen 1997; Overstreet 1982; Overstreet et al. 1983) (Figure 5.2). Known dingle-style camps generally predate 1910. Artifacts associated with food preparation and consumption indicate functional differences between the two sections of these camps. Starting in the late nineteenth century, loggers began building separate unconnected cookhouses and bunkhouses, probably in response to the increasing size of logging operations. Examples verified by excavation occur at a circa 1887–1897 Van Winkle and Montague camp in Northern Michigan (20DE272), the Trout Point camp in Wisconsin, and Bingham's camp in Oregon (Dunham and Branstner 1995; Horn 1987; Richner 1986).

As transportation networks expanded and camps became easier to supply (and potentially move), lumber frame construction became common (Figure 5.3). Archaeological excavations at sites in Michigan, Wisconsin, Washington, and California identified the location of wood frame structures based on evidence like nails, pane glass, tar paper, and lumber remnants (Boswell et al. 1990; Hardwick 2008; Miss et al. 2000; Rich and Roscoe

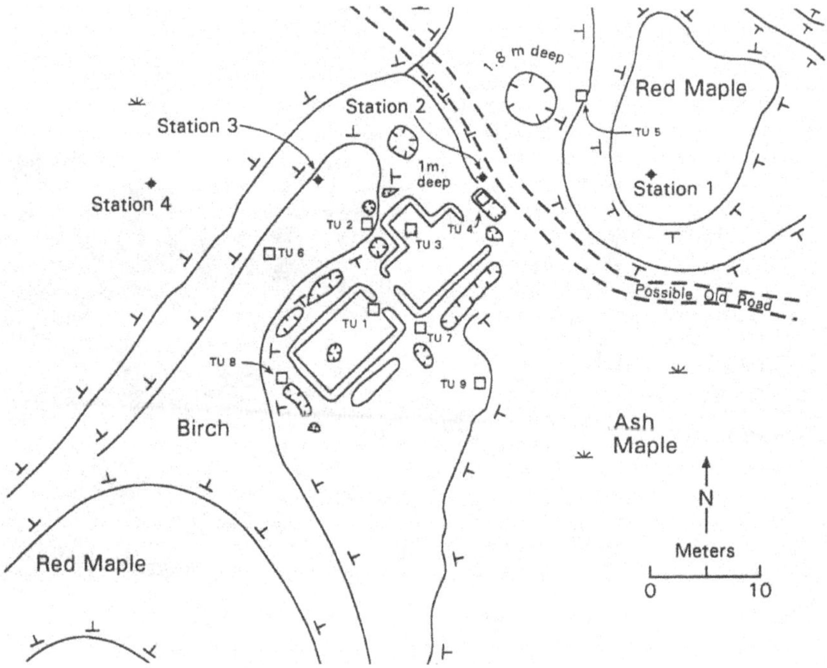

Figure 5.2. Site plan showing archaeological remains of circa 1875–1885 dingle-style logging camp (20DE234) investigated by Great Lakes Research. (Dunham and Branstner 1995; drawing [1995] by Great Lakes Research Inc., courtesy USDA Forest Service, Hiawatha National Forest, Gladstone, Mich.)

2009). Although it was eventually determined to be of limited value due to disturbance from highway and bridge construction as well as mixture with later refuse, test excavation in Oregon explored the collapsed remains of an unusual railroad logging camp built on top of a wooden framework adjacent to a railroad trestle crossing (Connolly et al. 2011). Sites with large quantities of structural debris suggest abandonment and in-place deterioration. Materials like nails, lumber, and tar paper are less abundant at locations where portable wood frame structures were removed after logging operations. At a large camp site in Oregon where families lived in portable dwellings transported by rail, bricks left from fireplaces and/or wood stoves marked former structure locations (Clark 2002). Several other sites in the West included archaeological evidence of portable housing (Bowyer et al. 1995; Hills et al. 1996; Vaughan 1990). At a circa 1903–1916 mill site in Louisiana, excavation documented locations of three portable single-family units (Whelan and Pearson 1999). Associated features included refuse deposits,

Figure 5.3. Railroad logging camp, Forest County, Wisconsin. (Photo [1937] by Russell Lee. Library of Congress, Prints and Photographs Division, FSA/OWI Collection, LC-USF34-010784-E [P&P] LOT 1112.)

privy pits, and brick concentrations representing foundation piers. Ceramics and container glass provided mean dates within the known period of the site's use, but dates based on the thickness of flat (pane) glass were 14 to 16 years earlier than the site's initial occupation, indicating that preexisting structures were moved to the site by rail to provide housing. This was a common practice of "cut and run" logging operations in the South. In West Virginia, leveled areas along railroad grades surrounded by refuse deposits showed where portable structures once stood at nine circa 1910–1927 logging camps operated by the Cherry River Boom and Lumber Company (Brashler 1991). At these locations, one to four (approximately 12 × 25 feet) wood frame "shanty cars" covered with board-and-batten siding were brought in by rail during logging operations and then moved to the next cutting area. The company railroad connected these camps to a much larger community called Dogway, a centrally located settlement that served a number of support functions, including railroad equipment repair and maintenance. Six railroad segments or spurs met at Dogway, which included as many as 60 portable shanty-car houses; but the only permanent structure was a combined hotel and company store.

Although tent camps may have also been used in the South, the only known archaeological example comes from the West. Wooden structures found at the Tate Creek logging camp in Northern California turned out to be the remains of tent floors (Elliott 1990). A total of 18 "tent flats" (12 × 14 feet) consisting of wood frames covered with tongue and groove flooring were left behind when the camp was abandoned. An inventory of property owned by the McCloud River Lumber Company in 1914 lists numerous tents, but by the time the Tate Creek camp was abandoned around 1922, the company may have been discontinuing their use and consequently left the floors behind. An undated historic photo of a McCloud River Lumber Company camp shows a row of tents labeled "poverty row" (Elliott 1990).

Some of the more unusual logging camp buildings were frame structures placed on barges in order to access stands of cypress in southern wetlands. Bratten and Booker-DeMonbreun (2014) tentatively identified structural debris submerged in Florida's Escambia River as the remains of a floating bunkhouse for loggers. A circa 1920 photo of a Wilson Cypress Company operation shows three houseboats: a large well-ventilated structure for field superintendents, a second smaller boat for white workmen, and a third even smaller structure for black workmen (State Library and Archives of Florida 192-). Cypress logging also left behind treeless swamps dissected by canals dredged for access and hauling logs. Where cypress cutovers have not regenerated, these old canal network patterns stand out in aerial or satellite photographs.

Archaeological evidence of spatial organization at logging sites reveals places where industrial and domestic activities overlapped or occurred in close proximity. Spatial and architectural patterns relate to the efforts of labor and management to further their separate but interdependent interests. Rather than living in a 100-man bunkhouse and perhaps indulging in weekly outdoor sponge baths, portable three- or four-man cabins near hot showers and a mess hall no doubt offered increased comfort for single men, but also less opportunity for union organization without being observed by management. Married workers obviously preferred living with their wives and children when small houses were available in camps, but companies no doubt appreciated downsizing communal kitchen and laundry facilities, with workers' wives assuming these duties. Architectural and spatial variation can express company policies, and differences are sometimes detected. In Michigan's central Upper Peninsula, late nineteenth-century camps operated by the Bay de Noquet Company included dingle-style structures with the cookhouse and bunkhouse connected end to end, while contemporaneous camps operated by the Van Winkle and Montague Company had separate bunkhouse and cookhouse structures (Franzen 1992; Dunham and Branstner 1995). Separating these functions may have been part of a strategy to increase production with larger crews or attract and retain workers by providing more space per man. There are indications that Van Winkle and Montague also provided cookhouses with fresh beef and ceramic tableware in accordance with worker preferences (Franzen 1992).

Landscape-Scale Spatial Patterns

In trying to understand the broader spatial relationships of logging sites, variations in the distribution of different tree species are of obvious importance, but the resulting locational patterns are sometimes more complex than might be expected. For example, white pine occurs in mixed stands located in a variety of different topographic settings. Before investing in a logging operation, companies estimated timber volume, logging and production costs, and market demand. Webster Marble's 1896–1897 cruise maps and notes provide examples of how pine logging proceeded over time in Northern Michigan (Franzen 1998). Comments describe some stands as "partly cut at least two different times, but still some pine" or "some cut many years ago, some recent, some pine left" (Marble 1896–1897, cited in Franzen 1998: 46). This sequential approach to pine logging resulted from the focus of early loggers on only the best (most profitable) trees, given existing production costs and market values. As pine became scarce, prices increased to the extent that it became profitable to harvest trees initially passed over. Whitney (1994: 179) refers to the earliest logging in the Great Lakes and Northeast as the "highly selective White Pine era."

Geographic factors also shaped the technologies needed for log transportation. Recreational visitors traveling through America's forests often follow routes once used to move logs by water or rail. Modern roads were built on old logging railroad grades, and rivers and lakes popular for boating once carried logs to downstream mills. Water bodies were abundant in the Northeast and Great Lakes, while the relatively level coastal plains of the southeastern states proved ideal for railroads. In the Pacific Northwest, rugged terrain, steep stream gradients, heavy precipitation, and the long distance to markets posed the greatest transportation challenges and ultimately required the most complex mechanized technology. To address locational decision-making, researchers in California used methods and theory developed by geographers to suggest that archaeological evidence of logging networks be compared to a "least cost" model that assumes rational decisions based on factors like distances between processing facilities and harvest areas, weights of the timber being transported, and expectations regarding costs and income (Tamez et al. 1988). A similar approach was suggested for studies in the Great Lakes region (Birk 1997). Both river driving and railroad logging involved networks of connected features, and locational patterns can only be understood within the context of these integrated systems.

Site catchment analysis was used to analyze the locations of some logging camps in Michigan. Dinsmore (1985) reviewed firsthand narratives describing Great Lakes pine logging and selected radii of 2.4 kilometers for non-railroad sites and 4.8 to 8 kilometers for railroad sites to identify the types of forest most likely exploited from these locations. The results showed non-railroad site catchments dominated by pine habitats, as expected, but railroad site catchments included mixtures of pine and hardwoods. This accords with documents suggesting that early non-railroad operations relying on draft animals and river drives focused on the most concentrated, accessible, and highest quality pine stands, while railroads enabled logging of more dispersed, mixed, and remote pine stands. Farther north in Michigan, Ferone et al. (1997) analyzed 62 pine-era (1880–1910) logging camp locations in the Ottawa National Forest. Correlations obviously existed between ecological zones and the location of various kinds of logging operations, but improved ecological mapping and larger site samples permitted a more detailed look at these patterns. Of the 22 different ecological zones that occur in this National Forest, three had higher frequencies of pine-era camps than would be expected by chance, one had lower, and this pattern conformed with the known soil and habitat preferences of white pine. However, these correlations failed to account for the location of all so-called pine-era camps. Because of unpredictable flow patterns and the uneven distribution of streams, much of this area's pine remained inaccessible until the construction of railroads. Using sites associated with the 1890s Choate Branch railroad logging system, Ferone et al. (1997) conducted further analysis using Dinsmore's (1985) catchment model to explain variations in camp locations. The main Choate Branch Railroad and the associated sawmill sites occupied the best pine areas, but not all the associated logging camps were similarly situated due to the fact that white pine can occur in small stands and mixed with other species. Pine-era camps that utilized railroads had more locational flexibility because wider catchments could be exploited from a single location.

Relying primarily on documents and oral history, Birk (1997) described the complex strategies devised to deal with environmental and cultural factors that facilitated or obstructed the harvest and transport of logs in north central Minnesota between about 1848 and the 1900s. Companies had to estimate the amount and value of available timber relative to the projected cost of obtaining it. Historical documents, oral history, and observations of surface features documented chronological and spatial variation in transportation systems that used various combinations of oxen, horses, tugboats, railroads, and flowing water to move logs. These systems included logging camps, dams, railroad grades, trestles, and mill settlements. One alternative conveyance method involved using a tug or a windlass powered by steam, horses, or even men, to pull rafts of logs across lakes that connected some river segments. By the time railroad logging flourished in Minnesota, standard- rather than narrow-gauge railroads were predominant. Other logging areas followed this trend, as companies determined that compatibility with main lines and the ease of transshipment warranted the extra expense of standard-gauge construction and operation. Birk (1997) argued that geographic and distance thresholds based on technology costs and market conditions determined the practical limits of harvesting. As technology developed and demand increased, the industry's reach extended. The most dramatic changes came with the eventual proliferation of railroad networks and associated environmental and social effects.

Another study focusing on networks rather than single sites relied on archaeology to define the elements of an 1890s logging operation in Montana (Knight 1981). Field surveys identified the locations of three splash dams, two log chutes, a hauling road, and seven decking areas. The areas previously harvested remained obvious in contrast with the surrounding old growth. Using written accounts from nearby areas to interpret features, Knight (1981) emphasized looking at related features as a single system and considering the influence of seasonal weather variations. The study confirmed that cutting occurred in both summer and winter. Logs driven down Sheep Creek in the spring ended up at a mill in Great Falls via the Smith and Missouri rivers. Given the ages of trees now growing in areas cleared during this original logging, he predicted that cutting was done in the mid- to late 1890s, and records indicate that it was the early 1890s. Knight's experimental approach used only archaeological evidence and historical accounts from other areas to make inferences and then tested these through detailed local historical research.

Logging in the western United States required technical and spatial strategies for dealing with rugged topography and very large trees. One solution involved moving portable steam-powered mills to the stands being cut. The Enterprise Sawmill near Mountain Home, California, processed giant sequoia from 1897 to 1901, and detailed mapping documented well-preserved remains of this operation (Dulitz 1998). Milling and transportation of sequoia logs posed special problems because of their size and the brittle nature of sequoia wood. Surface features included stumps of 283 sequoias felled using axes and crosscut saws (approximately four million board feet of lumber), as well as shattered or otherwise damaged logs left behind. Researchers reconstructed the spatial organization of the entire operation by mapping all 283 stumps, trails, skid roads, and the mill location. Many living trees remained in this stand, probably left behind because their diameters exceeded the mill's sawing capacity. Some historical information came from the maps and notes of dendrochronologists who visited the site in the 1920s to take samples; growth ring variation in sequoia stumps preserves many centuries of climate data. Stump height averaged 5 feet, but loggers perched on springboards cut some trees 12 to 14 feet above ground where the trunks narrowed (Figure 5.4). This operation may have violated an unenforced 1874 California statute banning the harvest of old-growth sequoia. Ironically, the sequoia's brittleness resulted in many of world's largest trees (by wood volume) being transformed into small products like pencils, fence posts, and stakes to support grape vines!

McKee (2009) looked at the nature and distribution of railroad tie production (tie hack) sites in the Sierra Madre Mountains of the Medicine Bow National Forest in southern Wyoming to reconstruct the locational strategies of the Carbon Timber Company, a circa 1889–1914 supplier of ties to the Union Pacific Railroad. Workers hewed logs into ties near the stands where they were cut. Teams of horses then hauled them to the banks of rivers or streams, which carried them downstream to landings where crews loaded them onto railroad cars. Relatively intact remains of log cabins occupied by tie cutters revealed their function and internal organization. This study recorded 46 tie-hack camps ranging from satellite camps with one or more small cabins to large multistructure sites that included barns, bunkhouses, mess halls, and blacksmith shops. All 46 sites occurred between 8,400 and

Figure 5.4. Giant sequoia stump remaining from tree cut in 1880s, Giant Sequoia National Monument, Sequoia National Forest, California. Notches show where loggers stood on springboards during cutting. (Photo [2017] by author.)

9,600 feet in elevation, which corresponds with the distribution of lodgepole pine, the local species preferred for tie-making. Larger camps were centrally located within watersheds relative to smaller and more numerous satellite camps.

Landscape-scale spatial analyses by archaeologists have also focused on charcoal production sites. In general, the heaviness of recently cut wood, especially the denser species with the most heat value, resulted in the location of processing sites relatively close to cutting areas. After burning, the much lighter charcoal was hauled away in wagons. Frye and Frye (1989) located 57 circa 1810–1840 charcoal "hearths" in a Maryland park. In plan view, the hearths were usually elliptical or circular, an average 38 feet long and 28 feet wide, and defined by deposits of charcoal on leveled areas cut into slopes. They are situated below likely cutting areas on more gently sloped plateaus or shelves surrounded by steeper topography. Researchers mapped a dendritic pattern of former roads used for carrying wood to kilns. A key variable was slope, with narrower features on steeper slopes where leveling was more difficult. Their distribution was both linear and tiered, illustrating how this technology adapted to local conditions. Other studies of charcoal production documented the spatial patterns of circa 1870–1890 operations that supplied smelters in the Eureka silver mining district in Nevada (Zeier 1987; Reno 1996). In this arid environment with sparse ground cover, dense circular concentrations of charcoal remained visible at kiln sites, which occurred in clusters around centrally located habitation sites. Although kiln locations clearly correlated with pinyon pine distribution, specific placement varied according to slope, wagon access, and soil type.

Besides archaeologists, other disciplines have studied charcoal production sites, including geographers, botanists, soil scientists, and geomorphologists. These studies show how strong demand for charcoal resulted in extremely high site densities. In a 1,170-square-kilometer forested area of northwestern Connecticut, LiDAR (light detection and ranging) revealed over 20,000 charcoal burning platforms approximately 3–8 meters in diameter as well as associated wagon roads, about 17 platforms per square kilometer (Johnson et al. 2015). Located in steeper areas where agriculture would have been difficult, these sites occur in linear patterns that follow topographic lines of similar elevation. The same distributional patterns also appeared in a LiDAR study that mapped over 500 charcoal-making features in a 40-square-mile area around blast furnaces in Pennsylvania (Sams et al. 2012). Detailed studies of soils at charcoal-producing sites provide a closer look at their environmental effects. Based on studying the stratigraphy and chemistry of soils at 24 approximately 150-year-old hearth locations in Connecticut as well as similar sites in Europe, Hirsch et al. (2017) determined that some platforms were reused and found they retained significant amounts of sequestered carbon.

Logging Archaeology and the Environment

Archaeological studies frequently employ natural science data to help understand spatial patterns, but archaeology also generates new information relevant to botany, forestry, ecology, soil science, and hydrology. This is especially relevant to the identification and explanation of environmental changes during an era many are calling the Anthropocene (see chapter 1) and to discussions about how altered or restored forests might be better managed. Crossing disciplinary boundaries also helps counter the illusion that industrial logging had separate effects on people or nature. Many of the studies cited in this book mention possible environmental influences when discussing technological and spatial characteristics, but some studies stand out by generating new information about past, present, and, possibly, future forests. These are worth pointing out because they bridge the perceptual divide often imposed between natural and cultural history and respond to calls for increased use of archaeology at industrial-era sites to address environmental topics (Hardesty 1999; Deagan 1988; Mrozowski 2006).

For example, archaeologists have employed dendrochronology in conjunction with investigations at several logging-related sites. At the Tate Creek camp in California, researchers sampled stumps and trees in or adjacent to key areas, such as the railroad grade and former structure locations. They identified stumps from trees cut during camp construction and trees that grew after the camp was abandoned. The resulting date estimate of 1919–1922 agreed with the ages of artifacts found at the site (Elliott 1990). Paullin (2007) also used tree ring data from in and around a logging site in Oregon to help map different activity areas and understand various processes that affected the area before, during, and after logging activity, especially forest fires and the construction of a landing strip. In western New Mexico, Towner and Kessler (2016) investigated a twentieth-century ponderosa pine–logging and milling operation that included a portable gas-powered sawmill and tent platforms for worker housing. The study used dendrochronology to analyze milling debris and samples from stumps on nearby hills to identify cutting dates as 1946–1947. Even though relatively recent, documents and oral history interviews yielded no information about this particular logging episode. Besides facilitating chronology, growth rings visible in milling debris indicated that 5,000–7,000 trees were harvested. The ecological effects of this harvest continue, with surrounding areas now either treeless or dominated by juniper instead of pine trees.

Burned wood found in archaeological excavations also provides environmental information. Charcoal samples from excavations at kiln sites in California and Nevada (Strachan et al. 2013) helped refine logging chronologies and revealed details of charcoal-making practices. Besides permitting the identification of tree species, some fragments were large enough for dendrochronology. These researchers sampled four sites, two in the mid-elevation Eastern Sierra mountains of California and two in central Nevada. Analysis of growth rings preserved in large pieces of charred wood revealed differences in the duration and extent of cutting episodes. This study documented vegetation change resulting from logging, especially decreases in pinyon pine and juniper trees and the expansion of open sagebrush grassland.

The persistence of logging effects on the environment has drawn attention from researchers interested in studying "cultural" or "historic" landscapes, although their research usually shows how both cultural and natural history shapes these areas. In Arizona's Kaibab National Forest, Cleeland (1995) evaluated the Barney Flat Historic Railroad Logging Landscape, the only "stump field" included in the National Register of Historic Places. Although they are relatively uncommon, stump fields provide iconic representations of "cut-out and get-out" logging (Figure 5.5). In most cutovers not converted to agricultural or urban use, reforestation occurred either naturally or with human help, and stumps eventually decayed. The Barney Flat landscape was created between 1899 and 1902 when the Saginaw and Manistee Lumber Company cut the area's ponderosa pine forest. Covering about 40 acres, the resulting open field contains about 300 stumps from trees between 150 and 300 years old when cut and the railroad grade used to transport the resulting logs. Stumps show trees were first notched with axes and then cut down with crosscut saws. When the Forest Service tried replanting Barney Flat with pine trees, none survived the following winter. It appears that both cultural and natural factors have hindered regeneration. Besides residual soil damage from logging, the area occupies a "frost pocket" created by surrounding topography. Barney Flat does not include the actual logging camp inhabited by the cutters, but Morris et al. (1994) conducted a major archaeological study of two camps operated by the Saginaw and Manistee Lumber Company at a different Arizona location.

Another example of a logging industry landscape illustrates the relationships between natural and cultural features (including archaeological sites): the Weyerhaeuser South Bay Log Dump Rural Historic Landscape along Puget Sound in Washington (Stevenson 1991). Covering about 260 upland acres and 190 acres of tideland, this area included one of the largest log transshipment facilities in the world, which operated between 1928 and 1984. After the Weyerhaeuser railroad delivered logs from interior areas and dumped them into the bay, this operation sorted and assembled them into rafts towed by tugs 99 miles to the company's mill in Everett. Over a billion board feet passed through this facility. Despite serious environmental effects, the company nonetheless protected this heavily modified property from subdivision and residential development. After the state of Washington acquired the site, toxic contaminants, especially creosote used as wood preservative, were removed. The clean-up effort necessitated the removal of many structures but left some in place for adaptive reuse by humans and wildlife. The site now includes the restored foreman's office, pier remnants

Figure 5.5. Stumps of pines cut during the 1890s, Kingston Plains, Alger County, Michigan. (Photo [2017] by author.)

left for bat habitat, and some pilings with attached log booms retained as pull-out habitat for harbor seals. High-quality informational signs cover the history and ecology of the area and provide a holistic context for logging-industry remains.

Although it has apparently not been the subject of archaeological study, Sugarloaf Cove along Lake Superior in northern Minnesota provides another example of a repurposed logging landscape where a new mix of more sustainable uses includes efforts to understand and interpret human history within an ecosystem context. Between 1943 and 1971, Consolidated Papers Company used the site for storing pulpwood and assembling logs into rafts towed by tugboats across Lake Superior to their paper mill in Ashland, Wisconsin (North Shore Stewardship Association 2016). It once included extensive support facilities for loggers and rafters. A root cellar, iron mooring rings anchored in bedrock, portions of a chute where logs entered the lake, and boom logs remain to illustrate the history of Sugarloaf Cove. Formerly cleared and filled areas have been restored with native vegetation, a small visitor center has been constructed, and the site is now used for research, educational, and recreational purposes.

Using archaeology to explore some of the human-influenced environmental changes that characterize the Anthropocene might seem complicated, but some phenomena, like catastrophic wildfires fueled by logging debris, left a conspicuous stratigraphic record. Such is the case at Williamsonville, site of a small community in northeastern Wisconsin that included a steam-powered shingle mill. In a region being cleared for agriculture, pine and cedar logs, ideal for shingle-making, supplemented the income of homesteaders. On October 8, 1871, the same day as the much better-known Chicago fire, the Peshtigo fire burned Williamsonville, along with 1.2 million acres of forest and cutover areas in Wisconsin and adjacent Michigan. Considered the deadliest wildfire in American history, an estimated 1,200 people died, including 59 of the 76 residents of Williamsonville. According to one survivor, "the woods and the heavens were all on fire, the smoke blocked the sun and the rising moon turned red" (University of Wisconsin–Milwaukee 2012).

Archaeologists excavated test units at Williamsonville in advance of a highway improvement project (Benchley et al. 1995; Sorensen 2005). Based on the distribution of charcoal and artifacts, they identified building locations, including some not mentioned in historic accounts. Remarkably, researchers noticed fewer than expected artifacts severely altered by heat. After experimentally burning glass and ceramic materials in a controlled setting, they noticed similar variation and concluded that even within a firestorm, differential heat and burning patterns existed. This corroborated certain historical accounts and the results of archaeology at other burned sites. They also identified an area with few artifacts or signs of burn damage that may have been a garden where many unsuccessfully sought shelter away from burning buildings; one person survived there, but 35 perished. The Williamsonville site provides an example of how archaeological remains can highlight the environmental effects of the logging industry. In fact, it illustrates that industrial endeavors seen as "improvements" can render places unlivable, at least temporarily. Although wind and drought contributed to the fire's rapid spread, branches, stumps, and other dry organic debris left behind after logging fueled this conflagration. In conjunction with highway reconstruction, a public website and interpretive signs provide information about Williamsonville and the Peshtigo fire.

A mix of archaeological and interpretive projects also took place at Falk, an abandoned mill settlement associated with railroad logging of redwoods from 1884 to 1937 by the Elk River Lumber Company in Humboldt County, California (Rich and Roscoe 2009). As many as 400 residents once lived in this company town. The U.S. Department of Interior, Bureau of Land Management (USDI BLM) now manages the site for interpretation and limited recreational development. Archaeological test excavation took place in conjunction with moving the intact portion of a steam locomotive engine house to be used as a visitor center, where signs, publications, and educational programs now interpret the area's natural and cultural features. Hiking trails enable visitors to pass through the Falk townsite and compare reforested cutover areas with a nearby uncut old-growth redwood forest.

A final example of how archaeology interfaces with other activities to help address the social and ecological effects of industrial logging comes from Northern Michigan's Hiawatha National Forest, where the Sandtown Project combined archaeology, outreach to descendant communities, ecological restoration, and public interpretation. Sandtown was a segregated American Indian community associated with the Bay de Noquet Lumber Company (1881–1951). Families of European descent lived on the other side of the Sturgeon River in the town of Nahma, where the mill, school, offices, store, and other public buildings were located. Even though the mill closed in 1951, Nahma still exists, but the structures at Sandtown were demolished and the residents dispersed. With the help of oral history, archaeologists surveyed and mapped the remains of this community. Besides the mill, Sandtown residents worked in logging camps, mainly for Native American jobbers. Former residents and descendants participated in archaeological excavations at one of these camps (USDA Forest Service 2017). They also joined with archaeologists, botanists, and other volunteers to plant native species like sweetgrass and milkweed in areas of Sandtown recently eroded by off-road vehicles. A series of interpretive signs now educates the public about this history.

These examples show archaeology playing a role in projects that include habitat restoration, preservation or reintroduction of threatened species, recreation, and education or interpretation. Besides tracing the roots of problems related to industrial growth, like climate change and the extreme concentration of wealth and power, these types of projects may ultimately contribute to more sustainable relationships between people and forests. The material evidence of radical forest modification and partial recovery is one of the values of contemporary forests, accessible through scientific investigations and interpretive or educational programs. Landscapes degraded by industrial resource extraction and processing have been called the "ruins of capitalism" (Tsing 2015). Archaeology addresses the denials, lack of memory, and oversimplifications that limit our ability to perceive past and present problems. It can also play a role in moving forward. The next chapter looks more closely at how the logging industry transformed spaces into places through practices that defined the daily life of workers.

6

Working in the Woods

Everyday Life in a "Roofless Factory"

> Situated in thinly settled forest regions, lumber camps are, to a great extent, cut off from civilization. The resulting conditions are a peculiar mixture of capitalism and feudalism, civilization and barbarism.
>
> IWW, *The Lumber Industry and Its Workers* (1922)

Archaeological studies focusing on the daily lives of working people reflect not only the anthropological background of most American archaeologists but the lingering influence of the 1960s New Social History movement. Besides the obvious value of historicizing the lived experiences of people usually not well represented in written records, the details of daily life reflect the power balance between labor and capital, the agency of workers, and differences in corporate policies. Daily life at logging industry sites has been studied by archaeologists in both descriptive as well as more problem-oriented ways. Chapter 7, which focuses on social organization, covers sites where researchers have emphasized daily life as it relates to ethnicity.

Foodways

From the loggers' point of view, the most important aspect of working conditions was the food provided by employers. As Thoreau (1988 [1864]: 173) described mid-nineteenth-century Maine loggers: "their minds ran chiefly on the hot bread and sweet cakes." In the Great Lakes, Louie Blanchard recalled: "good grub was about all we had to look forward to" (Blanchard et al. 1976). Supposedly, this led to camps that served the best food getting the "best men" (Conlin 1979). It may be impossible to determine who got the best workers, but concerns about food clearly contributed to high rates of worker turnover. Firsthand accounts like this recollection from former "lumberjack" Jem McKem (1921: 37) support this observation: "I have known a whole logging crew to quit work and the only reason given was that the cooks served a bad breakfast." The limited records available for early to mid-nineteenth-century logging in the northeast show the diet of loggers was influenced by the caloric requirements of hard labor in cold weather and by remote settings; it consisted heavily of beans, preserved pork, and bread. The quality and diversity of food began to increase around 1880 as the Great Lakes states assumed dominance as the leading lumber production region, and Conlin (1979) attributes this to increased competition for labor as well as increases in the scale of operations and improved transportation infrastructure. Systematic studies done by nutritionists in the early twentieth century estimate that loggers consumed from 5,000 to a little over 8,000 calories per day, depending on the season and type of work being done (Woods and Mansfield 1904; Mueller 1921: 243; Howd 1924: 42). Woods and Mansfield (1904) actually collected food and feces samples at a Maine logging camp. These were stored in glass jars and later transported to a university laboratory for analysis of their fat, carbohydrate, protein, and calorie content. Fortunately, the study took place during the winter so that samples could remain frozen between the times of collection and analysis!

Several archaeological studies argue that food played a central role in the relationship between labor and capital within the lumber industry (Franzen 1992; Dunham and Branstner 1995; Dunham and Franzen 1997). Lumberjacks also seem to have preferred ceramic rather than metal tableware. As one operator of a circa 1905 camp in Michigan put it, "any human being should have a dish worthwhile eating on" (Harding 1982). The desire for good food motivated workers as they traveled in search of employment. For researchers trying to understand this process, archival documents like actual menus or inventory lists of supplies are rare and usually associated with larger and more recent companies. However, certain types of generally well-preserved archaeological data provide information on this topic.

The following sections compare studies from different regions in order to explore two variables: meat consumption and tableware. Using historical documents and oral history to frame archaeological research questions both appropriate to these topics and realistic in terms of likely data sources, Franzen (1992) proposed that Great Lakes loggers preferred fresh over preserved meat, domestic species over wild, beef over pork and mutton, and ceramic over metal tableware. Even though this initial study was based on research in the Great Lakes, the migration of both workers and logging companies to other regions suggests that extending these comparisons might further represent the concerns, experiences, and agency of workers. Refuse deposits generated by institutional-style cooking and dining facilities operated by lumber companies provide most of these data. Sites in the Great Lakes and western United States are included in this exercise. No data sets were available from comparable sites in the South, where archaeological excavation at logging industry sites has focused on family housing rather than institutional settings like mess halls.

Meat Consumption

To determine whether workers were provided with the fresh domestic meats they preferred, sites with relatively large bone samples derived from excavation are obviously preferable to those without. Sampling bias is more likely if investigations are limited to surface materials or very small excavation areas. Faunal remains from the First Nahma Sawmill site (ca. 1848–1855) in Northern Michigan provide a look at meat consumption in a frontier setting where logging preceded the advent of railroads or regular shipping service (Blair 2001; Franzen and Drake 2010). Despite the presence of a variety of wild species, pork and beef still provided most of the available meat. Recovered swine and cattle elements are primarily vertebrae and rib fragments, suggesting salted meat was shipped to this isolated, nonagricultural settlement. However, differences expected between elements included in barreled meat and meats delivered as part of fresh or frozen whole carcasses or sides may be subtle. The only elements universally excluded from barrels would be pig snouts and perhaps the feet and heads of cattle (Tourigny 2016). At other frontier industrial settlements in Northern Michigan, residents considered the scarcity of fresh meat, especially beef, a significant hardship (Lankton 1997: 70, 87). The First Nahma Sawmill site also included remains of wild game and fish species, notable in their diversity if not for the amount of meat represented. These species may represent evidence of trade with local Native Americans. Ryan (1980: 35) mentions that logging camps in Minnesota obtained venison and moose meat from local tribes.

In the 1860s, regional shipping on the Great Lakes expanded, and logging companies established networks of "tote roads" to supply their camps from coastal mill settlements. Chapter 8 describes beef-dominated assemblages at two early camps in Northern Michigan that may have been preserved rather than fresh. By the 1880s, Great Lakes shipping networks had matured and railroads provided some settlements with year-round service. Even though meat was supplied by wagon or sleigh rather than railroad, excavation at the site of a circa 1887–1897 logging camp (20DE272) in Northern Michigan, operated by the partnership of Van Winkle and Montague, provided a large sample of faunal remains. The recovered assemblage included 3,767 specimens, and identifiable elements were dominated by beef (63% NISP [number of identifiable specimens]; 5 MNI [minimum number of individuals]), pork (18% NISP; 4 MNI), and white-tailed deer (17% NISP; 6 MNI), with at least one elk or moose also present. The relatively high frequency of venison suggests that it represents part of the company's provisioning strategy, rather than incidental sport hunting. Some camps procured venison from hired hunters or local Native Americans, but loggers generally preferred domestic meats (Franzen 1992). In fact, one early twentieth-century source indicated that venison was "not particularly appetizing" to loggers (Dye 1975: 47).

While it might not be possible to determine with any certainty whether a given domestic element represents preserved or fresh meat, one source describes the delivery by sleigh of freshly butchered beef to camps operated by Van Winkle and Montague (Tatrow 1982: 71). Nearly all logging operations in the Great Lakes states during this period took place during the winter, enabling the transportation and storage of meat without spoilage. Cattle bone at 20DE272 tended to be from low- to medium-value cuts, and although pork bones were less frequent, most elements came from relatively high-value cuts. If the men preferred beef, complaints may have been avoided by offering higher-value cuts when pork was served. Smaller assemblages from other Great Lakes sites raise questions about sampling adequacy. However, cattle remains also dominate these collections, with pork and venison consistently present but usually less abundant (Dunham and Branstner 1995; Richner 1986). Some camps in Great Lakes states kept pigs and allowed them to forage in the surrounding forest, an especially tasty option if acorns were present (Ryan 1973: 15).

Among western sites, a Manley–Moore Lumber Company camp in Washington, active 1912–1914, included faunal assemblages from two separate contexts: structures where workers with families resided and a railroad siding once occupied by an institutional kitchen and dining cars (Miss et al. 2000). The company's railroad network for hauling logs provided for the easy delivery of fresh meat. It appears beef arrived as sides or quarters, while pork and mutton arrived in wholesale or retail cuts (Miss et al. 2000). Refuse along the railroad siding generated by institutional-style cooking included elements representing three cattle, eight pigs, and two sheep (MNI).

However, the authors feel the MNI count for swine is inflated due to the popularity of pickled pigs feet! As in the Great Lakes, some western studies recovered only small samples, but these were still dominated by cattle remains (Morris et al. 1994: 115). At Bingham's Camp in Oregon (ca. 1890s) most remains came from cattle, but the site also included saw-cut horse elements and a beef bone fragment large and robust enough to be from a working ox (Horn 1987). This was the only archaeological site encountered with evidence of lumberers eating draft animals. Explanations might include food shortages, utilization of injured or sick animals, or the presence of an ethnic group that traditionally consumed horse meat.

At various times and places, logging operations included housing for families or small groups of men who did their own cooking. Some large sites included both an institutional-style kitchen and mess hall for single men as well as houses and cabins or shacks for certain workers allowed to have their families present. Family dining was still influenced by policies of the company store or commissary, in many cases the only source where camp residents could obtain supplies. Faunal remains associated with families or single men who did their own cooking may reflect ethnic differences (Hahn and Schwab 1998; Whelan and Pearson 1999; Drake 2003; Douglass 2000), which are discussed in chapter 7. Regardless of ethnicity, the faunal remains from deposits associated with family housing tend to be different from those associated with company-sponsored mess halls. Beef and pork are still predominant, but the family-related assemblages include more wild species. Refuse deposits associated with single-family housing at Shevlin-Hixon Company's Lava Caves camp in Oregon were dominated by medium-cost cuts of pork and beef, while a nearby all-male construction camp had far more high-cost cuts (Bowyer et al. 1995). Since both groups would have earned similar pay, the authors conclude that social composition (families to feed) and consumer preferences, rather than income, were responsible for this difference. At a Manley–Moore Company camp in Washington, features associated with the location of tar paper shacks occupied by families yielded bones representing a minimum of five cattle, one pig, two sheep, and one deer (Miss et al. 2000). With the exception of the venison, these proportions resemble those of faunal remains associated with the nearby institutional railroad-car kitchen and mess hall. However, far more of the highly fractured faunal specimens from the family area were burned or calcined, probably as a result of deliberate incineration prior to disposal, making them less odiferous than the unburned bones discarded next to the railroad-car dining facility. Loggers unaccompanied by families rarely cooked for themselves, with examples of this only seen at small decentralized operations or in distinctive ethnic settings. For example, faunal remains associated with the Italo-Swiss Carbonari, who cut wood for charcoal kilns in Nevada, include relatively expensive beef cuts but also reveal intensive bone processing (Zeier 1987). This may represent a "feast and famine" cycle: workers who purchased prime cuts had to eventually process bones to maximize calorie extraction as money and/or supplies dwindled.

Company-operated mess halls in both Great Lakes and western logging camps show the relatively consistent dominance of beef, but no comparable institutional dining facilities have been excavated in the South, where one might expect to see more swine use. Even though assemblage composition alone is an unreliable indicator of whether particular cuts arrived fresh or preserved, the predominance of beef at logging sites is more consistent with the delivery of fresh meats. The logging workers' preference for beef during the late nineteenth and early twentieth centuries is especially significant when compared to the early to mid-nineteenth century, when pork was the nation's preferred salted or barreled meat. In 1880, the average U.S. citizen still consumed more pork than beef (400 vs. 175 calories per day) (Bennett and Pierce 1961: 105–117, cited in Crass and Wallsmith 1992: 7). Nationally, the popularity of beef relative to pork increased as rail networks spread and fresh meat could be shipped in refrigerated cars during the warmer months (Drury 1966). The only archaeological reference to mutton remains found at a logging camp site comes from the state of Washington (Miss et al. 2000). A Minnesota camp operator who shipped in sheep from Montana supposedly served mutton every day and had a hard time keeping a full crew (Ryan 1973: 16). The frequency of venison remains at sites in Michigan and Wisconsin stands out as a notable regional difference. At early sites in the Great Lakes region without regular ship or railroad service, local procurement of venison could have reduced meat costs. None of the Great Lakes sites mentioned in this discussion of faunal remains were directly accessible by rail, while most of the western sites were. However, at one western site without rail service, loggers apparently consumed at least samples of horse and ox meat (Horn 1987).

Tableware

Loggers in the Great Lakes area during the late nineteenth and early twentieth centuries apparently preferred eating from ceramic rather than metal tableware (Franzen 1992). Metal tableware included coated (enamelware) and uncoated (tinware) vessels, but tinware corroded easily and, although the cheapest option, was probably the least desirable from the lumberjack's point of view. At a "modern" camp in the Pacific Northwest where portable camp structures were moved by railroad, Gibbons (1918) noted: "Heavy crockery dishes are used because they are easy to clean and have no enameled surface to chip off into the food." Enamel coatings containing antimony, arsenic, or lead could poison diners. A 1908 catalog guaranteed their enamelware "free from all poisonous or harmful ingredients" (Schroeder 1971: 462). As late as 1922, a Pacific Northwestern supplier of cookhouse and mess hall equipment advertised both "heavy china" and "white enamel ware" for logging camps (Four L Bulletin 1922: 22). Holbrook (1936) oversimplified this process when he wrote that "years ago" camp operators replaced "tin plates" with "crockery." The written record lacks specifics on how this process played out at different times in different places, but in the 1990s archaeological studies focused on Michigan began looking at tableware relative to the interaction between labor and capital (Franzen 1992; Dunham and Branstner 1995). In the following paragraphs, this approach is extended to consider additional archaeological evidence from the Great Lakes and other regions, especially the West.

No metal tableware was found at two relatively early logging camps (ca. late 1860s) excavated in Michigan (see chapter 8), and each site included only a single ceramic or metal vessel among the kitchen-related artifacts. This suggests potential sampling and preservation issues. Both included heavily oxidized fragments of sheet metal, and it seems likely that tin tableware deteriorated and became unrecognizable. More durable and better preserved metal tableware occurs at two Wisconsin camps occupied in the 1870s and 1880s (Overstreet et al. 1983; Bruhy et al. 1993). In contrast to logging camps where ceramics were absent or scarce, excavation at 20DE272 in Northern Michigan recovered over 1,700 undecorated white earthenware sherds representing 167 vessels (Dunham and Branstner 1995). Land ownership and tax records associate this site with the partnership of Van Winkle and Montague. Marks of both English and American manufacturers indicate activity there in the early to mid-1890s. Ceramics from surface collections at two other Van Winkle camps suggest a company-wide policy of providing ceramic tableware (Franzen 1992). Results of test excavation at three Northern Michigan logging camp sites operated by other companies between about 1875 and 1910 were less clear: they yielded no recognizable metal tableware, but ceramic samples did not seem large enough to represent institutional-scale use (Dunham and Branstner 1995). At some camps, if the foreman resided separately with his family, they may have also dined separately, and some operators may not have had a clearly defined policy for specific types of tableware. Besides undecorated white earthenware used for dining, Northern Michigan logging camps subjected to test excavation have included smaller quantities of earthenware and stoneware from vessels used for food preparation, storage, and serving (Franzen 1992; Dunham and Branstner 1995).

Other companies in the Great Lakes region no doubt stocked their mess halls with ceramic tableware, but metal tableware remained common in the early twentieth century (Figure 6.1). Richner (1986) reports that metal was used at the circa 1912–1920 Trout Point site, which is one of the latest camps in the Great Lakes region where significant amounts of excavation have taken place. Evidence of tableware at other Great Lakes logging camps occupied after ca. 1910 is limited to surface observations and/or very small excavation areas. Metal appears dominant at three sites in Michigan and one in Wisconsin occupied in the teens and early to mid-twenties (Franzen 1992; Stencel 2000). However, two Northern Michigan logging camps operated by the timber division of Cleveland-Cliffs Iron Company during the late 1920s included dense surface deposits representing numerous whiteware vessels, including some with the marks of Scamell China Company and Buffalo China (Franzen 1992). An earlier camp operated by Cleveland-Cliffs included abundant enamelware, with some found in a nested arrangement suggesting mass abandonment or disposal (Figure 6.2). It appears this company discontinued metal and adopted ceramic tableware during a period of worker shortages and labor unrest (Karamanski 1989; Ryan 1980: 6).

Archaeology at a series of railroad logging camps in the western United States provides additional evidence for increased use of ceramic tableware in the early twentieth century. Three camps occupied before circa 1910 included only metal tableware or a mixture of both metal and ceramic vessels (Horn 1987; Mack 2005; Morris et al. 1994), while a series of sites occupied after around 1910 included numerous ceramic fragments in excavation units or in dense surface deposits (Bass 2017; Elliott 1990; Hills et al. 1996; Miss et al. 2000; Morris et al. 1994; Paullin 2007). Researchers describe most of the white earthenware at these sites as thick, hard-paste "hotel china" with manufacturers' marks of American firms. In 1917, a lumber industry representative reported that "enameled ware" remained in use, but the "best camps"

Figure 6.1. Logging camp dining hall, Thief River Falls, Red Lake County, Minnesota, 1904. (Photo [1904] by E. S. Bruce. National Archives and Records Administration, USDA Forest Service Photograph Collection, Negative No. 54141. Washington, D.C.)

Figure 6.2. Enamelware on ground surface at Cleveland-Cliffs Iron Company Camp No. 3 (20AR33), area D, unit 3. Hiawatha National Forest, Michigan. (Photo [1989] by author, courtesy USDA Forest Service, Hiawatha National Forest, Gladstone, Mich.)

used "heavy hotel stone china" (Pacific Logging Congress 1917: 24). Two sites in Washington include evidence for the replacement of enamelware with ceramics. At the Hamilton Lumber Company Camp 6 (ca. 1912–1919) and the C. B. and M. site (ca. 1920s–1932), relatively large quantities of both fragmented hotel china and intact enamelware were found, and clusters of enamelware vessels in refuse deposits may indicate mass disposal (Hollenbeck 1983; Shong and Miss 2009).

Tableware assemblages associated with the residences of families or small groups of men who did their own cooking also occur at some sites. In contrast to refuse deposits located near institutional-style dining facilities, those related to smaller-scale dining tend to include more diverse ceramics in terms of pastes, glazes, and decoration. In the family housing section at the Lava Caves camp in Oregon, ceramics ranged from inexpensive tablewares to relatively expensive teawares (Bowyer et al. 1995). The abundance of bowls relative to plates suggested the consumption of more stews and soups compared to individual cuts of meat. Investigations recovered no enameled or tin tableware, but, unfortunately, the bunkhouse and dining areas for single men at the Lava Caves camp were not investigated. Other early twentieth-century lumber industry sites with family-associated deposits that contain ceramics include the Manley–Moore camp in Washington (Miss et al. 2000) as well as logging settlements in California (Raskin et al. 2014), Michigan (Howe 2015), and Louisiana (Hahn and Schwab 1998; Whelan and Pearson 1999). Researchers examining sawmill settlements in California, Nevada, and Washington also encountered imported Chinese and Japanese ceramics associated with housing for workers from these countries (Douglass 2000; Hartse 2017; Lee 2008; Solury 2004).

Although archival sources suggest some reasons for workers' tableware preferences, records contain few details about how companies made decisions about provisioning camps. Looking at purchase costs alone, a series of catalogs dating between 1895 and 1908 show that ceramic plates and cups actually tended to be less expensive than enamelware (Franzen 1992: 89). Given this difference, one might expect ceramics to be even more frequent in the archaeological record around 1900 than they are. However, breakage rates probably reduced or eliminated any cost advantage of ceramics. By 1922, ceramic tableware had generally become more expensive than enamelware (Cohen 1969: 516, 522; Franzen 1992). In later years, as ceramics became more expensive relative to other alternatives, their presence suggests accommodation of workers' demands for better camp conditions.

"Tin Can Archaeology"

Empty metal food cans might be the least glamorous artifacts encountered by archaeologists. Some even pejoratively call the discipline of historical archaeology "tin can archaeology" (Ascher 1974). Nonetheless, archaeologists remain wary of "writing-off" materials that might seem unattractive or unpopular objects for study, and cans possess both symbolic and concrete attributes of archaeological interest. As Ascher (1974) points out, not only are they "ubiquitous," they stand out as icons of "contemporary culture" related to topics such as industrialization, geographic mobility, disposability, and our alienation from locally grown foods and seasonality. In fact, Edgeworth et al. (2015) mention cans among the quintessential "index fossils" of the Anthropocene, a time when refuse deposits became "geological" in extent and influence. Although metal food cans became familiar to most Americans around the time of the Civil War, successive technological developments led to fully automated production and extremely high levels of use during the early twentieth century (Pearson 2016). Cans occur at late nineteenth-century logging sites (Gilbert/Commonwealth 1985; Horn 1987), but extensive surface middens containing thousands exist at early to mid-twentieth-century sites (Morris et al. 1994; Hills et al. 1996). In one of the earliest efforts to suggest research topics related to cans, Rock (1984) portrayed them as representing industrial and economic connections between widely separated geographic areas and populations. The reciprocal movement of logs and canned foods (and other supplies) by rail linked remote logging settlements to distant manufacturing centers and agricultural areas. Because of these connections, by the 1980s published literature recognized cans as a legitimate source of archaeological information (Busch 1981; Rock 1984). Archaeologists conducted historical research to provide the background information necessary for analyzing cans, focusing on the changes in manufacturing technology that make it possible to distinguish cans from different time periods (Rock 1984; Sandor and Rose 2017). Because different manufacturing techniques left distinctive markings and changed dramatically between the mid-nineteenth century and the early twentieth century, can types provide useful chronological markers.

Dumps containing empty cans also help identify the scale and location of food preparation areas. Although their exact contents usually remain unknown, embossed lettering identifies some products, such as lard and baking powder. In a few cases, their size and shape are diagnostic (e.g., sardines, potted meat). Evaporated milk cans exhibit distinctive manufacturing characteristics, and users almost always opened them by punching two small holes on opposite sides of the top. The way cans were opened also provides clues about the organization and provisioning of kitchens. Variable and/or crude cutting of lids might indicate the cooks did not have access to mechanical can openers. Reuse of cans as pails or strainers or as a source of sheet metal for purposes such as roof repair might indicate frugality or economic distress. Preservation issues related to climate also affect the condition of cans. At the Lava Caves camp in south central Oregon, good preservation resulted in legible brand names on many metal containers, while at a logging camp in rainy western Washington, only 28 intact cans were found among over 2,300 rusted can fragments (Bowyer et al. 1995; Miss et al. 2000: 64).

Research projects intended to recover information from threatened sites before earth-disturbing works such as road or pipeline construction have forced some archaeologists to confront these problematic artifacts. Several archaeological studies at logging camps in the western United States experimented with ways to count and analyze large numbers of cans (Elliott 1990; Morris et al. 1994; Hills et al. 1996). For example, the main refuse deposit at Saginaw and Manistee Company Camp 3 contained over 10,000 cans (Morris et al. 1994). Very few cans were actually collected during these studies: researchers examined samples in the field and left them on site. They determined it was unnecessary to collect, process, and store large numbers of cans in curation facilities in order to reveal their information potential.

An example of how to generate information through "tin can archaeology" is found in a report on data recovery at the Weyerhaeuser Camp 2 site in Oregon (Hills et al. 1996). The most abundant artifacts at the site were metal cans, and field crews estimated their frequency based on a series of 1 × 1 square meter "surface evaluation units," where they counted and classified cans by type and size, with the results used to extrapolate totals for various deposits (Hills et al. 1996). The combined estimates for all areas totaled over 12,000 cans, with the vast majority either evaporated milk (16- or 14½-oz. sizes) or No. 10–size (3 qt.) fruit or vegetable cans. Using archival sources, the researchers also estimated the total number of cans probably used based on the number of people at Camp 2, duration of camp operations (ca. 1928–1940), supplies purchased, typical menus, and food consumption rates. They then calculated that although cans were abundant, it is likely that those found around the camp represented only a fraction of those used.

As trash accumulated over time, the occupants may have started hauling it away by rail or truck for sanitary reasons. Although some aspects of this camp represented improved working conditions, disposal of refuse close to camp buildings was one practice that did not. This pattern of trash dumping shows how improvements in camp conditions progressed at different rates and involved trade-offs or strategies on the part of labor or management to advance their opposing interests. Another example of the dynamic relationship between the labor market and camp conditions can also be seen at Weyerhaeuser Camp 2. The company originally designed this state-of-the-art camp with many features desired by workers, such as hot showers, in anticipation of future labor shortages. However, when construction started, the labor market favored employers, so the company cut back on some of its planned improvements (Hills et al. 1996: 4-4).

Metal food containers provide evidence for variation in social organization at some logging settlements. Small- to medium-sized cans at the Lava Caves site in Oregon showed that individual families in separate structures did their own cooking (Bowyer et al. 1995). Although relatively common at this site, cans didn't occur in the densities seen near company-run cook houses. Bowyer et al. (1995) also calculated the ratio of metal food cans to home canning supplies (i.e., glass jars, lids, rims), showing a high incidence of home canning consistent with family rather than institutional cooking. At other logging settlements, deposits containing relatively large numbers of artifacts related to home canning occur near structures that accommodated families (Woodward 1975; Drake 2003; Raskin et al. 2014; Howe 2015). Besides attracting workers by providing family housing, companies may have hoped to save money: wives would be doing the cooking and purchasing food at the camp store or commissary. On the other hand, families could perhaps save some money through home canning compared to purchasing canned goods, even if canning supplies had to be purchased from company sources. Drake (2003, 2018) points out additional implications of home canning at some logging sites in Northern Michigan: Native American families canned wild foods that contributed to social reproduction by perpetuating traditional foodways.

Thus far, relatively few researchers have highlighted the ubiquitous but problematic "tin can." However, archaeology has documented the importance of canned food (milk, fruits, and vegetables) at early twentieth-century logging camps, even after railroad connections enabled more frequent food deliveries (Elliott 1990; Hills et al. 1996; Morris et al. 1994). For year-round operations, it is likely that the available refrigerated storage space restricted the amount of perishable foods used and contributed to the importance of canned food (Hills et al. 1996: 8–19). Meat probably had priority over products like fresh milk, fruits, or vegetables for the available cold storage space.

Concluding Thoughts about Foodways

Although larger and more numerous samples would be desirable, there appear to be two different contexts in which companies served food that conformed to worker preferences. During the nineteenth century, some of the era's highly independent owners and operators provided fresh beef and ceramic tableware, perhaps on the basis of a personal calculus that it was the "right thing to do" and would ultimately benefit their "bottom line" through worker quality and retention. Many company owners maintained close control over daily operations and made most of their decisions independently. However, during the early twentieth century, decisions about camp conditions became increasingly subject to external influences, including trade associations, labor unions that backed up their demands with strikes, and the policies of federal and state governments. During this era, company owners often delegated authority for various decisions and even sought input from outside specialists. Provisioning decisions therefore reflected systematic and collective efforts of both labor and management. This is illustrated, on one hand, by the various efforts of companies to reduce costs and, on the other, by labor's demands for specific improvements in camp conditions. In terms of foodways, archaeology suggests an overall level of responsiveness to worker preferences that contrasts with a power imbalance favoring capital over labor. However, the trend toward providing family housing for workers reduced the need for company dining facilities. Ongoing technological developments also reduced the demand for labor, encouraging some companies to end their logging operations and rely on independent contractors, and, as transportation infrastructure improved, the need for camp facilities ended altogether.

Archaeological evidence of foodways at logging industry sites contrasts with recommendations derived from a company-sponsored analysis of the industries' "feeding problems." In the *Journal of Home Economics*, Mueller (1921) described lumber camps in the Northwest from the perspective of company owners and managers, who provided all the background used to prepare the article. They identified ethnic diversity as one of their "problems." Company representatives described their workforce as made up of "every white race on earth," "hard to satisfy," and "infested with obstructionists" (Mueller 1921: 242). They also described workers as "unsteady," with the average length of employment in one camp being six months. Managers complained about being forced to meet worker demands vis-à-vis food quantity, variety, and quality in order to retain workers and that the resulting competition between companies increased costs. In keeping with early twentieth-century ideas about "scientific management," Mueller (1921) advised companies to get together and standardize less expensive menus, thereby eliminating culinary competition for labor and the resulting high turnover rate. He also recommended changing to cafeteria-style dining where men would be charged based on their choice of food items and portion sizes, but he acknowledged that this would "arouse opposition!" Given that loggers had already demonstrated a willingness to withhold their labor over food issues, this was indeed an understatement, and it appears that nothing like this was seriously attempted. Despite the desires of management as reflected in these proposals, archaeology shows that the influence of workers on foodways remained strong through the combined effects of the demand for labor and worker activism.

Intoxicants

Humans have an affinity for intoxicants, and there is a long tradition of social scientists and historians examining alcohol use by industrial workers (Crocq 2007; Barrows and Room 1991). As early as 1844, Engels (1958: 116) attributed high rates of alcohol consumption by English factory workers to the physical and emotional stress of adverse living and working conditions. An influential cross-cultural model developed in the 1940s suggested that in many settings, alcohol consumption represents an attempt to reduce anxiety resulting from unpredictable living situations (Horton 1943). Historical archaeologists in North America offer similar "environmental" explanations for alcohol use by workers and have documented high consumption rates at sites characterized by transient lifestyles such as those of soldiers, miners, fur traders, and, of course, loggers (Smith 2008: 98–99). The speed with which cutting depleted forests and the seasonality of operations in some areas limited the duration of logging jobs.

Artifacts related to intoxicants, including alcoholic beverages, patent medicines (which often contained alcohol and occasionally opiates), and tobacco are common at logging industry sites. Chapter 7, which focuses on ethnicity, describes paraphernalia for smoking opium associated with Chinese woodcutters in the western United States. Widespread archaeological evidence of alcohol use contradicts some common perceptions, including the overgeneralization that "liquor was strictly taboo" at logging camps (Lillard 1947: 219). Similarly, popular accounts that emphasize binges occurring in town neglect the role of drinking in daily camp life (Wells 1978; Holbrook 2016). Archaeology has identified many sites where significant alcohol use occurred in company-controlled settings, revealing details about living conditions and the balance of power between management and workers. As Troy Duster (1981: 326) succinctly pointed out: "Alcohol is to social science what dye is to microscopy."

In contrast to alcohol, all logging companies considered nicotine and caffeine compatible with the requirements of industrial work: they made tobacco available for purchase and provided ample supplies of tea or coffee. Companies sold patent medicines containing alcohol or opiates in camp stores and commissaries, but in limited quantities and at high cost. Large paternalistic companies usually tried to limit workers' access to alcohol. At Potlatch, Idaho, a Weyerhaeuser-affiliated company town with a large sawmill that began operations in 1906, officials encouraged "social order" and a "stable, sober" workforce by prohibiting alcohol (Petersen 1987). This long-standing issue transcended regional boundaries. During the winter of 1891–1892, Wisconsin lumbermen contributed funds to support a WCTU (Woman's Christian Temperance Union) missionary, who distributed temperance leaflets, newspapers, and magazines to 120 logging camps (Upham 1892).

Alcohol

Archaeological studies confirm the frequent use of intoxicants at many camps and mill settlements in the Great Lakes region. Franzen (1995) studied 220 glass containers from 86 late nineteenth- and early twentieth-century logging camps in the Upper Peninsula of Michigan. This analysis also reviewed oral history, published firsthand accounts, advertising claims, and documents revealing the actual contents of certain patent medicines. Embossing or distinctive shapes and closures showed that patent medicine, liquor, and beer containers dominated the sample. Alcohol seemed more prevalent than would be expected from written accounts, and many so-called medicines also contained alcohol or other intoxicants. Distilled liquor was the preferred alcoholic beverage, and rye whiskey appears to have been especially popular (Franzen 1995). Loggers apparently also preferred whiskey in northern Wisconsin, where a test unit at one camp yielded 26 bottles (Stencel 2000). Likewise, whiskey bottles dominated containers at the site of a small 1880s sawmill settlement in the western Sierra Mountains of California (Praetzellis and Praetzellis 1993). If workers had to conceal alcohol brought into camp or if the site was in a remote location with limited access, it makes sense that they would select beverages with the highest alcohol content. Evidence of alcohol use at lumber industry sites extends across a variety of geographic and ethnic contexts. Significant amounts of drinking occurred at charcoal processing sites in Nevada occupied by Italo-Swiss Carbonari (Zeier 1987). African Americans at a logging and milling operation in Louisiana consumed liquor, beer, and wine, and at a similar site nearby, Cajun workers preferred wine (Whelan and Pearson 1999; Hahn and Schwab 1998). A camp in Northern Michigan yielded wine bottles and a medicine bottle embossed in Croatian, and researchers suggested that intoxicants at this site might reflect ethnic preferences (Dunham and Branstner 1995). Merritt (2015) estimated that a railroad tie–cutting camp in Utah contained a minimum of 250 glass bottles in surface refuse deposits, and a large number once contained alcohol. Although archaeological work has focused on widely scattered sites or restricted geographic areas, alcohol use occurred at many lumber industry sites throughout the United States.

The intrasite distribution of containers illustrates variation in efforts by management to proscribe alcohol use and the reaction of workers to such policies. At one logging camp in Wisconsin and another in Arizona, abundant and widely distributed alcohol bottles led researchers to conclude that drinking was not only allowed, but alcohol may have been available for purchase (Stencel 2000; Morris et al. 1994). In contrast, drinkers concealed discarded bottles under floor boards or in privies at sites in California (Rich and Roscoe 2009) and Michigan (Hardwick 2008; Riordan 1980). The distribution of discarded, but not necessarily concealed, bottles near worker housing or along the edges of camp clearings characterized other sites in California (Elliott 1990; Praetzellis and Praetzellis 1993) and Michigan (Dunham and Branstner 1995). This pattern may indicate tolerance for drinking as long as it took place away from communal dining and administrative or work areas. An example of discreet but unconcealed drinking occurred at Tate Creek camp: adjacent to one worker's tent location was a cluster of 39 tobacco tins and three whiskey bottles (Elliott 1990: 41). One mill settlement exhibited differential disposal practices for alcohol containers:

beer bottles were found near dwellings, while liquor containers were discarded in more distant refuse dumps along an adjacent wetland (Whelan and Pearson 1999).

Skibo and Schiffer (2008: 34) suggested that logging camps provide an ideal "testing ground for understanding social power" through archaeological documentation of alcohol use. Similarly, Merritt and Ayres (2014) point out that numerous bottles found at Standard Tie Company camps in the mountains of Utah indicate resistance to a policy banning alcohol. Although drinking may be a direct response to physical and emotional discomfort, this does not preclude other influences. For certain immigrants with ethnic traditions involving alcohol consumption, drinking contributed to group identification and solidarity. Workers from different backgrounds sharing alcohol could strengthen bonds within an occupational group. Some camps or settlements active during federal prohibition included alcohol containers in enough abundance that authors concluded they were not "dry" operations (Riordan 1980; Elliott 1990; Bryant and Rich 2011). Although not always addressed by researchers, or even resolvable, analytic opportunities occur when archaeological evidence contradicts archival or oral history accounts. In studying one Northern Michigan logging camp, researchers interviewed a sawyer who worked there in 1926: he stated that drinking was strictly forbidden, and employees were fired for violations (Riordan 1980). When a shot glass and at least nine alcohol containers were recovered during archaeological testing, the author was unable to resolve this contradiction. Likely explanations for such occurrences include worker resistance to company control or reuse of the camp by squatters or sportsmen. Postdepositional factors affect archaeological evidence of alcohol use. Sawyers repurposed bottles to hold kerosene for sprinkling onto saw blades to speed cutting through resinous conifers (Horn 1987; Franzen 1995). At a 1907 logging camp investigated in Montana, a liquor bottle used for this purpose had a wire loop attached around the vessel's neck so it could hang from a branch (Hatlestad 2016).

Taking a closer look at bottles recovered from an African American residential area at an early twentieth-century sawmill settlement in a Louisiana cypress swamp demonstrates how documentary sources enhance archaeological analysis. This site included two bottles embossed "Devil's Island Endurance Gin," and Whelan and Pearson (1999: 186) suggested that "working [and] living in the swamp required or encouraged a higher level of alcohol consumption to insure [*sic*] endurance." The 1910 census listed the occupations of six men at this site as "swampers," perhaps the most difficult and undesirable work associated with cypress logging. These workers most likely waded through swamps without protective clothing or footwear. The wider context of alcohol consumption in the early twentieth century included a national discussion about alcohol use and debates about prohibition. As a result, we know that Devil's Island Gin was available "in the low dives of all the black belt from the Carolinas to Louisiana and Mississippi" and was never seen in establishments that excluded African Americans (Irwin 1908: 10). It was supposedly advertised using "Southern negro slang" that implied it had "aphrodisiac" properties. In this racist and anti-Semitic narrative, "cheap gin" produced by Jewish distillers, resulted in sexual crimes committed by intoxicated African American males (Irwin 1908: 10). Pianist and singer Roosevelt Sykes, who started his career playing in jook joints associated with southern logging and turpentine camps, made a circa 1932 recording called *Devil's Island Gin Blues,* expressing both the agency and anxiety that might be expected among African American loggers working in a Louisiana cypress swamp during the Jim Crow era (Hahn 2015; Sykes 2000):

> Give me one more drink
> Of that Devil's Island Gin
> I've been drunk once tonight
> And I want to get drunk, again . . .
>
> Oh yes, oh yes, I know
> Keep me worried and bothered
> Troubled ev'rywhere I go

Patent Medicines

So-called patent medicines provided loggers with a source of alcohol and, less frequently, opiates. Other intoxicants occasionally present in these products included cocaine, cannabis, chloroform, and caffeine. As of 1906, "immense quantities" of patent medicines were being sold at logging settlements in Northern Michigan (American Medical Association 1906). According to an IWW union leader, in order keep employees from seeking jobs elsewhere, southern companies that operated logging and turpentine

Figure 6.3. Van (store) at a lumber camp in Minnesota, circa 1905. Note patent medicine bottles and boxes containing jars of tobacco (snuff) on shelf. (Undated photo by H. A. Belier. National Archives and Records Administration, USDA Forest Service Photograph Collection, Negative No. 43105, Washington, D.C.)

camps "deliberately cultivated" intoxicant use by selling patent medicines containing cocaine, morphine, and heroin at "every company store" (Haywood 1983 [ca. 1929]: 243, cited in Green 1973: 167) (Figure 6.3). Product names embossed on bottles enable archaeologists to use archival sources for understanding particular advertising appeals. Because of concerns about their efficacy and potential for harm, in the late nineteenth and early twentieth centuries, investigators worked to identify the actual contents of such products, sometimes with the assistance of independent testing by chemists (Adams 1912; Cramp 1923; Oleson 1891). Besides intoxicants, patent medicines contained many other ingredients including capsicum, camphor, turpentine, thyme, wintergreen, myrrh, sassafras, lobelia, pine tar, peppermint, and kerosene. Changes in the contents and advertising of patent medicines occurred after enactment of the Pure Food and Drug Act of 1906.

Archaeological finds of patent medicine bottles at logging sites include a variety of products advertised as painkillers, cures, liniments, and laxatives

(Franzen 1995). Besides any desire for medical benefits, their popularity might be due to the alcohol present in most of these products. Many patent medicines were available in camps that prohibited alcoholic beverages. A Dr. Hornbogen of Marquette, Michigan, reported: "in many of the lumber camp stores Hinkley's Bone Liniment is as much a staple as tobacco and many of the woodsmen drink it in place of whiskey" (Wood 1905: 8). An early researcher, using various clues but no laboratory tests, surmised that the circa 1890 Hinkley's formula contained alcohol, wormwood, hemlock, thyme, turpentine, and capsicum (Oleson 1891: 93). Testing by chemists revealed that a later version of Hinkley's contained water, alcohol, camphor, and red pepper (Cramp 1923: 595). In a study of four Northern Michigan logging camps, the site with the most medicine bottles yielded the fewest alcohol bottles, and the site with the most alcohol bottles had no medicine bottles, suggesting the possibility of functional equivalence (Dunham and Branstner 1995; Dunham and Franzen 1997). Similarly, field work at an Oregon logging settlement called Old Palmer recovered only one alcohol bottle, but numerous fragmentary or intact patent medicine bottles represented a wide variety of products (Woodward 1975). Of course, in isolated camps or mill settlements, companies made money by selling these products in camp stores or commissaries.

Archaeological studies identified some products popular among loggers nationwide: Dr. Kilmer's Swamp Root, Hinkley's Bone Liniment, Dr. Kennedy's Medical Discovery, Hamlin's Wizard Oil, and Perry Davis Vegetable Pain Killer (Bryant and Rich 2011; Drake 2003; Dunham and Branstner 1995; Franzen 1995; Horn 1987; Howe 2015; Morris et al. 1994; Whelan and Pearson 1999; Woodward 1975). All of these contained alcohol as the primary ingredient, and an opium derivative enhanced the "pain killing" effects of Perry Davis (Oleson 1891; Sharrah and Bause 2017). In keeping with the Michigan origins of the Saginaw and Manistee Lumber Company and many of its employees, their Camp 3 in Arizona included Hinkley's Bone Liniment and Dr. Kilmer's Swamp Root, two of the most common products found at sites in Northern Michigan (Franzen 1995; Morris et al. 1994). At some sites, both alcoholic beverage and patent medicine containers exhibit similar distributions. For example, at the Tate Creek camp in California, both were closely associated with tent flats where workers resided (Elliott 1990). At sites where "medicines" essentially replaced "alcohol," there was apparently no need for concealment or discretion: at 20DE272, a nineteenth-century

Northern Michigan site with dense refuse deposits, numerous medicine bottles occurred in test units immediately adjacent to the cookhouse and bunkhouse (Dunham and Branstner 1995).

Although less common than intoxicants, some logging sites included glass containers that once held nonintoxicating medicinal substances predominantly marketed for respiratory problems and skin irritations: Vick's VapoRub, Musterole, Vasoline, Pond's, and Mentholatum (Drake 2003; Elliott 1990; Muckle 2016; Whelan and Pearson 1999). In general, their recommended uses address the expected effects of living in institutional settings and working outdoors handling logs and lumber. Given the lack of fresh fruit and vegetables, laxative effects may have been desired by some loggers. Sites in Michigan, Oregon, California, and Washington included containers for Fletcher's Castoria, Pitcher's Castoria, Hood's Sarsaparilla, and Scott's Emulsion (Franzen 1995; Horn 1987; Miss et al. 2000; Praetzellis and Praetzellis 1993; Woodward 1975). Hood's contained 16.5 percent alcohol and a laxative similar to senna (Cramp 1923: 597). Although its high alcohol content explains the popularity of Hinkley's Bone Liniment, one account of logging camp life in Michigan refers to it as "liquid dynamite" because of its "explosive" effects and cautions that "it had to be rationed out sparingly by the camp clerk if he wanted a full work crew the next day" (Reimann 1951: 37). This illustrates one reason why management attempted to control the types and quantities of intoxicants available in camps.

Tobacco

Given its New World origins and global role in colonization and economic development, tobacco is perhaps the quintessential American intoxicant. Companies offered tobacco products for purchase at camp stores or commissaries and clearly thought it was a stimulant compatible with production. Archival sources provide some details about tobacco use, but these sources are rare and unavailable for most sites. Nonetheless, artifacts associated with different forms of tobacco reveal variation potentially related to factors like chronology, ethnicity, consumer availability, and advertising. Smokeless tobacco could be used while working, and chewing tobacco was the most popular form of tobacco in America during the mid- to late nineteenth century (Rogozinski 1990). Fox (2015: 50) comments that as "ephemeral" tobacco uses became dominant after 1860, they left "little or no trace in the archaeological record." However, with favorable artifact preservation and adequate sampling, evidence of tobacco use besides pipe smoking persists, mainly as remnants of packaging or containers. Loggers generally favored pipes, chewing tobacco, and snuff, but apparently despised cigarettes. Legendary logger Jigger Jones supposedly told Stewart Holbrook (2016: 228), "A man who will smoke one of them pimp sticks won't stop at nothin'." According to Ryan (1973: 50), before World War I most camp foremen in northern Minnesota would not employ workers who smoked cigarettes.

Archaeologists working at logging industry sites seldom encounter the large numbers of ubiquitous and informative white clay pipe fragments found at colonial and early American sites. This is attributable at least in part, if not predominantly, to changing preferences during the nineteenth century as other forms of nicotine use became popular. White clay pipe fragments found at logging sites in Northern Michigan decreased from over 400 fragments at the circa 1848–1855 First Nahma Sawmill (Blair 2001; Franzen and Drake 2010) to fewer than 10 fragments at each of four circa 1870s–1910 logging camps tested in 1994 (Dunham and Branstner 1995). Pipe-smoking remained popular, but with increased use, after 1850, of more durable pipe materials much less common in the archaeological record (Bradley 2000). Chewing tobacco, snuff, pipe tobacco, and cigars dominated the tobacco market in the United States from the mid-nineteenth century until the rise of cigarette smoking in the early twentieth century (Rogozinski 1990). Snuff and chewing tobacco may not always be well represented in the archaeological record because some containers were perishable, and tin containers are often poorly preserved. Making provisions for recovering small-scale artifacts is important in documenting tobacco use because the only common nonperishable evidence of plug tobacco would be small, embedded metal tags that identified different brands. Tobacco tags have been recovered at logging sites in Arizona (Morris et al. 1994), California (Praetzellis and Praetzellis 1993), Oregon (Horn 1987), and Michigan (Gilbert/Commonwealth 1985; Dunham and Branstner 1995). The size and shape of these tags vary by brand. Examples include round tags marked "Lorillard's Climax Plug," American Tobacco Company's "Spearhead"-shaped tags, and a star-shaped tag from Ligget and Meyers (Horn 1987; Morris et al. 1994). Logging sites where tags have been found thus far predate 1910. Archaeological examples of devices for cutting plugs have been found at logging camps in Wisconsin and Arizona, probably associated with camp stores or company commissaries (Morris et al. 1994; Overstreet et al. 1983). Nationally, snuff was much less popular than chewing tobacco, but it was preferred by Scandinavians, especially Swedes, and, as a result, snuff containers are relatively abundant at some logging industry sites (Morris et al. 1994; Richner 1986; Rogozinski 1990).

Packaging changes and better preservation enhance the archaeological visibility of tobacco use at many logging sites occupied during the early twentieth century. Logging sites dating from shortly after circa 1900 up through the 1920s in California, Oregon, Washington, and Wisconsin include large numbers of tobacco tins (Clark 2002; Elliott 1990; Mack 2005; Richner 1986; Stencel 2000; Vaughan 1990). Counts of cans either collected or mapped at these sites range from 30 to over 500. Upright, flat, pocket-sized tins first used around 1907 dominate these samples (Rock 1984). Brand names still legible on some examples from these sites include Prince Albert, Stag, Velvet, Tuxedo, and Edgeworth. In the early twentieth century, some brands marketed the same cut tobacco for both smoking and chewing (Calumet News 1914; Ryan 1980: 59). The relative popularity of different products at the Tate Creek camp in California reflects national preferences around 1920: only three Copenhagen snuff cans were found in comparison to 112 cut tobacco cans. Snuff accounted for only 3–5 percent of American tobacco consumption between 1880 and 1930, while plug and cut tobacco (mainly used for chewing and pipe smoking) together accounted for 55–73 percent (Rogozinski 1990). Given that managers condoned its use, it is not surprising that tobacco-related artifacts seem more widely distributed than alcohol containers. Evidence of tobacco use (cans, tags, pipe fragments) are abundant around bunkhouses but not restricted to these areas (Blair 2001; Horn 1987; Mack 2005; Stencel 2000). At the Tate Creek site, pocket-sized tobacco tins were clustered around residential tent-flat areas but also occurred in refuse dumps (Elliott 1990). Personal items were almost totally absent in the sawmill and blacksmith areas of the Cole and Smith site in California, with the notable exception of metal tobacco tags (Praetzellis and Praetzellis 1993).

Comparing national trends with variations in tobacco use at lumber industry sites suggests possibilities for further research. Even though the physical effects of tobacco were not as dramatic as those of alcohol or opiates, loggers apparently also used it to cope with difficult working and living conditions. The unnamed author of an 1868 article on Minnesota's "pineries" emphasized the needful relaxation embodied in a bunkhouse smoking scene at an 1860s logging camp: "A large number puffed away at their meerschaums, or their short, black, clay pipes, looking a kind of quiet content, as if the weariness they brought in from their days work were really taking flight in clouds of smoke" (Harper's New Monthly Magazine 1868: 417). Tobacco played an important role in the daily routine of lumber industry workers, and additional consideration of its social-symbolic implications is warranted.

Intoxicants like alcohol, tobacco, and opiates could also contribute to maintaining ethnic or occupational bonds and solidarity. These functions would complement or supplement "environmental" interpretations and those focusing on resistance. Contextualizing archaeological evidence of intoxicants in ways that better reflect their functions in closely controlled industrial labor settings has been productive, and this approach could be developed and refined with larger samples and wider interregional coverage. Howe (2015) offers an example of artifact classifications that better reflect situations where workers essentially lived "on-the-job" and at least partially under company control. Even though found near residential structures instead of industrial work areas, many artifacts at the circa 1901–1912 Coalwood logging settlement in Northern Michigan are interpreted as representing both "productive" and "reproductive" activities (Howe 2015). For example, besides their role as "personal" items or "indulgences," alcohol and medicine bottles relate to "production" because they provided relief from work-related discomfort (Howe 2015).

Sanitation

Builders constructed most logging camps without any provisions for workers to bathe or wash their clothes. One notable result is the frequency with which firsthand accounts mention lice and bedbugs. In fact, a variety of "tall tales" recount incidents involving insect pests, such as the lumberjack who woke up in the night to see one of his unwashed shirts heading out the door under its own power (Bernhardt 1979: 15–16). Despite the wry humor, workers cited unsanitary conditions as justification for strikes. Even though companies improved conditions in northwestern camps during the early twentieth century, Gibbons (1918) admitted that "operators as a class do not seem to have given sufficient attention to camp sanitation." Even less progress occurred in regions where the logging industry was in decline. A logger active in Northern Michigan, Matt Savola, described conditions leading up to a 1937 strike:

> There were two-man wooden bunks with hay-straw mattress ticks made out of gunny sacks. The blankets were of cheap material, just like horse blankets. They weren't washed till the spring, and they were lousy. There was no place to wash. Washing facilities was just an iron pot. They'd save up underwear for a couple of weeks and Sundays they would "boil up"—kill the lice by boiling in an iron pot. The lack of bathing facilities was terrible. Some of the heartier ones would wash themselves with snow. . . . The ventilation and lighting was just terrible. A terrible stench came from the haywire strung around the woodstove where the men would hang their socks to dry. . . . It was these conditions that led to the strike and made the men very militant.
>
> (From June 30, 1977, interview with Savola by Bernhardt [1979: 15])

Debra Bernhardt (1979: 15) credited this leader of the 1937 timber workers strike in Northern Michigan with rallying strikers by paraphrasing Marx: "Lumberjacks, unite! All you've got to lose is your bedbugs!" Given the general lack of sanitation, any archaeological evidence of bathing or laundry facilities stands out. Archaeology at Bingham's camp in Oregon documented the remains of a relatively early (ca. 1890s) facility: a 9 × 11-foot frame building thought to be a laundry and/or bathhouse (Horn 1987). Instead of round logs, it was built using squared timbers and joinery supposedly resembling a technique used in China. Associated artifacts included patent medicine bottles, stove parts, buttons, a wire line with handmade hooks for hanging clothing, and large metal cans and buckets. In addition, shallow drainage ditches extended out from this structure. Chapter 7 discusses two other types of bathing facilities: Finnish *savusaunas* and Japanese *ofuros*. However, most companies did not provide bathing and laundry facilities until relatively late in the logging camp era, and these were restricted to larger corporate camps (Butler 1922; Hills et al. 1996).

Leisure Activities

Some aspects of daily life are difficult to study directly through archaeology because they produce few material remains or their remains are not preserved. This includes activities such as religious services, storytelling, stag dances, card games, music, and reading. Some of these activities may be nonetheless visible at sites with unusually good preservation or where larger samples are recovered. Archaeological excavations conducted by Michigan

Figure 6.4. Lahti Logging Camp, Alger County, Michigan, circa 1910. Lahti is a Finnish surname meaning bay or cove. Note patent medicine bottle and accordion. (Courtesy Jack Deo, Superior View Studio, Marquette, Mich.)

Technological University recovered large and diverse samples from Coalwood, a Cleveland-Cliffs Iron Company logging site active from 1901 to 1912 in the Upper Peninsula of Michigan (Wurst 2016, 2017). This enabled Durocher (2018) to address the role of music in this largely Finnish logging community consisting of family residences that frequently included boarders, based on cupreous and ferrous metal reed plates representing at least 20 different instruments (harmonicas, concertinas, and accordions). Their even distribution throughout residential areas (but not around the company store) led the author to conclude that, at one time or another, "there were people with reed instruments living in every house across the site" (Durocher 2018: 65). Speaking of camps like Coalwood where families were present, Robert Lustick (1995) recounted that "many of these guys . . . knew how to play the old button box. They'd have these little get togethers and dance" (Figure 6.4). Besides documenting recreational activities and leisure-time entertainment, combining both archaeological and historical information suggests the social-political context of this music. Durocher (2018) points out that music at Coalwood and other Finnish and Slovenian camps in the area reinforced ethnic identities and facilitated political expression, such as these lyrics (translated from Finnish) complaining about prices in a company store:

> While we're slaving over lumber work,
> That cock-eyed Mäkinen is fixing the prices.
> A dollar-and-a-half shirt he wants to sell for two and a quarter.
>
> (Similä 1938, from *Yli kymmenen vuotta Korpiinissa oli jo astuttu* [Over Ten Years We Have Lived in Corbin])

Everyday Life: Transience as a Tactic?

Variations in daily life and camp conditions suggest indirect or implicit negotiation of working and living conditions through worker mobility. Some conditions vary by company or even site by site, while other characteristics seem more consistent. As logger Matt Savola recounted based on his 1930s experiences in Northern Michigan camps, "Some camps had lousy food. . . . Men followed the camps where the food was good" (from June 30, 1977, interview with Savola by Bernhardt [1979: 16]). Regarding sanitation, he also recalled, "some of the jobbers, especially the Finns, had saunas. . . . They had more decent conditions and their camps were always crowded with men wanting to get in." For many years, job shopping based on camp conditions took place through decisions by individual workers. In later years, labor collectively advanced the same concerns through union activity. Future archaeological studies of lumber-camp life could benefit from early twentieth-century documentary sources that criticize camp conditions and make recommendations for improvements (Bryant 1923; California Commission of Immigration and Housing 1920, cited in Maniery 2002; Gibbons 1918). These sources provide information useful for developing models or hypotheses about what might be found archaeologically. In identifying areas needing improvement, critics provide the background needed to formulate research designs and analyze archaeological variation relative to particular social, environmental, and economic conditions. Recommendations for so-called modern camps specify details such as numbers of windows, floor space per man, distance of refuse dumps from camp structures, menus, and sanitary facility designs (Gibbons 1918; Bryant 1923). Archaeology can determine if a particular operation met certain standards and thus provide insight into more general questions regarding the relationship between workers, lumber companies, and government agencies.

7

Savusaunas, Opium, Dolls, and Snuff

Social Organization at Logging Sites

> The men are of many shades and many tongues. . . . The work in the woods is almost exclusively in the hands of what might be called the northern type, the American, German, and Swede predominating. . . . [T]he grading crew, the lowest class of unskilled workers, consists of five Greeks, one Italian, and two Americans.
>
> Frederick Mills, "Work in a Sierra Lumber Camp" (1914)

Race, ethnicity, gender, and class have become important research topics in historical archaeology, and studies of the lumber industry reflect this trend. Both participants in historic logging and firsthand observers emphasized various forms of identity, and these categorizations defined many social, political, and economic relationships. However, intersecting systems for determining identity were routinely conflated. Some groups were "racially" classified on the basis of their "whiteness" without regard to their physical appearance. Diversity defined the late nineteenth- and early twentieth-century industrial workforce, and immigration is linked to the expansion of many industries, including logging. Workers coming from nonindustrial agricultural backgrounds adapted to new settings. Since the "factory regime" desired by companies emphasized standardization, it conflicted with the expression of traditional identities, especially in areas like language and foodways. Homogenization did occur, but some accounts overemphasize the effectiveness and speed of this process. One historian described lumber industry workers as a "cross section of the American melting pot" (Maybee 1960: 27). Archaeology permits us to highlight diversity and document it in geographic areas or time periods not covered by written records. In identifying different social groups within logging camps and settlements, it is important to examine how ideology shaped these identities.

Based on historical records and oral history, Rock (1986) describes various ethnic groups involved in Northern California logging. He recommends further archaeological exploration of this topic but warns that material culture differences might not always be visible because corporate pressure for standardization suppressed the expression of ethnic identities. Other research topics suggested by Rock (1986) include the causes and effects of the change from "stag" camps to those with women and children present and of recreational drinking before, during, and after prohibition. When available, oral history and documents play an important role in researching social organization, but archaeology also provides clues about gender, age, race, class, and ethnicity. Many archaeologists working on logging industry sites infer the presence of women and children based on decorated ceramics, jewelry, and toys. Features and artifacts closely associated with particular ethnic groups include Chinese opium-smoking paraphernalia and group-specific bathing facilities, such as Finnish *savusaunas* or Japanese *ofuros*. On rare occasions, immigrants' native languages occur on consumer products or coins. However, archaeologists are generally cautious in evaluating archaeological evidence of identity. Few traits are as clear and unequivocal as those noted above, given the mass production and national distribution of affordable consumer goods in the late nineteenth and early twentieth centuries. However, identity is also expressed in less direct ways.

Gender and Age

Many early camps were all-male, but this led to stereotypes: "A logging camp in the Michigan woods was no place for weaklings or the ladies" (Maybee 1960: 19). However, families accompanied foremen and other high-status employees at some sites, and females often worked in key support roles such as cooking. Personal accounts and oral histories document the presence of women and children, especially after about 1900. Archaeologists soon realized this when they began finding artifacts that appeared out of place, like porcelain fragments of dolls, at remote logging camps (Figure 7.1). In fact, some researchers wisely addressed gender, even when they encountered no evidence of women or children. Elliott (1990) specifically mentions that no evidence of women was present at the Tate Creek site, calling it a "stag camp." Other sites designated "all-male" by researchers include camps in Arizona (Morris et al. 1994), California (Vaughan 1990), and Washington (Miss et al. 2000). More frequently, researchers have inferred the presence

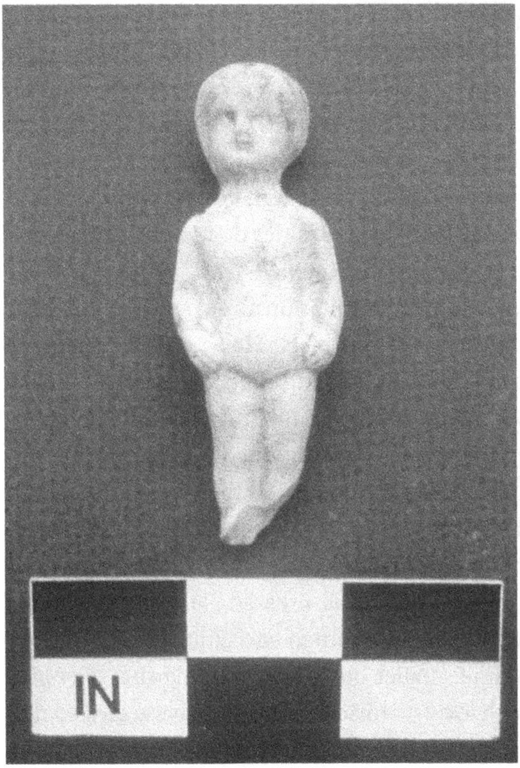

Figure 7.1. Porcelain doll (Frozen Charlotte) from archaeological testing at the Salling-Hanson logging camp (20CR53), Hartwick Pines State Park, Michigan. (Photo [1992] by Dean Anderson, courtesy State of Michigan Archaeological Site File, Lansing.)

of women and children based on the finding of jewelry and small-sized footwear (Clark 2002; Horn 1987; McKee 2009; Morris et al. 1994), toys like marbles, porcelain doll fragments, and doll china (Clark 2002; McKee 2009; Miss et al. 2000; Raskin et al. 2014; Wettstaed 2003), and decorated ceramics or glassware (Bowyer et al. 1995; Brashler 1991; Woodward 1975). In some cases, written records and oral history aided in these attributions, but in others the only evidence of gender or age diversity came from archaeology.

After around 1900, families accompanied nonsupervisory workers more frequently as companies gradually responded to labor shortages by offering better housing. Besides identifying the presence of families, several studies offer more detailed discussions of gender. At a Shevlin-Hixon Company railroad logging camp in south central Oregon, researchers compared the frequency of gender- or age-specific artifacts: 125 male, 113 female, 9 children (Bowyer et al. 1995). Compared to a nearby all-male railroad construction camp, the family housing area at this logging camp exhibited less evidence of tobacco use and a greater number of decorated ceramic fragments.

Every residential feature included an associated refuse dump, indicating that each household prepared meals separately. Research in Michigan at the logging settlement of Coalwood included excavation and controlled surface collection from extensive refuse deposits associated with family housing for workers. Arguing that residential contexts at industrial sites are too narrowly defined as domestic, Howe (2015) looked at material culture patterns in terms of the social relations of capitalism. Besides documenting the presence of women and children, he regarded artifacts and features in these deposits related to cooking, sewing, and sanitation as evidence of domestic labor used in the production of forest products. Howe (2015) concluded that the Cleveland-Cliffs Iron Company logging division preferred hiring "family men," not just for workforce stability, but because family members, especially wives, contributed to production without compensation.

Brashler (1991) examined gender in the context of the West Virginia railroad logging industry, with oral history and documents providing background for archaeological analysis. An abundance of decorative items at a logging settlement called Dogway, including pressed glass and decorated ceramics, was interpreted as evidence of women and children. In contrast, similar items were scarce at nine smaller but related logging sites occupied by all-male crews. Even though local historical references characterized mill towns as the only locations with families present, the author concluded that family life also played a key role at intermediate settlements such as Dogway during a period when a "rural subsistence economy" was changing to a "rural industrial economy" (Brashler 1991: 66).

Ethnicity and Race

Even though the documentary record contains many spatial and temporal gaps, scattered references highlight the ethnic diversity of various logging regions. Reinhardt (1983: 76) claimed that, in this respect, the number of different groups present in Upper Great Lakes logging settlements rivaled that of New York's Lower East Side. Likewise, in 1913 the *Bangor Daily News* headlined, "Congress of all nations in Maine's lumber camps: Russians, Poles, Finns, Swedes and Lithuanians Have Succeeded the Canadians Who Displaced Native Loggers." The headline's ethnic sequence indicates how companies lowered labor costs by employing the most recent immigrants. Based on his experiences at a logging camp in the Sierra Mountains of California in 1914, Frederick Mills (1992) described both ethnic diversity and "division of work by nationalities," with Americans from New England and Kentucky, Swedes, and Germans doing most of the actual logging, while railroad and grade construction crews consisted primarily of "less skilled" (non–English speaking) immigrants from Greece and Italy. One interviewee told Mills that Italians and Greeks were replacing "white men" at a nearby sawmill because they worked harder and would tolerate more abuse from bosses (Mills 1992: 52). In 1909, a supervisor for a company in the Pacific Northwest described a plan to replace troublesome Finns with "white men" (Rajala 1993: 102). In what could be called color-blind racism, whiteness tropes supported hierarchical social divisions that facilitated exploitive employment practices and the exclusion of immigrant groups likely to espouse socialist ideologies. Shortly after a major 1907 strike on the Minnesota Iron Range led by Finns, a district attorney in northern Minnesota tried to reject citizenship applications from 16 Finnish immigrants because they were supposedly "Mongols," not "white persons" (Huhta 2014). He based this denial, which a court later reversed, on his interpretation of the 1882 Chinese Exclusion Act, linguistic differences between Finnish and other European languages, and Finns' supposed inherent incivility (Huhta 2014). Clearly, elements within the "melting pot" did not always integrate smoothly on industrial frontiers. Although many logging crews were mixed, discrimination and/or self-identification sometimes resulted in camps or crews dominated by a single ethnic group.

Although companies maintained strict segregation at all settlements, the southern lumber industry depended on African American labor. As a result, the policies of large companies in the South could be both racist and paternalistic. African Americans usually received lower pay and endured poorer living conditions than white workers, but lumber companies often opposed violent racist groups, who could disrupt their operations by intimidating or attacking their employees. Even though companies opposed instances of racial violence, they could also benefit from increased control of the workforce. Despite abusive practices like debt peonage and convict leasing, as the twentieth century progressed, increased numbers of African Americans created relatively stable working-class communities based on permanent employment in the lumber industry (Jones 2005). Sawmill communities in the South studied by archaeologists represent some of the experiences of both African American and European American workers.

Enslaved African Americans labored at the mid- to late nineteenth-century Van Winkle Sawmill in northwest Arkansas, which included the archaeological remains of an entire community (Brandon and Davidson 2005; Brandon 2013). Instead of resembling a company town, it was clearly modeled on plantations of the lowland south; even though founder Peter Van Winkle originally came from New York, he became the main supplier of lumber for a large area in northwest Arkansas. The site consisted of industrial and segregated residential zones, with the owner's house strategically placed with views of all areas (Brandon and Davidson 2005). The owner, whose home was burned during the Civil War, supported the Confederate cause and advocated the modernization of local infrastructure. The industrial use of slaves combined with an emphasis on modernization challenge the stereotype of the Ozarks as poor, white, and agricultural. Van Winkle rebuilt the settlement after the war and, as a result, this site includes antebellum and postbellum deposits. At the former slave quarters, material culture was relatively sparse and included mostly kitchen and architecture-related items. In contrast, a house later occupied by freed workers showed a dramatic increase in mass-produced consumer goods, including personal items and toys.

Enslaved African Americans also labored at the circa 1840–1870 Brown-Cozzens Sawmill in Natchez-Under-the-Hill, Adams County, Mississippi (Cramer 2003; Hahn et al. 2005). The most notable features found during archaeological excavations include a brick-lined well and a brick foundation associated with a chimney or furnace. The brick well feature contained a mixture of industrial, personal, and food related items, and the authors make a good case that domestic inclusions represent workers (Figure 7.2). Faunal remains dominated by pork were consistent with other sites occupied by African Americans, and historical documents confirm that the mill owner used slave labor. Lower value utilitarian ceramics (undecorated white earthenware) exhibited cut marks, and saucers were apparently used as plates. In this same deposit, higher status items such as champagne bottles appeared out of place, but the authors suggest workers repurposed them as drinking water containers.

Archaeological data recovery took place in an African American housing area associated with the 1903–1916 Good Land Cypress Company Mill along Chacahoula Bayou in Louisiana (Whelan and Pearson 1999). The sawmill location itself was not part of this data recovery, and the study covered social aspects of worker housing rather than industrial technology. Cypress swamp dominates this area, and the site is low and frequently flooded, with the water table only 20 centimeters below the ground surface. Although

Figure 7.2. Interior of brick-lined well at McFadden-Sisloff-Cozzens Sawmill (22DA993), Natchez-Under-the-Hill, Adams County, Mississippi (Hahn et al. 2005: figure 9-27). Note sash saw blade and mid-nineteenth-century blue-edged whiteware plate. (Photo courtesy Coastal Environments Inc. and U.S. Army Corps of Engineers, Vicksburg District.)

not emphasized in the original report, besides the 17 men with sawmill occupations, the 1910 census lists six men as "swampers" (workers who felled trees and skidded logs along railroad grades and spurs) and three as railroad workers. These men either traveled back and forth by railroad each day to participate in harvest operations or stayed in some kind of floating bunkhouse during the week. Undecorated (60%) and molded (34%) whiteware dominated the ceramic sample. Bone preservation was only "fair," with pork and beef dominant. Numerous wild species were present, including elements representing 10 raccoons, but their relative biomass contributions were small in comparison to domestic species. Pork bones came mainly from larger or wholesale cuts, and beef came from more diverse and carefully butchered mid-range value cuts. Of the pork specimens, 57 percent represent picnic shoulders, and although this may be an "ethnic indicator" of African Americans, it is also consistent with low socioeconomic status in general.

About two miles down the railroad tracks from the Good Land Cypress Company Mill described above, the Dibert, Stark, and Brown Cypress Company constructed a mill town called Donner. Hahn and Schwab (1998) investigated this circa 1900–1938 settlement, and while documentary evidence indicated that Cajun laborers lived in an area where many wine bottles occurred, most of the assemblage resembled the African American material from the Good Land site. The authors point out the difficulty of separating the material culture effects of ethnicity from those of socioeconomic status. The bone assemblage associated with the Cajun workers at Donner resembled that from the African American housing area at the Good Land Company just down the tracks: pork and beef supplemented by small but diverse quantities of game and fish. Among pork cuts, picnic shoulder also dominated at Donner, and chuck was the most common beef cut. The authors believe that the similarities in food remains between the Cajun area at Donner and the African American area at Good Land resulted from socioeconomic status and limited availability rather than ethnicity (Hahn and Schwab 1998).

African Americans provided almost all the labor for producing naval stores, an industry represented in southern states by archaeological remains of tar kilns, pine gum collection, and turpentine stills (Forney 1985; Healey and Kirkland 2015; Southerlin 2013). Fragments of mass-produced unglazed earthenware vessels used to collect pine gum are numerous and widespread in southern pine forests (Figure 7.3). Called Herty cups, they were invented in 1903 as part of an effort to develop less destructive collection methods. Prior to this improvement, deep cavities chopped into trees served as reservoirs for accumulating gum. Although many naval stores industry sites have been located, very little excavation has taken place, and their research potential remains relatively unexplored (Healey and Kirkland 2015). Exceptions include a limited investigation at Camp Dantzler in southern Mississippi's Pine Hills region, where African American loggers and turpentine workers lived from about 1910 to 1920 (Reams and Cramer 1998, cited in Young 2004: 75). In the residential area of this site, test units encountered tin cans, kerosene lamp parts, barrel hoops, a wash basin, and a pitcher. Features included a structural "drip line" and an outdoor hearth. The overall scarcity of material suggested poverty, portable residences, and/or a short duration of site use. An adjacent industrial area associated with a turpentine still yielded Herty cup fragments. Artifacts were more abundant at a 1919–1928 turpentine camp called Nalaka in Polk County, Florida (Ziel

Figure 7.3. Mass disposal or abandonment of earthenware Herty cups for collecting pine gum, mainly used to produce turpentine. Cups are about seven inches high; hole near rim is for hanging on a nail below the area cut to stimulate flow of gum. Osceola National Forest, Columbia County, Florida. (Photo [2017] by author.)

2013). The 1920 census showed this settlement consisted of 26 whites and 231 blacks or mulattos. In an attempt to determine if a "jook joint" was present, numerous surface artifacts exposed by a controlled burn were described and mapped using GPS (Global Positioning System) and GIS (Geographic Information System). A possible jook joint location along the edge of the segregated African American section included harmonica reeds, a tobacco tin, buttons, bottle glass, a costume jewelry bead, and a broken human tooth (Ziel 2013).

African Americans also worked in the lumber industry outside the South. The Elmwood site in the western Upper Peninsula of Michigan on the Ottawa National Forest represents a logging camp occupied 1926–1930 by African Americans from Chicago, who cut pulpwood in hopes of generating enough income to purchase land and start farming (Bastian 1999; Bastian and Rutter 1987). Local newspapers indicate their supposed employer never paid for the wood they cut. Police later arrested all 20 adults at the camp for making moonshine; 15 pled guilty and agreed to return to Chicago with train fare paid by county authorities. Newspaper articles contained racial slurs, and eventually the entire group left the area. Archaeological data recovery at the site provided an opportunity to examine these events from multiple perspectives: documents, oral history, and archaeology. Researchers located and interviewed two former residents of this camp. Their accounts suggested life at Elmwood was neither as destitute nor as desperate as portrayed in local news articles. The residents raised vegetables, chickens, and rabbits; hunted deer, fished, and had a milk cow. They denied moonshine production but admitted some of the group purchased alcohol from local whites. Although excavation recovered only one "ethnic" artifact (a McBrady's Hair Pomade jar lid), researchers identified deposits associated with this group based on chronological and stratigraphic evidence. Archaeology supported oral history in providing a more positive depiction of life at Elmwood than obtained from newspapers. Excavation showed they added a substantial structure to the camp, and faunal remains show a varied and nutritious diet. Copper tubing, a cache of reusable bottles, and an outdoor hearth indicated liquor production, but even if the African Americans, in fact, violated prohibition laws, they experienced discriminatory enforcement. Newspapers mention locals arrested for this offense, but they had not been forced to leave the area as a result. The Ku Klux Klan was active in nearby communities during this period.

In some southern logging-related communities, memories of racism and violence connect the past and present, and this can challenge researchers. As William Faulkner wrote in *Requiem for a Nun*, "The past is never dead. It's not even past." This was illustrated when researchers proposed an archaeological project to study a vanished African American community associated with lumbering and turpentine production in Rosewood, Florida. Racially motivated attacks destroyed this settlement in 1923, resulting in eight deaths and the burning of 18 homes, a church, a store, and the Masonic hall (González-Tennant 2010; Davidson and González-Tennant 2008). Surviving residents abandoned their properties, which were later acquired by neighbors of European descent. After many years of silence, survivors recounted these events and journalists covered the story in the 1990s. Consultants prepared a detailed historical report, and the Florida legislature authorized compensation to survivors and descendants because of negligence by state and local authorities during the incident. A proposal for archaeological research was formulated to facilitate historical awareness and public education about Rosewood, but researchers could only access a small portion of the destroyed community, and some local residents opposed recognition or commemoration of its existence. A historical marker about the events at Rosewood has been repeatedly vandalized. As a result, the Virtual Rosewood project digitally re-created the town, based on documents and oral history, as it existed in 1923 prior to its destruction (http://www.virtualrosewood.com/). González-Tennant (2010) describes the project as a "simple act of remembering in the face of overwhelming and deliberate forgetting."

The experience of Scandinavian immigrants working in the lumber industry contrasts with that of African Americans. James Ayres (1983, 1996), a pioneer in early archaeological studies of logging, identified evidence of Swedish ethnicity at sites in Utah with partially standing log structures occupied from about 1867 until 1930. Logging there provided railroad ties, bridge timbers, and fuel wood for the transcontinental railroad. Based on names carved or written on structure walls, documents that mention the site, and remains of Swedish language newspapers used for chinking, he attributed architectural variation to an influx of Swedish and other Scandinavian workers in the early twentieth century. Morris et al. (1994) also examined ethnicity and found numerous metal and ceramic snuff containers at the Saginaw and Manistee Company's Camp 3 in Arizona. Knowing from records that many Swedes worked there, the authors surmised that they preferred snuff for economic or other pragmatic reasons. However, there is actually a long-standing and well-documented Swedish tradition favoring snuff over other forms of tobacco, and from the late eighteenth century until the 1930s it dominated tobacco sales in Sweden (Goodman 2005: 90).

Distinctive and well-preserved archaeological features associated with ethnicity at Great Lakes logging sites include the remains of Finnish *savusaunas* (smoke saunas): small log or frame buildings without chimneys where a wood fire heated a mortarless stove-like stone structure (*kiaus*). Floor plan dimensions of intact *savusaunas* at Finnish American farmsteads in northern Minnesota ranged from 8 × 10 feet to 13 × 24 feet, depending on whether a dressing room was attached. Two functioning *kiaus* recorded in northern Minnesota measured about 5 feet x 5 feet x 2 feet high (Kaups 1976a: 12; 1976b: 36). Scrap metal or short segments of repurposed steel rails supported rocks above a space that served as a fire chamber within the rock pile. After the *kiaus* was hot, the fire was allowed to die, smoke cleared through vents, and the building was closed up. Water for bathing was heated in a metal vessel atop the *kiaus*. Finnish farmers abandoned or converted

Figure 7.4. Remains of *savusauna* (smoke sauna) at early twentieth-century Cleveland-Cliffs Iron Company Camp No. 4 (20AR199), Hiawatha National Forest, Michigan. (Photo [2015] by author.)

most *savusaunas* to saunas with chimneys in the 1920s or 1930s (Kaups 1976a: 12). Because of the amount of rock used, *kiaus* remain visible long after wooden portions of structures have disappeared (Figure 7.4). Besides their practical utility for bathing, users attributed restorative and healing properties to saunas. According to a Finnish proverb, "Sauna is a poor man's pharmacy" (*Sauna on köyhän apteekki*) (Ganter 2011: 35). Medicine bottles embossed with the words *Suomen Verenpuhdistus* (Finnish Blood Cleanser) associated with the remains of *savusaunas* at the Coalwood logging settlement in Michigan highlight this function (Franzen 1992; Howe 2015). Several historical studies document the social and symbolic importance of saunas in both Finland and North America (Edelsward 2001; Johnson 1951; Lockwood 1977).

Franzen (1992) used the archaeological remains of *savusaunas* in Northern Michigan to argue that workers' ethnic backgrounds and preferences had a greater influence on camp conditions than is often acknowledged. A stark contrast existed between Finnish camps with saunas and other contemporary logging camps, which usually lacked any facilities or indoor space specifically reserved for bathing. Finns played a major role in logging in the upper Great Lakes states and Ontario, and many joined labor unions and socialist organizations (Kero 1973). In fact, archaeological and historical research focusing on early twentieth-century Finnish logging camps in Northern Michigan suggests that *savusaunas* became "politicized" and represented the tensions between labor and capital over camp conditions (Drake et al. 2006; Drake and Drake 2007). Future archaeological research on logging camp *savusaunas* might consider the influence of different regional traditions within Finland and variation related to whether or not logging companies cooperated in sauna construction (Drake et al. 2006; Drake and Drake 2007). In his study of the Coalwood logging settlement, Howe (2015: 7) identifies *savusaunas* as an "excellent example of the material and political expression of ethnic identity within labor camps." At least one other ethnic group active in logging built traditional structures for bathing (the Japanese *ofuro*), and future comparative research on the *savusauna* and the *ofuro* might be informative.

Besides the Scandinavians and Finns often associated with logging, several other European groups are possible subjects for archaeological research on ethnicity in the lumber industry. Excavation in an 1860s–1920s residential area next to a Minnesota sawmill revealed features associated with former boardinghouse locations where French Canadian and Irish workers lived. Terrell (2005) cites the archaeological potential for documenting their daily lives relative to sanitation, hygiene, health, diet, consumer choice, and religious practices. For example, a nearly complete porcelain holy water font decorated by an image of the Christ Child in relief was found in a privy presumably used by Irish workers who lived in a nearby boardinghouse (Terrell 2005). At a sawmill settlement in Vermont, residential remains clustered in two separate areas, and researchers hypothesized that this demarcation represents the segregation of French-speaking from English-speaking employees (Lacy and Charles 2000). Unfortunately, they were unable to pursue this idea but highlighted it as a research topic for future exploration.

Only one archaeological study in this literature survey specifically focused on a Native American logging camp, even though Native Americans played a significant role in the Great Lakes lumber industry (Drake 2003, 2018). The Moses Camp (20DE537) was an early twentieth-century *Anishinaabe* site in Northern Michigan. Documentary and oral evidence identify the camp foreman as Pete Moses, a Bay De Noquet Lumber Company jobber, who often employed kin and other members of the Nahma Indian community. Located on the company's main rail line, the site consists of eight structure locations outlined by earthen berms, nineteen pits (including six within the confines of structure outlines), and extensive refuse deposits. One test unit bisected a subfloor pit with complex stratigraphy that contained a high density of artifacts (Figure 7.5). Fill zones represent separate episodes of use, with a layer of tar paper in place from a refurbishment effort. This feature contained a wide variety of domestic and industrial artifacts, including beads, tobacco tins, white clay pipe fragments, an alarm clock, 57 buttons (multiple sizes and types indicating disposal and/or caching of clothing), safety pins, a thimble, five sharpening files, and five U.S. coins with dates ranging from 1891 to 1925. Identifiable glass containers included Hamlin's Wizard Oil, Vicks Vapor Rub, Musterole, Davis Vegetable Pain Killer, and Sauer's Extract. Although liquor bottles were present, the assemblage seems to reflect health concerns and physical stresses more than recreational drinking. Abundant evidence of women and children included a marble, a rubber nipple, a baby powder tin, a child's glove, and a woman's shoe. A clause in the logging contract between Pete Moses and the Bay De Noquet Lumber Company specified that any services provided by a jobber's

Figure 7.5. Stratigraphy of subfloor storage pit, showing tar paper layer separating seasonal episodes of use. Test unit 6, Moses Camp (20DE537). (Photo [2002] by Eric Drake, courtesy USDA Forest Service, Hiawatha National Forest, Gladstone, Mich.)

Figure 7.6. Artifacts from Moses Camp (20DE537). *Clockwise from left*: fragment of canning jar, clock, milk glass cap with zinc band, gauge for pressure cooker. (Photo [2004] by Eric Drake, courtesy USDA Forest Service, Hiawatha National Forest, Gladstone, Mich.)

wife or minor children would be considered services provided by the jobber and that the company would not be responsible for claims or demands related to their work. Moses Camp also included an abundance of jars, lids, and caps for home canning (Figure 7.6). Although cattle and swine remains represented the majority of available meat, wild species included snowshoe hare, raccoon, porcupine, white-tail deer, grouse, and burbot.

Archaeology, oral history, and documents indicate that some people remained at Moses Camp year round. The 1920 census lists 15 family members representing three generations. This camp thus reflects social processes different from those of most other logging camps: the transformation of an industrial setting into a more family-oriented space despite the proximity of industrial and domestic activities. This permitted an extended Native American family to stay together during a period of boarding schools, assimilation pressures, and economic hardship. The sharing and consuming of traditional foods, the hiring of family members, and the contributions of

Figure 7.7. Chinese ceramics associated with James Canyon cabin sites, TY-3590, Toiyabe National Forest, Douglas County, Nevada. Chinese workers at these sites cut wood for the Carson and Tahoe Lumber Company to supply the Comstock mining district, circa 1873–1898. (Photo [1995] by Larry Kingsbury. Library of Congress Prints and Photographs Division, Washington, D.C.)

women and children functioned to maintain kinship bonds and facilitated social reproduction.

Chinese workers played a major role in the western logging industry, even though past historical and archaeological research focused on their participation in railroad construction and mining (Chung 2015). They specialized in providing wood for heating, cooking, and firing steam boilers that powered engines used by mills, mines, and railroads. Small numbers of Chinese-origin artifacts at some sites suggest their presence as cooks, launderers, or as workers in other support roles at camps where they were probably the only Asians present (Horn 1987). Other sites with more numerous Chinese-origin artifacts may have been exclusively Chinese (Figure 7.7). Historical records document a predominantly male Chinese population in the West. Archaeologists explored an 1870s or 1880s Chinese logging camp in the eastern Sierra Nevada Mountains of California that supplied various wood products to the mining settlements around Virginia City, Nevada

(Solury 2004). A late 1890s camp in Dog Valley, Sierra County, California, may represent the last Chinese camp in the area (Lee 2008). The Chinese had been working for many years in the mining, railroad construction, and logging industries of California and Nevada, but starting around 1886, vigorous anti-Chinese efforts and well-organized "total boycotts" ended both their employment and trade opportunities, and most Chinese left the area. The Dog Valley site apparently postdates this exodus, and Chinese workers there must have been either independent sellers or clandestinely employed by a local company.

In larger settlements, Chinese men lived in boardinghouses or barracks, but in remote resource extraction camps, they lived together in small groups. Outdoor cooking hearths constructed from rocks are conspicuous features at some sites (Lee 2008; Solury 2004). Faunal remains associated with Chinese workers at an 1870s redwood sawmill in northern California varied more than nearby deposits thought to be linked to non-Chinese workers: besides bird, fish, and mammal remains, they included abalone and mussel shells (Douglass 2000). Chinese ceramic fragments found at logging-related sites came from bamboo-pattern porcelain rice bowls, celadon bowls and cups, and brown stoneware storage jars for soy sauce or other liquids (Lee 2008; Douglass 2000; Solury 2004). Although not as numerous as ceramics, opium-smoking paraphernalia, including cupreous metal "Beautiful Origins"–brand containers, provide consistent evidence of ethnicity. These items reveal "self-medication" related to the physical and psychological stresses of harsh working and living conditions. Chinese coins used for gaming or as keepsakes are also found. Chinese merchants and middlemen, acting as both labor contractors and suppliers, provided the abundance of Chinese-origin artifacts seen at sites in the West. Work-related artifacts included files, axes, shovels, saw blades, and saw handle parts. Remains of rubber boots at one site suggest that flume-tending occurred along with timber-cutting and hauling (Solury 2004). Evidence for adaptive reuse of consumer goods is relatively common at Chinese sites, including strainers and shingles made from metal food or kerosene cans and a leaf spring modified for use as a bark peeling spud. Researchers regard such examples of reuse as demonstrating both adaptability and frugality, necessitated by low wages, discrimination, and the desire to accumulate savings. Archaeological studies of Chinese loggers transcend disciplinary boundaries. At least one historian of the Chinese in North America credits archaeology as a primary source of both information and inspiration (Chung 2015).

People of Japanese ancestry also worked in the lumber industry in western North America. Recent projects explored the archaeology of segregated *Issei* (first generation Japanese American) settlements associated with early twentieth-century sawmills in the state of Washington (Campbell 2017; Carlson 2017; Hartse 2017). Documents and oral history depict these communities in the context of both racial discrimination and vibrant social and economic activity. Besides housing for workers and their families, accounts mention tea houses, gardens, public baths, an ice cream parlor, a photo studio, and places of Buddhist and Christian worship. In one community, collective negotiations with mill management took place through a representative elected by workers. Archaeological findings illustrate the persistence of traditional practices and material culture as well as adaptation to living and working in a North American industrial setting. Researchers concluded this process involved the development of "trans-national" identities (Hartse 2017) and resistance to racial discrimination (Carlson 2017). Perhaps the most notable archaeological findings thus far reported are assemblages of Japanese and non-Japanese ceramics, showing both maintenance of ethnic identity and a willingness to integrate locally purchased American and European merchandise. Fragments of Japanese ceramics represented soup bowls, rice bowls, small pickle and sauce plates, tea cups, tea pots, and sake cups. Campbell (2017) analyzed 194 fragments of Japanese pottery from the circa 1903–1930 Japanese Gulch site in Mukilteo, Washington, using a typology based on Japanese terminology. This assemblage included at least 58 vessels associated with specific centers of the Meiji- and Taishō-era ceramic industry, mainly vessel forms for serving noodle and rice dishes and sauces (Campbell 2017).

Although multiple researchers have been studying Japanese communities associated with sawmills, the literature survey encountered only one study of a Japanese logging camp. Muckle (2016) conducted archaeology at a circa 1920–1924 British Columbia site that probably focused on cutting cedar used to make shingles. Crosscut saw blades, files, and axes confirmed the logging function of this site. Indicators of ethnicity included products of Japanese origin as well as the remains of a rock hearth feature that formed a base for heating a large tub of water, possible evidence of a Japanese-style bathhouse (*ofuro*). Gender- and age-specific artifacts confirmed the presence of families. Concentrations of nails and window glass revealed the locations of cabins or small houses. Artifacts were not described in detail, but 28 glass jars marked "Pond's" once contained skin moisturizer, a product apparently well suited for easing skin damage associated with logging and other outdoor occupations.

Occupation, Status, and Class

Spatial patterns at many logging sites reflect differences in occupational status. At the most basic level, social distinctions resulted in housing workers separately from higher status individuals such as foremen, clerks, and cooks. For example, at the Tate Creek camp, the cooking crew and management occupied several tents separated by a creek and railroad from those of workers (Elliott 1990). Because no evidence of ethnic differences was found, this separation appeared to reflect occupational status. In contrast, at a much smaller and earlier site in California, researchers observed relatively little evidence of social differentiation and attributed this to its small scale (12–16 employees), lack of bureaucracy, and relatively flat hierarchy (the owner was probably also the on-site manager) (Praetzellis and Praetzellis 1993). Additional examples of spatial patterns based on social stratification are included in the section of chapter 5 dealing with small-scale settlement patterns. The following discussion highlights more detailed archaeological analysis of social organization based on occupational and/or economic status differences within logging sites.

Corporate officials designed Weyerhaeuser Camp 2 in Oregon, and a 1932 site plan shows separate residential areas for single men, men with families, and managers (called "brass row") (Hills et al. 1996). This layout contrasts with less complex linear arrangements with camp structures situated on railroad cars parked on sidings or in rows paralleling railroads. Frame structures at Camp 2 were portable and transported by rail. A few structures (kitchen and dining cars) remained on a railroad siding, but Camp 2's segregated residential areas clustered back from the rails. Although it does not appear on the original company design, archaeological researchers identified an extensive "tent town" where workers lived when housing was unavailable or if they preferred to avoid having rent deducted from their pay. Open spaces and roads separated the four main residential areas. Lines of rocks demarcated yards around some households. The offices, store, community hall, and dining cars were adjacent to cabins for single men and brass row, while garages, shops, and other industrial buildings formed a separate cluster. Major changes in labor relations had taken place since the turbulent World War I era: companies preferred hiring men with families, and many women and children lived at this camp, which also included a schoolhouse and a teacher. Instead of housing single men in large bunkhouses, Camp 2 included 40 separate four-man units near a bathhouse with hot showers. Single men ate in dining cars parked on a railroad spur, but families cooked and ate separately. Although workers no doubt appreciated improved housing, separating the workforce into smaller groups may have made union activity more difficult.

Although the site is more recent than others covered in this book and was not studied using traditional archaeological methods, Pappas (2004) analyzed social organization at Soap Creek Pass, a large railroad logging settlement operated by the Pickering Lumber Company between 1955 and 1965 in California's Sierra Nevada Mountains. Pappas examined the physical remains of the camp, which included both extant and collapsed structures, and utilized company records and oral history accounts. His research focused on the material expression of relationships between capital and labor and could be relevant to archaeologists studying older work camps or company towns. Soap Creek Pass provides a late example of corporate paternalism, a philosophy most companies had abandoned by the 1950s. The camp included a central area with a mess hall and three-man cabins for single men, clusters of larger cabins around the edge of the camp where workers with families lived, and industrial structures related to railroad operations and equipment maintenance. The superintendent and his assistant, who lived in houses overlooking the central area, strictly enforced values of cleanliness, hard work, and cooperation. Mandatory deductions from single men's wages paid for housekeepers to wash their bedding and clean their cabins. Pappas (2004) interprets the camp as being organized to emulate the hierarchical structure of a family. Management treated single men like children, monitoring them more closely than married men, and tried to correct behaviors like rudeness and bad table manners. In contrast, families enjoyed more privacy and management allowed them to personalize their cabins and yards. The company store, with prices similar to those in towns, offered cash advances in the form of company scrip so that workers would not spend on items like alcohol, which was not sold. Pappas (2004) describes management as "authoritarian" relative to single men and as a "benevolent patron" toward families (Pappas 2004). Architecture and spatial organization represented an attempt to naturalize power relations in a way designed to minimize resentment from the more desired workers (men with families). Although the superintendent and assistant superintendent lived in larger and more permanent structures, these buildings resembled the style and materials of the family cabins. Social, managerial, spatial, and architectural patterns at Soap Creek Pass expressed an overarching paternalistic metaphor based on "fictive kinship" (Pappas 2004).

Summary: Celebrating Diversity, Fighting Racism

By emphasizing the diverse identities of people living in logging settlements, the archaeological studies described in this chapter contradict any impressions of homogeneity within the lumber industry. Recent research highlights the roles played by non-European groups such as African Americans and Chinese, but other groups, such as Native Americans and Hispanics, are less well represented in archaeological studies. Historical sources mention Native American involvement with logging in multiple regions but, with the exception of Drake's (2003) study, this has not been fully explored by archaeologists. Much potential exists: for example, Stein (1993) mentions an Arizona logging camp site that includes remains of Navaho hogans. The role of Hispanic workers in the southwestern lumber industry has been touched on by historians but has not yet been the focus of archaeology. Morris et al. (1994) document the presence of Mexicans in Arizona logging camps, and early twentieth-century sawmill towns like McPhee, the largest lumber mill town in Colorado, included housing segregated into Hispanic and non-Hispanic sections (Smith 2001). Additional opportunities also exist for archaeology to document the experiences of African Americans who worked in lumbering both within and outside the South, including some known sites in the Pacific Northwest (Marsh 2015; Trice 2018).

Despite evidence for ethnic differences, there may also be broad similarities between widely separated sites as a result of industry-based ethnogenesis. This potential is suggested by Holbrook's description of wealthy lumbermen moving their operations from the eastern United States to the Northwest:

> . . . they fetched their crews, often whole trainloads of them, together with their saws, axes, habits, speech, folkways, and snuff, and built them villages in the woods. Thus the Northwest received sealed cargoes of logging-woods culture intact, untainted by contact with either farms or cities.
>
> (1948: 87)

Tentative archaeological evidence for this process may include similarities in foodways and intoxicant use among sites in the Great Lakes and the western states (see chapter 6).

Archaeological research on the social organization of lumber industry workers can hopefully do more than satisfy our intellectual curiosity. As one archaeologist concluded after watching a Ku Klux Klan rally in his hometown during the 1990s: "It seems too simplistic, but archaeology's purpose today is to play a role in ending racism. Everything follows from this fact" (Kelly 1998). By focusing on how people responded to the challenges posed by industrial work settings, we hopefully gain some appreciation of our shared humanity even as we celebrate diversity. On this score, a former lumberjack from British Columbia with both Native American and European ancestry, Hank Pennier, described how in certain times and places, occupational identity united loggers with different ethnic or racial backgrounds: "Way back in the bush amongst the big trees doing a man's work, I wasn't a half-breed, I was just good old Hank. . . . we were all buddies and we watched over one another." He goes on to describe his hope for the future: "Why shouldn't there be just people now? No Indians. No Eskimos. No whites. Just people" (Pennier 2006: 89). Other workers may have shared this desire to be seen as "just people" rather than as ethnic or occupational stereotypes. Because of chronological and geographic gaps in both the archaeological and historical literature of industrial logging, the agency and experiences of many groups remain unrecognized. The next chapter begins filling in one of these gaps: it presents a case study of distinctive camps associated with the earliest industrial logging operations.

8

Archaeology of the Camboose Shanty in Northern Michigan

A Case Study of Two Nineteenth-Century Lumber Camps

> The whole interior is one large room. The most conspicuous object is a huge log fire-place or platform, like an ancient altar, in the centre of the floor. It is covered with earth and blackened embers. . . . Immediately over it is an opening in the roof giving vent to the smoke . . .
>
> William H. Withrow, *Our Own Country* (1889), 394

Two recently discovered late 1860s lumber camp sites in Michigan's Upper Peninsula included the archaeological remains of a distinctive hearth feature called a camboose (or cambuse). These consisted of earthen platforms framed by wooden timbers or logs where an open fire was maintained for both cooking and heating (Figures 8.1 and 8.2). Smoke exited through a large hole in the roof (Figure 8.3). Accounts of mid-nineteenth-century logging camps in the northeastern United States and adjacent Canada often mention camboose shanties (Fraser 1883: 23; Harper's New Monthly Magazine 1868: 412–415; Springer 1851: 72; Ward 1936: 301–302). Numerous Canadian sources refer to them and George S. Thompson describes one in Ontario:

> A large opening, about eight feet square, was left in the center of the roof and a wooden tapered chimney, about six feet high, built up to carry off the smoke from the fire place or camboose, which was built of sand and stone in the center of the shanty. . . . Sometimes a floor of logs was put in, but just as often none. . . . The cookery outfit of a camboose shanty, in the early days, consisted of half a dozen bake kettles for baking bread, and one for baking beans . . . , which is done by covering the kettles with hot ashes.
>
> (1895: 22)

Figure 8.1. Interior of camboose shanty. (Photo [ca. 1905] by W. M. Harmer, labeled "Waiting for dinner in the cook shanty at a logging camp in the Ottawa Valley." Copy Negative PA-106194, courtesy Library and Archives of Canada, Ottawa.)

Figure 8.2. Interior of a Canadian shanty. (Photo [1900] by Charles Macnamara, Digital Image No. 10010814.jpg, courtesy Archives of Ontario, Toronto.)

Figure 8.3. Camboose shanty, Arnprior, Ontario. (Photo [1900] by Charles Macnamara, labeled "McL.B's last camboose shanty, Black River, Nov. 1900, Paul Kittner, cook." Digital Image No. 10010813, courtesy Archives of Ontario, Toronto.)

Only two sites with these features have been found on public lands in the Hiawatha National Forest: the Mason's Purchase site (20DE649) and the Trespass Camboose site (20DE648).

Because of the potential for gaining additional information about logging during this period and the threat sites like these face from relic hunters, the USDA Forest Service initiated test excavation and evaluation. Although historical accounts portray the camboose as a defining characteristic of early logging camps, this study represents the first archaeological investigation in the Great Lakes states to focus on these features. Based on historical sources, the following questions were formulated:

How were camboose features constructed and used, and in what specific context?

How do camboose shanties documented through historical archaeology compare to firsthand descriptions from the nineteenth century?

Why were camboose features constructed and used after cast-iron stoves became widely available?

What can archaeological remains tell us about the everyday lives of workers at these early camps?

Investigations consisted of shovel tests and test excavation units screened through ¼-inch mesh as well as surface scrapes to expose shallow material often present at the forest duff–topsoil interface. A metal detector guided the placement of some units.

Historical Background

The Mason's Purchase and Trespass Camboose sites provide a baseline for understanding the increases in scale, mechanization, and standardization that took place later in the nineteenth century in association with the expansion of the white pine lumber industry. Starting during the Civil War and ending with the Panic of 1873, this industry experienced what lumberman Henry Sage called "11 fat years" (cited in Cox 2010: 133). In fact, the occupation of these sites coincides with the beginning of Michigan's dominance from around 1870 to 1900 as the nation's leading lumber producer (Defebaugh 1970 [1906]: 491). During this period, Canadians comprised "the largest single group of foreigners" working in the lumber industry of the Great Lakes states (Engberg 1948: 241). Although English-speaking workers from Canada, especially Scots, also crossed the border seeking work, the majority of migrating loggers spoke French (Cox 2010: 139). Engberg (1948: 239–241) calls French-speaking Canadians "pioneers" of the industry. Similarly, Lower (1968: xix) suggests that the flow of both labor and ideas across the border enabled the white pine lumber industry to reach "the apex of its qualities and growth" in Michigan. Although the border meant little to mid-nineteenth-century workers, it apparently presents an obstacle to some researchers. Few have made use of Canadian sources in tracing the roots of Great Lakes lumbering. Much has been made of the connections between the Great Lakes and Maine, and this accurately reflects the contributions of some workers and certainly a majority of foremen and company owners (Stephenson 1915: 79). In describing buildings with the characteristics of camboose shanties, some Great Lakes sources refer to them as the "old State of Maine type" (Harper's New Monthly Magazine 1868; Holden 1916: 2). However, the geographic specificity of this attribution obscures the influence of French-Canadian workers and the flow of people and ideas entering the Great Lakes–states lumber industry by way of Quebec and Ontario.

An 1880 French-Canadian glossary defined the word *cabousse* as a corruption of *cambuse*, loosely translated as "a kitchen and dining area for servants attached to the rear of a house" (Dunn 1880: 230). One reference cites the Dutch *kombuis* or *kabuis* (the cook's cabin aboard a ship) as the mid-eighteenth-century origin of the English "caboose" or "camboose" and the French *cambuse* (de Vries 1916: 107). Besides appearing in nineteenth-century accounts of logging in Maine, the Maritime Provinces, Quebec, Ontario, and the Great Lakes states of Michigan, Wisconsin, and Minnesota, the term also occurs in nautical contexts. *Webster's Revised Unabridged Dictionary* (1913) defines camboose as a variation of caboose, meaning "a house on deck, where the cooking is done." Nineteenth-century accounts frequently refer to logging camp structures as shanties, with loggers called "shantymen" as early as 1821 (Lee 2006: 163). The term "shanty" comes from the French *chantier*, referring to a "workshop, work site, or a rough working camp" (Hammond 1994: 100).

Anecdotal histories contain exaggerations, like the following, about the crudeness of shanty life: "early camps were more primitive abodes than those of the cave dwellers" where the oxen used to haul logs "lived better than the men" (Holbrook 2016: 44). However, firsthand accounts include both positive and negative descriptions of camboose shanties. Most mention the good food cooked in cast-iron pots buried in hot coals and the potential for eye irritation caused by smoke (Fraser 1883: 23; Harper's New Monthly Magazine 1868: 412–415; Springer 1851: 72; Thompson 1895; Ward 1936: 301–302). Four accounts that mention ethnicity identify cooks at camboose camps as French Canadian (Fraser 1883: 23; Harper's New Monthly Magazine 1868; Thompson 1895; Ward 1936: 301–302). The challenges of camboose construction appear substantial: one source indicates they had to carefully locate the camp in a "sheltered nook" to avoid drafts that might divert smoke from exiting out the chimney (A.J.H. 1867: 149). After describing how smoke could be a problem, Ward (1936: 348) points out that constructing a camboose required "very considerable mechanical ingenuity and practical experience."

Etymological, historical, and demographic information support an association between camboose shanties and logging operations that included French-speaking Canadian workers. The large numbers of recent Canadian immigrants in Michigan during the 1860s probably made it easy to find workers who could build and operate such a feature as well as workers who would perhaps appreciate, or at least tolerate, living conditions in a camboose shanty. Although proffered as a source of "color" in anecdotal accounts, some researchers neglect ethnicity as a factor in the overall evolution of the lumber industry. While it does not specifically mention ethnicity, the following explanation for the circa 1900 persistence of camboose features along the Ottawa River in Canada *does* refer to a period when French-Canadian workers made up a high percentage of most crews: "This old style has been abandoned on almost all other streams for the American style—the cooking range and box stove, which is considered more up-to-date and economical but there are still concerns who prefer to keep up the old style on account of its being more cheerful for the men and because they think it more cleanly and healthful" (Canada Lumberman 1903: 19).

The two camboose camps discussed here date to a period when stoves would have been readily available in northern Michigan. Scholars have described the development and diffusion of cast-iron stoves during the nineteenth century as well as the various factors that influenced the change from fireplaces to stoves (Brewer 1990). Iron stove production increased in the mid-1800s and prices decreased. Estate inventories show that many mid-nineteenth-century homes in New England and the Midwest used both iron stoves and fireplaces, with stoves most often located in kitchens and fireplaces usually found in parlors. Although Brewer's (1990) observations relate to domestic residences, domestic life and industrial activity shared the same space at early lumber camps, possibly leading to concerns about the influence of technology on domestic values. Lee (2006: 168) suggests that some logging operations continued to use the camboose instead of stoves in order to reduce their expenses (Lee 2006: 168). However, building a camboose and using it for cooking required special expertise, and it consumed more firewood than stoves. In fact, iron stoves were considered "more economical" than a camboose (Canada Lumberman 1903: 19). This suggests that anachronistic occurrences of these structures might represent worker preferences, especially at camps operated by established companies that could definitely afford stoves.

Firsthand accounts of early logging camps based on observations and reminiscences of Anglo-American or Anglo-Canadian journalists, tourists, and company owners or managers, often stress the health and happiness of workers, despite the hard work and primitive accommodations. Some accounts also include humorous anecdotes involving French-Canadian or Irish workers (Macnamara 1959; Stephenson 1915; Fraser 1883; Springer 1851). According to Macnamara (1959: 76), a French-Canadian shantyman once stated, "At night we sit around the fire and everyone is gay." In 1867, writing in the *New Dominion Monthly* (149), "A.J.H." describes a camboose camp as a place of "light hearted happiness." The hyperbole continues as he argues that "a healthier, heartier, happier, rougher, more careless, reckless, jollier lot of dogs, could scarcely be found in any other employment the world over, than our own bold, fearless, generous, warm-hearted shanty-men" (A.J.H. 1867: 150). The only translated example we found showing the perspective of a non-English–speaking shantyman in a nonsupervisory role comes from a French-Canadian logger who worked in a circa 1900 *chantier* dominated by English speakers: "it was not the work that was difficult, but the language," and "it's aggravating not to understand anything" (Miner 1963: 279).

Comparing historical accounts from the Great Lakes states and Canadian provinces shows major differences in the chronological and cultural context of the camboose, including the persistence of these features in certain areas. Stoves appeared in Canadian logging camps as early as 1850 (Lower 1968: 310), but 20 years later 5 out of 15 Ontario camps operated by Rathbun and Son still used a camboose (Sherwood 1872: 573). A systematic survey of 64 camps conducted by Ontario public health officials in 1901 still found two in use (Ontario Legislative Assembly 1902). Likewise, Macnamara (1959) indicates that the last cambooses remained in use until about 1900 to 1905. As Osborn (1919: 197) points out, "the Canadian lumberjack was hard to wean from the camboose."

In contrast to the situation in Canada, historical evidence from the U.S. Great Lakes states shows a different progression, with cast-iron stoves replacing the camboose in the 1870s (Rosholt 1980: 84). Various sources from this period describe the camboose as an outmoded, obsolete, or "old-fashioned" technology (Larson 1949; Fitzmaurice 1889). Thus far, the latest reference to a camboose shanty in Michigan mentions an "old-fashioned style" camp with a camboose along the Rifle River in 1883 (Fitzmaurice 1889: 54). Although there are, no doubt, other late examples, these hearth features apparently did not persist in the United States as they did in Canada. As large numbers of immigrants from Scandinavia and Eastern Europe arrived in the Great Lakes states during the late nineteenth century, the percentage of workers with a knowledge of or desire for camboose shanty living decreased rapidly. Around 1900, even as a few remained in use, Canadians recontextualized the camboose as a symbol of a bygone era based on nostalgic literary and popular culture revisions of lumber industry and ethnic history, a process that began with contemporary perceptions in the mid-nineteenth century and no doubt continues. Rather than representing a recent reinterpretation, the romanticized image of early lumbering originated in written accounts, in English, by firsthand observers. This includes descriptions of French Canadian and Irish workers written by Anglo-Canadian travelers, clerks, and foremen. A similar process took place in the United States, but without the camboose's playing a major role and with Scandinavians as one of the major "ethnic characters."

The Trespass Camboose Site

The Trespass Camboose site (20DE648) is located along a small stream flowing into the Sturgeon River in Delta County, Michigan, and a sawmill was present at the mouth of the Sturgeon on Lake Michigan as early as 1848. In 1849, General Land Office (GLO) surveyors noted that the area around the site contained abundant large white pine. An 1869 timber cruise notebook identifies this site as a "lumber camp" occupied by trespassers cutting timber on lands claimed by the Chicago and Northwestern Railroad. This company obtained a large land grant in return for constructing a rail line from the Marquette Iron Range to the Wisconsin state line. The occupants of 20DE648 cut timber around their camp and on another parcel owned by the railroad about 1.5 miles west. They no doubt hoped to float their logs to a mill at the mouth of the Sturgeon River. Although not patented by the railroad until 1874, acts of Congress in 1864 and 1865 approved and reserved parcels selected by the company (USDA Forest Service 1967).

Massive earthen berms outline a structure that would have been about 19 × 5.25 meters (Figure 8.4). These berms are approximately two meters wide and rise about 40–50 centimeters above the surrounding ground surface. A series of linear borrow pits parallels the outside edge of the berms. A 1.5-meter gap in the berms at about the midpoint of the structure's long axis separates this feature into two sections. Centered in the southeast section is a mound about 2.5 meters in diameter that rises to about 44 centimeters above the adjacent ground surface. Test Unit 2 encompassed about one quarter of this camboose feature and a small adjacent area. Additional units sampled dense refuse deposits outside the structure (Test Units 1 and 3) and a much smaller raised area (probably from a sand platform for an iron box stove) within the other section of the structure (Test Unit 4).

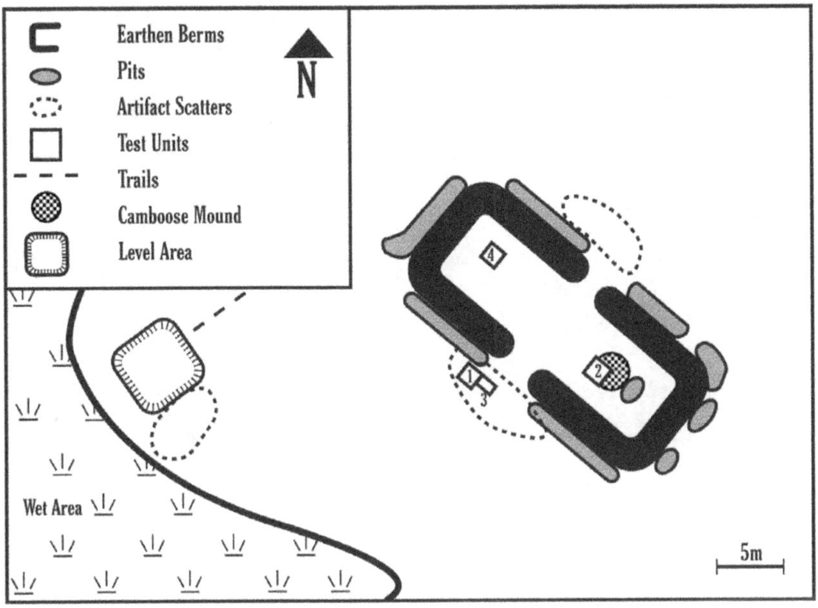

Figure 8.4. Site plan, Trespass Camboose site (20DE648). (Original by Franzen and Drake [2013], redrawn by Brady Ray Nelson, Genesis Graphics.)

Cut nails dominated the artifacts found at site 20DE648 (n=378, no wire nails present), followed by glass fragments (n=103, including both container and pane fragments), and white clay pipe fragments (n=64). Test Units 1 and 3 sampled a dense refuse midden immediately adjacent to the structure. This deposit varied from about 10 to 30 centimeters in thickness, with the deeper areas representing the filling of low areas or borrows along the outside of the berm that surrounds the structure. It contained decaying wood and charcoal and a wide range of refuse—dominated by animal bones, glass, and nails—as well as cast-iron stove lids and three iron keys.

Excavation within the camboose revealed at least 20 separate depositional units consisting of sand, ash, charcoal, decayed wood, and duff (Figure 8.5). Heat partially cemented or fused some ash deposits. Profiles show multiple episodes of use and evidence of burying and removing cooking pots along the perimeter of the feature. The most common inclusions in the feature matrix consist of small calcined bone fragments. Cut nails most likely represent the construction, maintenance, and deterioration of a wooden hood-like structure above the camboose that directed smoke up

Figure 8.5. Profile of camboose feature, Trespass Camboose site (20DE648), test unit 2, east wall. (Photo courtesy USDA Forest Service, Hiawatha National Forest, Gladstone, Mich.)

through an opening in the roof. Some nails may also remain from wooden portions of a crane used to suspend cookware over the fire, and a heavy iron hook and chain links probably relate to this apparatus. Stem and bowl fragments of white clay pipes represent the second most common manufactured objects within this feature. Nearly all clay pipe fragments occurred at deeper levels. Descriptions of smoking at logging camps usually place this activity around the bunkhouse heat source (Harper's New Monthly Magazine 1868: 417). The vertical distribution of pipe fragments within the camboose feature suggests initial use by a logging crew, followed by less intensive use by a smaller number of trappers or hunters.

The four iron single-bit axe heads recovered included one marked "Hibbard" and "68." Hibbard, Spencer, and Company operated in Chicago from 1865 until 1882 (Chicago Historical Society 2005). The three relatively intact axe heads each weighed between 4.2 and 4.8 pounds. Fragments from four different grindstones or whetstones were also found. Other metal tools included a wood plane blade and a crosscut saw blade fragment. This saw blade had triangular cutting teeth but lacked raker teeth to remove chips and dust from the cut. As a result, it was suitable only for bucking logs into segments after a tree was cut and lying in a horizontal position. Saws lacking rakers would bind when used to cut into a standing tree. Introduced during the 1870s, crosscut saws suitable for felling became widespread by the 1880s (Davis 1983).

Firearms-related artifacts included five lead balls (.316 to .458 inches in diameter) and three brass rimfire cartridge casings (.32, .44, and .56 caliber). Smith and Wesson introduced the .32 caliber rimfire cartridge in 1861, and Benjamin T. Henry patented the .44 cal Henry rimfire in 1860 (Barnes 1997: 385; Chicoine 2004: 11). The .56 caliber Spencer was also patented in 1860 and used during the Civil War (Marcot 1983). A .38 caliber bullet had a crude lead jacket wrapped around its base, apparently an attempt to enlarge it for use in a .50 caliber or larger muzzle loader. Revolvers and sporting rifles in .38 caliber became popular immediately after the Civil War (Barnes 1997: 386). This variety reflects the transition from muzzle-loading to breech-loading arms during this period.

The button assemblage (n=17) included the following materials: 7 ceramic (prosser), 3 iron, 3 brass/iron composite, and 4 bone. Four holes perforate all 15 unbroken buttons. Test units in the outdoor refuse deposit contained 13 of the 17 buttons. Other clothing-related items included 5 buckles: a single-loop D-shaped frame, a double prong with a rectangular frame, a brass suspender clip, an oval double-loop frame, and a single-loop rectangular frame with a double tongue. Footwear remnants include several fragments of leather soles and boot "uppers" with brass eyelets. These items reflect the heavy wear and frequent disposal of clothing and footwear associated with logging.

Identifiable iron nails and nail fragments included both cut (345) and wrought (2) examples. Compared to the exterior refuse deposits, far greater nail density occurred inside the structure. Complete nails accounted for 36 percent of the assemblage and were classified according to their size. The nails in Test Unit 2 (camboose unit) averaged 5.2d (d=denarius [penny], larger number=larger nail) while other units averaged between 7.3d and 7.6d. Some of the smaller nails may represent the burning of nonarchitectural items such as barrels or boxes. Nail sizes in Test Unit 2 varied by strata, with the upper levels averaging 8.8d and the lower levels averaging 4.9d. This difference may result from the repair or collapse of structural elements above the camboose during the later period of use or after abandonment. Historic accounts mention that builders used very few nails in the construction of log "shanties" during this period (Rector 1953: 70).

A small number of table and kitchen utensils occurred throughout the site, including three-tined forks, iron spoons, an iron table knife, and bone scale handle fragments. The ceramic assemblage represents only three vessels: one white earthenware bowl with molded (ribbed) decoration and two conical salt-glazed stoneware ink bottles (probably related to record keeping). As the most frequent material found in excavation units, the mammal bone from this site included a distinctive mix of domestic and wild species. In order from most to least frequent based on the number of identified specimens (NISP), the following were present: white-tailed deer, beaver, muskrat, cattle, swine, marten, and rabbit or hare. A timber cruiser passing through this area in November 1855, noted: "Saw a good many signs of beaver, otter, and mink in the stream" (Brotherton 1855). Although representing minimal biomass, ruffed grouse, hooded merganser, black bass, and northern pike remains also occurred. The presence of furbearers, including one not commonly eaten (marten), and an animal trap found nearby, raises the question of possible reuse of the structure by trappers. However, given the presence of deer remains in the lower levels of the camboose feature, even if trappers later reoccupied the site, the loggers also ate wild game (venison).

The total NISP counts for each of the three different areas reveal a pattern of intrasite variation. Although beaver and deer occurred in all areas tested, the absence of domestic species in the northwest section of the structure, which was inferred to be the scene of wild game processing, supports the inference of reuse by trappers. It seems unlikely that the loggers would have left animal carcasses to rot within their bunkhouse. The greatest contrast was between Test Units 1, 3, and 4, with abundant wild species, and Test Unit 2 (camboose), where wild game remains other than deer rarely occur. If we only consider commercially important furbearers (beaver, muskrat, and marten) the contrast becomes clear: the camboose feature included only one individual compared to 12 individuals in other units. This suggests that trappers reoccupied the camp, but that they made little use of the camboose area for disposal of animal remains. Early camps often augmented their meat supply with wild game, and historical accounts from other areas do mention loggers who supplemented their pay by trapping (A.J.H. 1867: 296; Oxley 1895: 267). However, the distribution of faunal material in Test Unit 2 suggests reuse of the camboose feature occurred after the loggers departed: two faunal assemblages within the feature are stratigraphically distinct. All wild game and fish (with the exception of deer) occurred in levels 1–3, while all domestic animal remains came from levels 5 and 6. The sizes of unidentified mammal bones conform to this scenario. The majority of large or very large mammal elements (74%) occurred in levels 4–6, while the majority of medium or medium-large mammal remains appeared in levels 1–3 (65%). This size distribution is consistent with the consumption of cattle and pork during the initial logging occupation, the processing and consumption of wild game (other than deer) during the latter occupation, and the utilization of deer during both periods.

Historical accounts describe camboose features within square or rectangular log structures where sleeping, cooking, eating, and tool maintenance shared a single open space. However, the camboose at 20DE648 is located within a "dingle-style" structure. These consisted of two separate sections placed end to end and connected by a small breezeway or storage area (the dingle). They gradually replaced camboose shanty–style camps in the mid- to late nineteenth century as part of the trend toward larger logging operations where various activities became more specialized and spatially segregated. From the perspective of nineteenth-century observers, the combination of a camboose and a dingle-style double structure represented "old-fashioned" heating and cooking technology within a more "up-to-date" type of structure.

Comparison of material from the two sections of the structure indicates that dining and cooking took place in the southeast portion, while tool maintenance, wild game processing, and refuse disposal occurred in the northwest portion, which included fragments of a metal stove. It also appears that the southeast section may have had a floor and/or was regularly cleaned, whereas the northwest section may not have had a floor and was littered with debris. However, this pattern may be influenced by the cumulative effects of two different occupations. The northwest section may have initially been used by the loggers for sleeping, with additional activity related to later reuse of the structure. Unlike deposits within the camboose, this area lacked stratigraphic evidence of separate occupations.

Trespassing lumberers at this camp employed different technologies and cost-saving practices. By doing things like combining a dingle-style structure with a camboose and utilizing locally available wild game (venison in the camboose's lower strata), they call into question linear models of technological progress. Many mid-nineteenth-century homes used both iron stoves and fireplaces, and, during this period, writers lamented losing the benefits of open-fire cooking and heating, especially social interaction around a localized source of warmth and light. Brewer (2000: 124) notes this phenomenon was part of the "compromise between tradition and innovation" that characterized the mid-nineteenth century. The mixed characteristics of the Trespass Camboose camp also highlight the limitations of technology-based historical chronologies and typologies of lumber industry sites. People such as trespassers stealing timber from a large corporation are almost invisible in the written record and peripheral to narratives celebrating technological progress.

Mason's Purchase Site (20DE649)

The Mason's Purchase site (20DE649) provided another opportunity to study a camboose shanty. It included earthen berms outlining an 8 × 8-meter (26 × 26 feet) square structure (Figure 8.6). Centered within this structure is the camboose, a 2 × 2-meter mound of ash, charcoal, rock, and oxidized soil that rises about 38 centimeters above the adjacent ground surface. On the south side of the shanty, an earthen berm outlines the footprint of an attached shed. Iron ox shoes indicate that less distinct berms in the northwest portion of the site represent an oxen hovel. About 10 meters northeast of the main structure are two water holes. One test unit encompassed about a quarter of the camboose. Other locations selected for test excavation based on positive metal detector readings included refuse middens just outside the structure and in the gap between the camboose shanty and the smaller structure behind it that may have been used for storage. According to the 1847 GLO (General Land Office) survey notes, an extensive forest of hemlock and white pine surrounded this area, which is about one mile from the Whitefish River (Comer et al. 1994).

The Mason's Purchase site is located on lands patented by the St. Mary's Falls Ship Canal Company in 1855 specifically to obtain white pine (Delta County Register of Deeds 1855). The company considered pinelands within a mile of rivers suitable for floating logs the most valuable of their holdings (St. Mary's Falls Ship Canal Company 1863: x). Ownership and tax records suggest that the Mason Lumber Company logged pine from this locale between 1867 and 1872 (Delta County Register of Deeds 1855–1888; Delta County Clerk 1871–1884). Richard Mason arrived in the area in 1852 and by 1860 operated a steam-powered sawmill in Masonville, located on Little Bay De Noc near the mouth of the Whitefish River about nine miles south-southwest of the site (Escanaba Tribune, June 11, 1870). The 1860 industrial census shows that Mason employed 30 men and 5 women in producing four

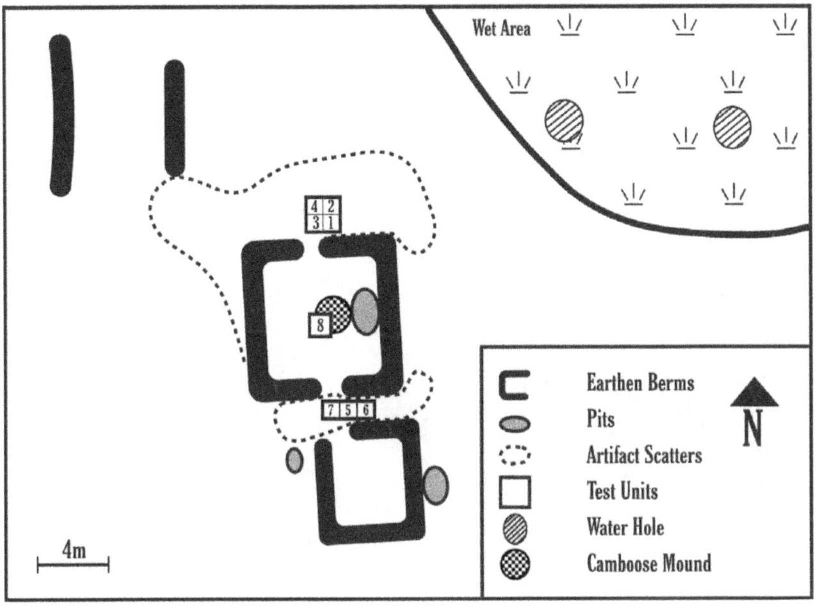

Figure 8.6. Site plan, Mason's Purchase (20DE649). (Original plan by Franzen and Drake [2013], redrawn by Brady Ray Nelson, Genesis Graphics.)

million board feet of pine lumber worth $25,000 and shipped it by schooner to Chicago, where city directories list him and his son as lumber dealers (Hotchkiss 1894: 62, 565). In 1870, the company advertised for "Choppers, Swampers, Sawyers," at wages varying from $25–$35 per month, "according to ability to earn same" (Escanaba Tribune, December 30, 1870). Richard Mason Sr. died in 1870, and Richard Jr. carried on the business until the mill closed as a result of the 1873 financial panic (Sawyer 1911: 1,348).

Test excavation within the camboose feature revealed a stratigraphic profile documenting at least two activities: maintaining a bed of coals in the center of the feature and burying iron pots along the edges (Figure 8.7). The main firing surface consists of a compact ash and sand layer containing a dense concentration of small burned bone fragments. High temperatures in this central area probably destroyed many artifacts. Resting upon the outside margins of this compact zone are large rocks. Outside these rocks lies a zone of charcoal and sand mixed by burying and uncovering iron kettles used for baking. The majority of artifacts recovered from the camboose feature occurred in this mixed zone, including bones and a variety of discarded personal items.

Figure 8.7. Profile of camboose feature, Mason's Purchase site (20DE649), test unit 8, east wall. (Photo courtesy USDA Forest Service, Hiawatha National Forest, Gladstone, Mich.)

Artifacts, including an 1866 two-cent U.S. copper coin from the midden north of the shanty, suggest a late 1860s or early 1870s date for the site. The following firearms-related items support this estimate. Two slightly deformed lead bullets could have been fired from a .32 caliber pistol; Smith and Wesson introduced the first .32 caliber cartridge in 1861 (Barnes 1997: 385). A deformed lead ball found in Test Unit 1 and a brass percussion cap found in Test Unit 8 represent older style firearms. The button assemblage consisted of 19 whole buttons and one button fragment. Test Unit 8 contained 11 buttons or 55 percent of the assemblage, suggesting sewing and/or clothing disposal in and around the camboose. The six buttons from Test Unit 2 may relate to disposal of refuse from camboose cleanouts. Four two-piece brass-and-iron buttons with loop attachments included one with a "spread eagle" in relief. Buttons like this one were issued between 1855 and 1884 by the U.S. Army for use on cuffs, vests, or jackets (Herskovitz 1978: 39).

Flat or pane glass was limited to 159 fragments, 88 percent of which came from Test Units 1–4. Much lower counts occurred in test units within or adjacent to the structure, suggesting that perhaps a shipment of pane glass, broken in transit to the camp, was discarded en masse. Other glass was scarce: most was burned or melted. Glass was unlikely to survive the heat within cambooses. Unburned container glass represented only three vessels. Two fragments of light green panels marked "VEG . . ." and " . . . KILLE . . ." (Test Units 7 and 8) may be from Perry Davis Vegetable Pain Killer. This product was popular with loggers over a long period and advertised locally around the time the site was occupied (Franzen 1995: 323; Mining Journal 1869). Four fragments of an olive-green wine or champagne-style bottle exhibited a pronounced basal kickup and a fire-polished lip with a laid-on ring. These neck and lip traits generally date between 1840 and 1870 (Newman 1970). A third vessel was represented by a black opaque fragment (Test Unit 7, Level 1) with a double ring–style applied lip characteristic of circa 1850–1870 (Newman 1970).

The cut nail assemblage was evenly divided between whole nails and nail fragments. Small sizes dominate, suggesting derivation from roofing or nonarchitectural uses such as boxes, barrels, and furnishings. Of the whole nails recovered, 75 percent were 6d or less, and of the nails larger than 6d, 29 percent came from the upper levels (1–3) of Test Unit 8 where they may represent the deterioration of wooden structures associated with the camboose. Although scarce in Test Units 5–7 (n=10), 50 percent of these nails were large and may represent the framing of a storage area. Ferrous sheet metal fragments common in the refuse deposit south of the shanty may represent small cans that contained dry items like tobacco or baking powder. Although very fragmented and corroded, the sheet metal assemblage included four round friction caps.

A large proportion of the metal tool assemblage related to the cutting and transport of logs. Among the 11 single-bit axe heads recovered, 10 complete specimens weighed between 4.2 and 5.4 pounds each. Some of these American-style felling axes exhibited seams or cracks resulting from the forging of two slabs of iron together with a wedge of steel, added for a durable bit (Kauffman 1972: 23–24). Stamped maker's marks on two identify the Douglas Axe Manufacturing Company in East Douglas, Massachusetts, which operated between 1836 and 1897 (Nelson 1999). Crosscut saws and double-bit axes replaced single-bit axes as the dominant felling tools during the 1870s and 1880s. Earlier loggers only used saws for bucking logs into shorter lengths after trees had been cut down with axes. In fact, Mason's 1870 newspaper advertisement (Escanaba Tribune, December 30, 1870) seeking both choppers and sawyers shows the company still used axes rather than saws for felling. A massive (3.25 lbs.) wrought-iron pointed tool bit was found with two loose iron bands that probably once held it in place at the end of a wooden handle or shaft. This object, one inch square in cross section, tapered to dull points at each end. It could be either an unusually large peavey tip ("peavey pike") or the tip of a "setting pole" used to push watercraft upstream (Springer 1851: 62). The letters "MXI" scratched into the side of this tool could represent a mark used by the Mason Lumber Company to identify logs and other company-owned property. Company marks were apparently limited to straight lines in "early years" before the use of special marking hammers so they could be easily cut into bark with an axe (W.P.A. 1942: 8).

Evidence suggests this camp used both oxen and horses, but the only definite horse-related item found was a full cheek snaffle bit from Test Unit 8. Excavation also recovered nine iron shoe nails as well as three ox shoes. Other items associated with draft animals included a harness snap, a harness buckle, and heavy chain links. All chain links found were either broken or cut. Three "cold shuts" and one "open link" (both used to replace broken chain links) were also found, along with three grabhooks. Most of the chain links, cold shuts, and grabhooks exhibited cracks or breaks that seemed to follow obvious seams or flaws arising from defective fabrication or ineffective repair techniques, but excavations encountered no forge, clinkers, or blacksmithing tools. Four iron files represent tool maintenance, including a complete specimen with the stamped mark, "JOHN . . . OTHERY." Greeley (1872: 453) identifies a John Rothery from England who started making files by hand in Mattewan, New York, in 1845. Because of the many wooden components needed for sleighs and other equipment, much woodworking took place at logging camps. One of the two wrought-iron adze heads recovered exhibited many seams and cracks suggestive of manufacturing defects. Another woodworking item, a 13-inch-long auger with a .52-inch-diameter bit, drilled holes that could have accommodated most of the heavy iron fasteners or connectors (such as bolts, rods, and pins) found at the site.

Kitchen and dining items were almost all made of iron, except for handle remnants of bone or wood. All ceramic fragments recovered apparently came from a partially reconstructable two-gallon salt-glazed gray stoneware jug with blue-painted floral decoration. Conjoining fragments of a cast-iron kettle represent a vessel similar to those shown in historic photos of camboose cookery (Figure 8.8). This vessel measured approximately 32.4 centimeters (12.75 in.) in diameter at its rim. Eating utensils included a three-tine

Figure 8.8. Cast iron kettle fragments from Mason's Purchase site (20DE649), MD 22, 10-6. (Photo [2012] by author, courtesy USDA Forest Service, Hiawatha National Forest, Gladstone, Mich.)

fork and fragments of bone scales from other handles. A complete iron-and-brass folding pocket knife retained intact wood scales that may be cocobolo (*Dalbergia retusa*), a decay-resistant tropical hardwood used for handles during the nineteenth century (Bultman and Southwell 1976). One historical account mentions a shantyman eating with "the aid of his clasp knife" (Oxley 1895: 267).

Test units encountered more than 500 pounds of angular rock fragments (536 lb./243 kg), and most of this rock showed signs of heat stress. Rock appeared in two contexts: within the camboose feature and in the refuse deposit north of the shanty where material from periodic cleaning was dumped. Rock placed to retain or direct heat within the camboose broke down over time from repeated thermal stress. Accordingly, larger-sized fragments occurred within the camboose compared to those in the north refuse area. During cleaning episodes, larger rock fragments likely remained in place, with smaller fragments frequently removed with ash and other debris. Heat also created the highly fragmented faunal assemblage at the Mason's Purchase site, which included 2,531 individual bone specimens with an average weight of only 1.4 grams. This reflects the frequent disposal of food refuse into the camboose, where a large percentage of bone fragments appear to be calcined (converted to ash but retaining their form). Spatial variation in average bone fragment weight and the relative frequency of burning defined different activity areas. Higher average weights and lower burning frequencies (10%) occurred in the south midden, which is interpreted as a refuse deposit dominated by waste produced during food preparation rather than food consumption. The lowest average weights occurred within the camboose, where 100 percent of the bone was burned. The north midden appears to be a mixed deposit that includes debris from periodic cleaning of the camboose, based on low average bone weight and a high frequency of burning (77%). The remains of large to very large-sized mammals (probably cattle) dominated the identifiable specimens, along with a small number of fish bones derived from a single walleye or sauger (*Sander sp.*) and a second unidentified fish species. Mammal bones identified below the level of class included cattle, swine, and white-tailed deer. Cattle bones represented a minimum number of four individuals; swine and white-tailed deer bones each represented at least one individual; and 26 percent of the cattle bones—along with one swine bone and two unidentified large or very large mammal bones—exhibited saw cut marks. The absence of foot bones or teeth suggests that beef and pork came into the camp already butchered. The presence of foot bones from white-tailed deer indicates on-site butchering. Overall, faunal remains depict a pattern of logging camp subsistence where camp crews relied on periodic shipments of prebutchered beef and pork that may have been preserved by salting. Supplementing the diet of loggers with wild game such as deer or even fish was not uncommon; however, given that nearly all the white-tailed deer bones came from the camboose feature and not the exterior middens, the case could be made that game was only eaten during the later stage of the camp's use, perhaps a result of late-season shortages or as part of cost-cutting measures associated with decreasing profitability. Another group could have briefly reused the camp, but there are no indications of any function for the site other than logging.

Counts of selected artifacts in different functional categories provide a way to compare the three areas tested at 20DE649. The camboose feature (Test Unit 8) and the north refuse scatter (Test Units 1–4) had similar densities of buttons and white clay pipe fragments. Large quantities of fire-cracked rock (FCR) in both areas show that the camboose was periodically cleaned out and the debris discarded outside the shanty's front door. Dominated by larger mammal bones and tin fragments, the south refuse scatter just outside the back door (Test Units 5–7) contrasts with the other two areas. In a simplified version of South's (1977, 1978) technique, researchers sorted artifacts into three categories for additional analysis of spatial organization: architectural (mainly nails and window glass), domestic (kitchen, tobacco, clothing, and personal items), and industrial (mainly tools and other logging-related items). The results show industrial artifacts relating to the maintenance and repair of logging equipment both within the shanty and in the refuse deposits to the north. They also show that refuse in the north midden included a mix of both domestic and industrial material, with the second refuse deposit to the south limited more specifically to kitchen materials. Besides domestic items, the camboose contained a high density of cut nails, probably related to the construction, repair, and deterioration of a wooden framework that guided smoke through the roof opening. Both the composition and spatial distribution of the artifact assemblage at 20DE649 speak to the use of the camboose shanty as combined cooking, eating, and sleeping quarters where both domestic and industrial activities occurred. Broken or partially repaired hand-forged items, such as iron chain links, were recovered from the north midden along with many personal items such as white clay pipe fragments and buttons. This spatial comingling of work and leisure under a single roof defines the character of logging camps during the middle 1800s.

Conclusions

Archaeology at the Trespass Camboose and Mason's Purchase sites revealed details about everyday life in early logging shanties and provides the first archaeological description of camboose construction and use. Lumberjacks usually focused on food as the most important aspect of working conditions, and owners and managers sometimes accommodated worker preferences (Conlin 1979; Franzen 1992). Slow cooking in cast-iron pots buried in ashes and coals was likely responsible for the perceived quality of camboose cookery, and stratigraphic evidence shows how this was accomplished. Cooking at both sites involved maintaining a fire in the center of the camboose and burying iron pots along the edges of the feature where they were easier to manipulate. Profiles of both features include baked or fused ash-dominated central deposits and looser mixed deposits along edges. It appears that cooks exercised care in maintaining a continuous central fire and not disrupting it by digging too deeply when moving coals toward the edges to bury pots. This would make sense in that the central fire would continue to provide heat, light, and rising hot air currents for ventilation as food slowly cooked along the periphery. Without the draft created by a robust central fire, smoke drifting laterally from a bed of coals might make a shanty uninhabitable.

Although both features functioned in similar ways, differences existed between the two camps. A camboose was, in a sense, "folk technology": built from locally available materials by loggers with previous knowledge and experience of these features. One obvious difference is the use of large rocks to retain or direct heat at the Mason's Purchase site and their absence at the Trespass Camboose site. If builders or cooks added rocks in order to increase heat retention, they may have been used on the basis of availability and, perhaps, personal preferences. Their presence or absence could have influenced the amount of firewood necessary or the frequency with which wood was added, but there may have been no difference in the basic way cooking was done or in the quality of the food prepared. Another difference between the two camboose features is their structural context. One was situated within a rectangular space in one section of a dingle-style camp, while the other was located in a square structure more typical of camboose shanties described in historical literature. Descriptions and historic photographs of camboose shanties show variations in form, materials, and associated features. For example, the vent hood/chimney could be built with either lumber or sticks and clay, while the roof could consist of log "scoops," lumber, or shakes. Archaeological sites offer more complete contextual data, even if some perishable components of the built environment do not survive. These two sites reflect the social-historical practices and processes leading up to logging camps where cooking and eating became segregated from other camp activities. The increasing spatial separation, standardization, and corporate control of various activities highlights the physical and symbolic importance of the camboose shanty; and this, in turn, may help to explain why it persisted in some situations even though the cast-iron stove was considered more efficient and "modern."

Camboose features tend to preserve archaeological information. Because they are nonportable and usually do not contain reusable materials, they would seldom be damaged by later salvage efforts. At the time of abandonment, they would retain evidence of activities that had taken place since the last cleanout, and it is unlikely the crew cleaned them frequently or completely during their use. Another key factor contributing to the archaeological potential of camboose features involves the concentration of various activities in and around them. They provided light, heat, and a convenient location for the disposal of unwanted items. Many smaller items dropped on the surface near the camboose would remain in place due to the absence of flooring or to large gaps between flooring members.

Although written sources attribute the popularity of the camboose to various subjective factors such as "cheerfulness" and tasty food (Canada Lumberman 1903; Osborn 1919; Fraser 1883), the camboose offered at least one objective physical benefit—a properly constructed camboose that didn't fill the shanty with smoke, that is. Two sources described cambooses as more healthful than stoves because they provided better ventilation (Osborn 1919: 197; Canada Lumberman 1903: 19). There may be some truth to this claim. Because of the Severe Acute Respiratory Syndrome (SARS) outbreak in 2003 and concern about a possible avian influenza epidemic, researchers conducted a systematic review of 40 studies on the relationship between ventilation and airborne transmission of infection (Li et al. 2007). Based on "strong and sufficient" evidence, the spread of diseases like influenza, smallpox, tuberculosis, and SARS is associated with inadequate building ventilation (Li et al. 2007). A survey of 62 logging camps heated by stoves conducted by Ontario Public Health workers during a smallpox outbreak in 1901 noted "an almost complete absence of any provision whereby fresh air can gain entrance to the dwellings," and 38 percent did not allow at least 300 cubic feet of air space per man (Ontario Legislative Assembly 1902). Resisting the imposition of stoves may have been an adaptive response to health threats. Osborn (1919: 197–198) stated that "ordinary lumber camps are not much better than black holes of Calcutta" but explained that in a camboose shanty, good ventilation resulted in "torrents of stinking breath passing up the hanging wooden chimney." Despite these potential advantages, there is good reason to assume that managers still wanted to discontinue their use. Increased profitability required increases in the scale and speed of logging and consequently required larger crews and cooking facilities. Dependence on workers with the specialized expertise required to construct and operate a camboose conflicted with the desires of managers to increase productivity and reduce costs by standardizing equipment and labor practices. Deskilling through imposed technological changes is one hallmark of "scientific management" (Rajala 1999). Cooks always ranked among the highest paid workers in logging camps. Using cast-iron cooking ranges instead of camsbooses expanded the pool of potential hires to include cooks with experience in more common institutional settings.

At least one aspect of camboose cookery persisted after "modern" logging camps replaced mid-nineteenth-century shanties. Although not well documented, some cooks at later camps equipped with cast-iron cooking stoves still cooked beans in an outdoor "bean hole." Early twentieth-century newspapers in Maine and the Great Lakes states indicate that cooks located their bean holes near the cookhouse, often in a "log shed or other rude shelter" (Von Schneidemesser et al. 2012). This tradition remains alive and well in Maine, where bean hole beans are prepared at church suppers and other events such as museum fundraisers. In the Midwest, Pequot Lakes, Minnesota, has conducted its annual Bean Hole Day since 1938, using "Paul Bunyan's secret recipe."

People like the loggers who lived in the camboose shanties at the Trespass Camboose and Mason's Purchase sites remain almost invisible in the written record and marginal to "march of progress" narratives. However, the distinctive and well-preserved features they left behind give them a place in the archaeological record independent of their financial success. Future archaeological investigations could no doubt yield additional information about how these workers adapted to the Great Lakes industrial frontier. Historical archaeology gives them visibility and reveals some of the cultural contingencies of technological change. Historical geographers Ennals and Holdsworth (1998: 223–225) refer to the "folk quality of much shanty building" and recommend further research into the interplay of techno-economic factors and "human agency" that led some operations to retain the camboose. González-Ruibal (2019: 128) points out that folk architecture resists forced chronological classification and contributes to heterochrony as a result of "non-modern materialities" refusing to disappear and providing connections to the past.

Archaeological analysis of the Trespass Camboose and Mason's Purchase sites in Northern Michigan challenges narratives that stress the linear progression of the logging industry within well-defined stages of technological development and economic expansion. These two sites also happen to be located in timber stands probably resembling those originally cut around them about 140 years ago. Both have a relatively open understory and include large hemlock and white pine that are over 100 years old. Many cutover areas, even if they remain forested, do not include trees of the same age or species as those originally harvested. These two areas illustrate the potential resilience of forests, their interrelated natural and cultural history, and a possible role for archaeology in more sustainable relationships between people and trees.

9

Logging, Archaeology, and the Anthropocene

> To track the histories that make multispecies livability possible, it is not enough to watch lively bodies. Instead, we must wander through landscapes, where assemblages of the dead gather together with the living. In their juxtapositions, we see livability anew.
>
> Elaine Gan, Anna Tsing, Heather Swanson, and Nils Bubandt, "Introduction: Haunted Landscapes of the Anthropocene" (2017), 5

Between the mid-nineteenth and mid-twentieth centuries, the American experience for many workers and their families involved industrial labor that produced immense but unequally distributed wealth. Research restricted to written documents and oral history, however, excludes many people and places from this narrative. Studies based only on written sources usually lack the multidisciplinary perspective, physical and locational details, and the "grounding," if you will, provided by archaeology. At logging-related sites, archaeology provides details about an industrial, but largely rural, American experience that can be discussed under four major domains: technology, the environment, daily life, and social organization. Archaeological studies reestablish suppressed, forgotten, or ignored connections between people and specific landscapes, a "practice of resistance" that some consider redemptive (González-Ruibal 2016b: 15). In fact, a book like this (involving critique while seeking more knowledge about the past) represents an example of how Americans address logging and other industries through a combination of analysis, debate, conflict, and politics. As early as the mid-nineteenth century, arguments developed between those justifying utilitarian "cut out and get out" extraction and others concerned about noncommercial values and conservation.

However, there is also a context for the archaeology of industrial logging in America that goes beyond our continent, beyond the nineteenth and twentieth centuries, and beyond an exclusive concern with human affairs: the so-called Anthropocene, a time of human-induced global change that some call an "Age of Destruction" (González-Ruibal 2018). Archaeology can address this topic through its material focus and the ease with which it articulates with other disciplines, especially those in the physical and biological sciences. Archaeology has also shown resistance to forces that obscure or naturalize the effects of humans on global life support systems. Archaeological efforts go beyond pointing out the negative effects of past practices; they are relevant to present-day issues and can help identify opportunities for alternative futures. Paradoxically, the archaeological record of forest exploitation can thus play a role in forest resurrection as part of research and educational projects involving multiple disciplines. Optimism about the regenerative possibilities of sustainable connections between people and trees inspired Springer and Turpin (2017) to paraphrase Ursula Le Guin (1972) for the title of a book that proclaims, despite the prevalence of human impacts and a scarcity of old-growth timber, "The Word for World Is Still Forest."

Recommendations

In light of contemporary circumstances, perhaps the highest priority for all archaeologists should be participation in multidisciplinary efforts to address topics like inequality, climate change, and pollution. Whether or not the Anthropocene concept provides an effective framework for accomplishing this charge remains to be seen, but there is a growing consensus among archaeologists that it must be addressed (Solli et al. 2011; Mrozowski 2018; Rick 2017). According to Edgeworth (2018a), even if it is problematic, this concept may be too important to ignore. Thus far, archaeology has engaged mainly over temporal, terminological, and theoretical discussions of the Anthropocene. It is still unclear what forms more on-the-ground involvement might take. Attaching events or processes to their physical traces in specific settings, even if they are otherwise well known, brings Anthropocene realities home: exploited, diminished, but potentially resilient forests that include newly created assemblages of natural and cultural features. This perspective makes it easier to see humans and various "things" as "mixed" in a way that erodes misleading conceptual divides between nature and culture without obscuring the ontological distinctions that encourage human responsibility and accountability (Solli et al. 2011: 51–52, 60; Malm 2018).

Myers (2018: 53) warns those of us inclined toward historical-material perspectives not to be distracted by the search for "physical markers and temporal boundaries" of an era defined by geological-scale human impacts and to focus instead on helping create a more "livable" environment. Rather than merely commenting on chronology or terminology, it is time for archaeologists to more actively participate in discussions of the Anthropocene or risk being seen as "fiddling" or "dithering" while the planet "burns" (Braje 2018: 216; Edgeworth 2018b). This requires selecting appropriate contexts for archaeological engagement. Some think urgency demands an even broader context that goes beyond research and includes the creative arts (Tsing et al. 2017). Clearly, scholarly articles or presentations may not have enough impact or reach to help mobilize broad support for necessary political changes, and popularized versions alone often lack the force and rigor necessary for persuasion. Referencing the Anthropocene concept, even while criticizing it, offers an expansive context, multidisciplinary opportunities, and potentially wider audiences for archaeological studies that focus on logging and the lumber industry.

Green Temples or Commodities?

Logging remains a contentious issue in the United States and around the world. Disputes range in scale from arguments over preserving remaining old-growth timber stands to deciding how forests should be managed to ameliorate rising levels of atmospheric carbon dioxide. The archaeological evidence described in this book supports a critique of logging operations that cause unnecessary damage to living things, humans included. Archaeological remains can play a role in new relationships between people and forests that are more balanced and include noncommodity-based values. If done at the right times and in the right places, timber harvest is compatible with these values. There is nothing inherently wrong with cutting down trees and using wood. However, this book has not taken a celebratory approach to logging history. Numerous popular and scholarly narratives, including corporate histories and biographies of lumber barons, have already provided ample coverage of the lumber industry's benefits and achievements. Nonetheless, much of the physical labor accomplished was difficult, dangerous, and not always well compensated. Timber workers deserved, and still deserve, not only dignity, respect, and a decent living, but also more realistic portrayals that put their efforts into broader contexts. The nature of both old-growth and recently regenerated forests also needs to be better understood.

Central to the American experience of logging is the still-unresolved conflict over the different values of forests. Trees and wood can be both beautiful and useful. Seeing both aspects is foundational, not just to the American experience but to the human experience. Besides lumber, some more recently developed wood-based products have progressed from utility to necessity, such as toilet paper. Whether different forest uses can be reconciled to everyone's satisfaction is doubtful, but examples showing how some influential Americans balanced these values might be helpful. Henry Thoreau (1862: 665) wrote, "In Wildness is the preservation of the world," but he also enjoyed looking at his wood pile: "the more chips the better to remind me of my pleasing work" (Thoreau 1981 [1854]: 188). No one can question John Muir's love for wild nature ("The clearest way into the Universe is through a forest wilderness"), but he also ran at least two different sawmills: "I like the piney fragrance of the fresh-sawn boards" (Muir and Badè 1924: 207–208, 211). Poet Gary Snyder (1990: 128) refers to an ancient forest as "a palace of organisms, a heaven for many beings, a temple where life investigates the puzzle of itself," but he also loved cutting logs with a crosscut saw: "the clean swish and ring of the blade, the rhythm, the comradeship, the white curl of the wood that came out with the rakers, the ritual of setting the handles, and the sprinkle of kerosene (to dissolve pitch) on the blade and into the kerf" (1990: 118). In 1954 Snyder worked as a "choker setter" for a mechanized logging operation in Oregon that selectively cut old-growth ponderosa pine. His job involved attaching cables to logs that D-8 Caterpillar tractors dragged from cutting areas to centralized landings for loading onto trucks. He recalled having "no great problem with that job" (Snyder 1990: 120). With credentials as both a logger and a poet, why not also quote him on sustainability: "With good practices North America could maintain a lumber industry and protect a halfway decent amount of wild forest for 10,000 years" (1990: 134).

Resilience, Resurgence, or Extinction?

We have previously argued for wider comparison between regions when studying archaeological remains of the American logging industry and proposed using an even broader context to address the global-scale environmental and social effects highlighted in Anthropocene narratives. Tsing et al. (2017) acknowledge how we are pressured to "forget" both social and environmental effects of industrial activity. In reforested areas, especially those without obvious traces of past logging, many people remain unaware of how existing forests (including archaeological sites within them) reflect changes, losses, and potential futures. This naturalizes the present situation, resulting in a spurious "baseline" for gauging future change. In other cases, people reject altered forests as sources of wild or nonhuman values, especially in cases like monoculture plantations with trees set in rows and depauperate understory vegetation. As a response to situations like this, Tsing (2017: 7) recommends multidisciplinary "noticing" of the traces of both natural and cultural history in unexpected places as the key to understanding the present situation and adaptively moving forward. Archaeology is nothing if not an advanced form of "noticing" things that are not readily apparent. Despite the losses they represent, multiple values exist within the second or third growth ruins of cutover ancient forests and, sometimes, even in tree plantations. These values can include, but are not limited to, commercial timber, solitude, scenery, wildlife, berries, mushrooms, archaeological sites, and opportunities for rewilding or establishing new relationships with other organisms and our surroundings.

Henry David Thoreau's perceptions of wildness within a landscape altered by logging provide useful guidance for moving forward in our relations with contemporary American forests. Thoreau (1988 [1864]: 29, 146, 196) was able to appreciate the Maine woods during three mid-nineteenth-century visits, even though he complained that essentially all of the large white pine were missing. His descriptions of logging camps and logging dams highlight their remoteness and wild surroundings because most had been abandoned, at least for the season. He uses the terms "wilderness" and "wildness" 68 times in this book, and oddly credits the loggers with leaving "a wilderness as they found it" (1988 [1864]: 312). This speaks directly to twenty-first-century concerns about reclaiming industrial landscapes, restoring nonhuman nature, and to the role of humans, both past and present, within so-called natural areas. The fact that "wildness" can persist in landscapes altered by humans is a viewpoint advocated by critics of the "wilderness concept" (Cronon 1995). If true "wildness" only exists in the tiny areas of pristine "wilderness" that remain, then it becomes harder to argue for preserving valuable aspects of nature outside of these areas. As put by one forest ecologist: "In many parts of the world, the forests of the future are not going to resemble the forests of the past. Let's move on" (Chazdon 2017: 88). We need to better understand how these changes occurred, but future steps could combine research with mitigation, restoration, and adaptation to (re) establish a mutually beneficial relationship between people and forests that accommodates wildness. According to Chazdon (2017: 90): "restoring the world's forests will also restore humanity."

Thoreau (1988 [1864]: 47) described the shore of Maine's North Twin Lake shore as "covered with forests," even though the best white pine timber around this remote lake had been cut. Early white pine logging was highly selective, and he reports that loggers supposedly constructed over three miles of road just to cut a single large pine worth $90. Logging at this time was seasonal in the extreme, and no logging or log driving was going on during Thoreau's summer visits. This no doubt increased the contrast between remote wildness and signs of humans: "it was always startling to discover so plain a trail of civilized man there. I remember that I was strangely affected, when we were returning, by the sight of a ring-bolt well-drilled into a rock, and fastened with lead, at the head of this solitary Ambejijis Lake." Chains connected to these rings would have anchored booms (a series of large logs attached end to end) that confined floating logs gathered together for temporary storage and eventual transport across lakes or wide sections of rivers (Figure 9.1).

Thoreau's "startled" response illustrates the contradiction between dichotomized views of nature and culture and his firsthand experience of their integration. He sometimes criticized logging and advocated preserves, but he was able to find both the "wild" and the "wilderness" while following in the footsteps of Maine loggers. However, the alteration of global systems by humans has progressed in ways unimaginable from a nineteenth-century perspective, and many people find themselves unable to conceptualize environmental changes in ways that acknowledge we still exist in "nature," along with nonhuman "others," who retain agency and require accommodation if we are to survive. Perhaps archaeology can help us be "strangely affected" like Thoreau by revealing the juxtaposition of natural and cultural features in ways that highlight the persistence of wildness and our continued dependence on earth systems that resist our control. This is a goal that can satisfy our intellectual curiosity and possibly contribute to our survival. Historical

Figure 9.1. Ring bolt embedded in rock, Lake Superior shore. This anchored a boom that extended to the opposite point and confined floating logs within the bay, shown on the right side of photo. Sugarloaf Cove, Cook County, Minn. (Photo [2016] by author.)

archaeology depicts industrial logging as a significant part of the American experience but a relatively short episode in the long history of humans and trees. If we better accommodate all the values of our forests and accept that we influence but do not control them, perhaps the Anthropocene can become an age of destruction *and* renewal, rather than a linear path toward mass extinction.

References Cited

Adams, Kramer A.

1961 *Logging Railroads of the West.* Bonanza Books, New York.

Adams, Samuel H.

1912 *The Great American Fraud.* American Medical Association, Chicago.

Adams, William H. (editor)

1980 Waverly Plantation: Ethnoarchaeology of a Tenant Farming Community. Resource Analysts, Inc., Bloomington, Indiana. Submitted to U.S. Army Corps of Engineers, Mobile District, Contract No. C-55026. Available from Defense Technical Information Center.

A.J.H.

1867 Stories around the Shanty Fire. *New Dominion Monthly.* December: 149–150. Montreal.

American Medical Association

1906 Patent Medicine and the Lumberjack. *Journal of the American Medical Association* 46(12): 898.

Anderton, John B., Sean B. Dunham, and Mark C. Branstner

1996 1995 Cultural Resource Surveys: Hiawatha National Forest. Great Lakes Research Associates, Williamston, Mich. Submitted to USDA Forest Service, Hiawatha National Forest, Escanaba, Michigan.

Angus, Ian

2016 Facing the Anthropocene: Fossil Capitalism and the Crisis of the Earth System. Electronic document, http://www.environmentalhumanities.ed.ac.uk/audio-test-lecture-deep-time-4/, accessed April 12, 2017.

Arnott, Sigrid, Douglas A. Birk, and David Maki

2013 Evaluating Minnesota's Historic Dams: A Framework for Management. Archaeo-Physics, LLC. University of Minnesota Digital Conservancy, http://hdl.handle.net/11299/189230, accessed November 11, 2017.

Ascher, Robert

1974 Tin Can Archaeology. *Historical Archaeology* 8: 7–16.

Atack, Jeremy, Frederick Bateman, and Robert A. Margo

2007 Steam Power, Establishment Size, and Labor Productivity Growth in Nineteenth-Century American Manufacturing. *Explorations in Economic History* 45(2): 185–198.

Auerbach, Daniel, and Brett Clark

2018 Metabolic Rifts, Temporal Imperatives, and Geographical Shifts: Logging in the Adirondack Forest in the 1800s. *International Critical Thought.* DOI: 10.1080/21598282.2018.1430603, accessed January 12, 2019.

Ayres, James E.

1983 Historic Logging Camps in the Uinta Mountains, Utah. In *Forgotten Places and Things*, edited by Albert E. Ward, pp. 252–255. Center for Anthropological Studies, Albuquerque, New Mexico.

1996 Standard Timber Company Logging Camps on the Mill Creek Drainage, Uinta Mountains, Utah. *Proceedings of the Society for California Archaeology* 9: 179–182. Chico.

Bajema, Carl J.

1991 First Logging Railroads in the Great Lakes Region. *Forest and Conservation History* 35(2): 76–83.

Bajema, Carl J., and Janet G. Brashler

1997 Blendon Landing: A Middle Nineteenth-Century Logging Railroad, Sawmill and Shipyard Village in West Michigan. *Michigan Archaeologist* 43(2–3): 44–58.

Baker, Suzanne M., and Laurence H. Shoup

1979 An Historical and Archaeological Study of the M.A. Burns and Castle Crag Lumber Companies, Shasta-Trinity National Forest. Archaeological Consultants, San Francisco, Calif. Submitted to USDA Forest Service. Available from California Historical Resources Information System, State Historic Preservation Office, Sacramento.

Barber, Jacob

2018 Disciplinarity, Epistemic Friction, and the "Anthropocene." PhD dissertation, Department of GeoSciences, University of Edinburgh, United Kingdom. https://www.era.lib.ed.ac.uk/bitstream/handle/1842/33153/Barber2018.pdf, accessed March 19, 2019.

Bardon, John A.

1934 Early Logging Methods. *Minnesota History* 15(2): 203–206.

Barile, Kerri S.

2004 Race, the National Register, and Cultural Resource Management: Creating an Historic Context for Postbellum Sites. *Historical Archaeology* 38(1): 90–100.

Barnes, Frank C.

1997 *Cartridges of the World.* DBI Books, Northfield, Illinois.

Barrows, Susanna I., and Robin G. Room

1991 *Drinking: Behavior and Belief in Modern History.* University of California Press, Berkeley.

Baskin, Jeremy M.

2015 Paradigm Dressed as Epoch: The Ideology of the Anthropocene. *Environmental Values* 24(1): 9–29.

Bass, Kayley M.

2017 The Hidden History of Western Washington Logging Camps: St. Paul and Tacoma Lumber Company's Camp #5 ca. 1934–1947. MS thesis, Department of Cultural and Environmental Resource Management, Central Washington University, Ellensburg.

Bastian, Beverly E.

1999 Elmwood: The Archeology of Twentieth-Century African-American Pioneers in the Great North Woods. In *I, Too, Am America*, edited by Theresa A. Singleton, pp. 283–298. University Press of Virginia, Charlottesville.

Bastian, Beverly E., and William E. Rutter

1987 Documentary, Oral Historical, and Phase III Archeological Investigations at Elmwood Logging Camp (20IO58), Iron County, Michigan. Gilbert/Commonwealth,

Inc., Jackson, Michigan. Submitted to USDA Forest Service, Ottawa National Forest, Ironwood, Michigan.

Beaudry, Mary C.

2005 Concluding Comments: Revolutionizing Industrial Archaeology. In *Industrial Archaeology, Future Directions*, edited by E. C. Casella and J. Symonds, pp. 301–314. Springer, New York.

Beidle, Jacqueline

1992 Railroad Logging Sites of the Sacramento Mountains, New Mexico. National Register of Historic Places Multiple Property Documentation Form NM 64500427. U.S. Department of Interior, National Park Service, Washington, D.C.

Benchley, Elizabeth D.

1997 Nineteenth-Century Logging along the Indian River in the Upper Peninsula of Michigan. *Michigan Archaeologist* 43(2–3): 153–174.

Benchley, Elizabeth D., Frederick A. Copes, Michael F. Kolb, Norman P. Lasca, Paula J. Porubcan, Mary J. Schabel, and Linda G. Whitman

1993 *Investigation of the Influence of Late Nineteenth–Early Twentieth-Century Logging on Fluvial Geomorphology and Fisheries Habitat on the Indian River, Hiawatha National Forest, Michigan.* University of Wisconsin-Milwaukee Archaeological Research Laboratory Reports of Investigations No. 113. Milwaukee.

Benchley, Elizabeth D., Gathel Weston, and Carrie A. Koster

1995 *Preliminary Report of 1995 Archaeological Investigations State Highway 57 Improvement Project Brown, Kewaunee, and Door Counties Wisconsin.* University of Wisconsin-Milwaukee Archaeological Research Laboratory Report of Investigations No. 126. Milwaukee.

Bennett, Merrill, and Rosamond H. Peirce

1961 Change in American Diet, 1879–1959. *Food Research Studies* 2(2): 95–119.

Bernhardt, Debra E.

1979 *We Knew Different: The Michigan Timber Workers' Strike of 1937.* Mid-Peninsula Library Cooperative, Iron Mountain, Michigan.

Birk, Douglas A.

1997 Outta the Woods and into the Mills: Shifting Timber Harvest Strategies on Minnesota's Early Lumbering Frontiers. *Michigan Archaeologist* 43(2–3): 51–86.

1999 Commercial Logging in Minnesota. National Register of Historic Places Multiple Property Documentation Form MN 64500278. U.S. Department of Interior, National Park Service, Washington, D.C.

Blair, Julia

2001 Nothing but Woods to the World's End: Archaeology at an Industrial Frontier. MS thesis, Industrial Archaeology Program, Michigan Technological University, Houghton.

Blanchard, Louie, Walker D. Wyman, and Lee Prentice

1976 *The Lumberjack Frontier: The Life of a Logger in the Early Days on the Chippeway.* University of Wisconsin-River Falls Press, River Falls.

Blanton, Paul, and W. Andrew Marcus

2009 Railroads, Roads and Lateral Disconnection in the River Landscapes of the Continental United States. *Geomorphology* 112(3): 212–227.

2014 Roads, Railroads, and Floodplain Fragmentation Due to Transportation Infrastructure along Rivers. *Annals of the Association of American Geographers* 104(3): 413–431.

Borden, Anna C.
1995 Four Walls, Two Timbers, and a Flood: Investigation of Lewis Wernwag's Nineteenth-Century Sawmill in an Industrial Community. *Journal of Middle Atlantic Archaeology* 11: 69–75.

Boswell, Sharon A., Sarah K. Campbell, L. C. McConaghy, and Christian J. Miss
1990 Pratt River Logging Camp Evaluation. Northwest Archaeological Associates, Inc., Seattle. Submitted to USDA Forest Service, Purchase Order 43-05M6-9-0445, Mt. Baker-Snoqualmie National Forest, Marblemount, Washington.

Bowyer, Gary C., Lou Ann Speulda, Lynda J. Sekora, and Lester A. Ross
1995 Archaeological Investigations, PCT-PG&E Pipeline Expansion Project, Idaho, Washington, Oregon, and California, Volume 3. INFOTEC Research, Inc., Fresno, Calif. Submitted to Pacific Gas Transmission Company, San Francisco.

Bradley, Charles S.
2000 Smoking Pipes for the Archaeologist. In *Studies in Material Culture Research*, edited by Karlis Karlins, pp. 104–133. Society for Historical Archaeology, California, Pennsylvania.

Bradley, Nickolas S.
2017 Geomorphic Effects of Logging Railbeds on an Ozarks Headwater Stream, Mark Twain National Forest, Missouri. MS thesis, Department of Geospatial Science, Missouri State University, Springfield.

Braje, Todd J.
2018 Comment on Andrew M. Bauer and Erle C. Ellis, "The Anthropocene Divide: Obscuring Understanding of Social-Environmental Change." *Current Anthropology* 59(2): 215–216.

Brandon, Jamie C.
2013 Reversing the Narrative of Hillbilly History: A Case Study Using Archaeology at Van Winkle's Mill in the Arkansas Ozarks. *Historical Archaeology* 47(3): 36–51.

Brandon, Jamie C., and James M. Davidson
2005 The Landscape of Van Winkle's Mill: Identity, Myth, and Modernity in the Ozark Upland South. *Historical Archaeology* 39(3): 113–131.

Branstner, Mark C.
1999 The Carp River Sawmill Company (20CH99): A Pre–Civil War Settlement on the South Shore of Lake Superior. *Michigan Archaeologist* 45(2): 36–57.

Branstner, Mark C., and Sean B. Dunham
1997 The Upper Great Lakes Lumber Industry: An Interdisciplinary Perspective. *Michigan Archaeologist* 43(2–3): 45–50.

Brashler, Janet G.
1991 When Daddy Was a Shanty Boy: The Role of Gender in the Organization of the Logging Industry in Highland West Virginia. *Historical Archaeology* 25(4): 54–68.

Bratten, John, and Rebecca Booker-DeMonbreun
2014 An Influx of Yankee Dollars and Ingenuity: The Archaeological Remains of Northwest Florida's Cypress Logging Industry. Paper presented at the Society for Historical Archaeology, Quebec City, Quebec.

Brewer, Priscilla J.
1990 Homefires: Cookstoves in American Culture, 1815–1900. In *House and Home*, pp. 68–88, edited by J. M. Benes and R. W. Beales. Dublin Seminar for New England Folklife, Boston.

2000 *From Fireplace to Cookstove: Technology and the Domestic Ideal in America.* Syracuse University Press, Syracuse, New York.

Brotherton, Charles E.

1855 Timber Cruise Notes. Delta County Historical Society, Escanaba, Michigan.

1869 Timber Cruise Notes. Delta County Historical Society, Escanaba, Michigan.

Brown, Marley R., and Charles M. Elling

1981 An Historical Overview of Redwood Logging Resources within the Hume Lake Ranger District, Sequoia National Forest, California. Sonoma State University Academic Foundation, Inc. Porterville, Calif. Submitted to USDA Forest Service.

Bruhy, Mark E., Kim L. Potaracke, Loxley A. Newell, and Randall E. Rohe

1993 Historical-Geographical and Archaeological Investigations of an 1870s Logging Camp: The Sherry and Gerry Camp. In *Heritage Resources Management 1990, Nicolet National Forest,* edited by Mark L. Bruhy, Kim L. Potaracke, and Loxley A. Newell, pp. 175–236. Cultural Resource Survey Report No. 8, USDA Forest Service, Rhinelander, Wisconsin.

Bryant, Jeff, and William Rich

2011 Archaeological Investigations at Locus 12 (Bachelor's Cabin), Elk River Mill and Lumber Company's Town Site of Falk, Headwaters Forest Reserve. Cultural Resource Facility, Humboldt State University, Arcata, Calif. Submitted to U.S. Department of Interior, Bureau of Land Management, Humboldt County, California.

Bryant, Ralph C.

1923 *Logging: The Principles and General Methods of Operation in the United States.* J. Wiley and Sons, New York.

Bultman, John D., and Charles R. Southwell

1976 Natural Resistance of Tropical American Woods to Terrestrial Wood-Destroying Organisms. *Biotropica* 8(2): 71–95.

Busch, Jane

1981 An Introduction to the Tin Can. *Historical Archaeology* 15(1): 95–104.

Butler, Ovid M.

1922 Henry Ford's Forest. *American Forestry* 28(348): 725–730.

Butters, George

1896 *The genealogical registry of the Butters family, including the descendants of William Butter, of Woburn, Massachusetts, 1665, and the families of New York, Pennsylvania, West Virginia, Ohio, Iowa and others bearing the name, who settled in America.* D. Oliphant, Chicago.

California Commission of Immigration and Housing

1920 Rules for Labor Camps. Commission of Immigration and Housing for California, San Francisco. California State Printing Office, Sacramento.

Calumet News (Calumet, Michigan)

1914 "Advertisement for Peerless Tobacco" 16 April: 7. *Chronicling America: Historic American Newspapers,* Library of Congress, http://chroniclingamerica.loc.gov/lccn/sn86086633/1914-04-16/ed-1/seq-7/, accessed August 1, 2019.

Campbell, Renae J.

2017 Reanalysis of Japanese-Manufactured Ceramics Recovered from Japanese Gulch Village (1903–1930), Mukilteo, Washington. *Archaeology in Washington* 17: 62–89.

Canada Lumberman

1903 The Food Supply for Lumber Camps. May, 23(5): 19–20. Toronto, Canada.

Carlson, David R.

2017 The Issei at Barneston Project: An Investigation into Issues of Race and Labor at an Early Twentieth-Century Japanese-American Community. *Archaeology in Washington* 17: 30–62.

Casella, Eleanor C.

2006 Transplanted Technologies and Rural Relics: Australian Industrial Archaeology and Questions that Matter. *Australasian Historical Archaeology* 24: 65–75.

Chazdon, Robin L.

2017 Forest Succession and Human Agency in an Uncertain Future. In *Living in the Anthropocene: Earth in the Age of Humans*, edited by W. John Kress and Jeffrey K. Stine, pp. 87–90. Smithsonian Institution Press, Washington, D.C.

Chicago Historical Society

2005 *Hibbard, Spencer, Bartlett, and Co. Electric Encyclopedia of Chicago*. Chicago Historical Society. Electronic document, www.encyclopedia.chicagohistory.org/pages/2700.

Chicoine, David R.

2004 *Smith and Wesson: Sixguns of the Old West*. Andrew Mowbray, Lincoln, Rhode Island.

Chin, Anne, Rong Fu, Jon Harbor, Mark P. Taylor, and Veerle Vanacker

2013 Anthropocene: Human Interactions with Earth Systems. *Anthropocene* 1: 1–2.

Chung, Sue F.

2015 *Chinese in the Woods: Logging and Lumbering in the American West*. University of Illinois Press, Champaign.

Clark, Jorie

2002 The Archaeology of Railroad Logging in Central Oregon: The Lumberman's Last Frontier. In *AOA Occasional Papers No. 7*, pp. 89–107. Association of Oregon Archaeologists, Eugene.

Clark, Thomas D.

2004 *The Greening of the South: The Recovery of Land and Forest*. University Press of Kentucky, Lexington.

Clawson, Marion

1983 *The Federal Lands Revisited*. Resources for the Future, Washington, D.C.

Cleeland, Teri A.

1995 Barney Flat Historic Railroad Logging Landscape, Arizona. National Register of Historic Places Registration Form, Reference No. 95000155. U.S. Department of Interior, National Park Service, Washington, D.C.

Cleland, Charles E.

1988 Questions of Substance, Questions that Count. *Historical Archaeology* 22(1): 13–17.

Clouse, Robert A., and Elizabeth K. Steiner

2000 *Archaeology at the Marine Mill Site, Marine-on-St. Croix*. Department of Archaeology, Minnesota Historical Society, St. Paul.

Cohen, Hal L. (editor)

1969 [1922] *Montgomery Ward Catalog*. Reprint of 1922 edition. H. C. Publishers, New York.

Comer, Patrick J., Barbara L. Hart, Heather A. Wells, Teresa R. Leibfried, Kraig M. Korrock, and Dennis A. Albert

1994 Pre-European Settlement Landscape of the Eastern Half of Northern Michigan. Michigan Natural Features Inventory, Michigan Department of Natural Resources, Lansing.

Conlin, Joseph

1979 Old Boy, Did You Get Enough of Pie? *Journal of Forest History* 23(40): 164–185.

Conners, Pamela A.

1997 Sugar Pine Railway: History of a Sierran Logging Railroad. USDA Forest Service, Stanislaus National Forest, Sonora, Calif. Available from California Historical Resources Information System, State Historic Preservation Office, Sacramento.

Connolly, Thomas J., Richard L. Bland, and Ward Tonsfeldt

2011 Tracking the Kerry Line: Evidence from a Logging Railroad Camp in the Nehalem Valley, Oregon. *Journal of Northwest Anthropology* 45(2): 199–208.

Cox, Thomas R.

1974 *Mills and Markets: A History of the Pacific Coast Lumber Industry to 1900*. University of Washington Press, Seattle.

2010 *The Lumberman's Frontier: Three Centuries of Land Use, Society, and Change in America's Forests*. Oregon State University Press, Corvallis.

Cramer, Jerame J.

2003 Logs, Labor, and Living: An Archaeological Investigation of African-American Laborers at the Upper and Middle Landing Sawmills at Natchez-under-the-Hill. MA thesis, Department of Geography and Anthropology, Louisiana State University and Agricultural and Mechanical College, Baton Rouge.

Cramp, Arthur Joseph

1923 *"Patent Medicines": The Nostrum and the Public Health: Truth in Advertising Drug Products*. American Medical Association, Chicago.

Crass, David C., and Deborah L. Wallsmith

1992 Where's the Beef? Food Supply at an Antebellum Frontier Post. *Historical Archaeology* 26(2): 3–23.

Creel, George

1915 The Feudal Towns of Texas. *Harper's Weekly* 60: 76–78.

Crocq, Marc-Antoine

2007 Historical and Cultural Aspects of Man's Relationship with Addictive Drugs. *Dialogues in Clinical Neuroscience* 9(4): 355–361.

Cronon, William

1991 *Nature's Metropolis: Chicago and the Great West*. W. W. Norton, New York.

1995 The Trouble with Wilderness; Or, Getting Back to the Wrong Nature. In *Uncommon Ground: Rethinking the Human Place in Nature*, edited by William Cronon, pp. 69–90. W. W. Norton, New York.

Crutzen, Paul J., and Eugene F. Stoermer

2000 The "Anthropocene." *Global Change Newsletter* 41: 17–18.

Davidson, James, and Edward González-Tennant

2008 A Potential Archaeology of Rosewood, Florida: The Process of Remembering a Community and a Tragedy. *SAA Archaeological Record* 8(1): 13–16.

Davis, Richard C.

1983 *Encyclopedia of American Forest and Conservation History*. Macmillan, New York.

Day, Grant L., Jonathan P. Kerr, and Jeffery G. Mauck

1997 Footprint of an Historic Sawmill, Archaeological Investigations of the Crawford-Nurre Sawmill in Williamsburg, Kentucky. In *Current Archaeological Research in Kentucky*, vol. 7, edited by Charles D. Hockensmith and Kenneth C. Carstens, pp. 281–304. Kentucky Heritage Council, Frankfort.

Deagan, Kathleen A.

1988 Neither History nor Prehistory: The Questions that Count in Historical Archaeology. *Historical Archaeology* 22(1): 7–12.

Defebaugh, James Elliott

1970 [1906–1907] *History of the Lumber Industry of America*. 2 vols. American Lumberman, Chicago.

Delle, James A.

2008 Review of *The Archaeology of Class in Urban America* by Stephen Mrozowski, Cambridge University Press. *Cambridge Archaeological Journal* 18(1): 122–123.

Delta County Clerk

1871–1884 Tax Records. Delta County Courthouse, Escanaba, Michigan.

Delta County Register of Deeds

1855–1888 Land Ownership Records. Delta County Courthouse, Escanaba, Michigan.

Demeter, C. Stephan, Nancy Ford Demeter, and Kathryn C. Egan-Bruhy

2010 Minertown-Oneva, Carter, Wisc. National Register of Historic Places Registration Form, State Site No. 47FR0112. U.S. Department of Interior, National Park Service, Washington, D.C.

Denton, Mark H.

1999 Dealing with Late Nineteenth- and Early Twentieth-Century Sites. *Cultural Resource Management News and Views* 11(1): 13–14.

de Vries, Tiemen

1916 *Holland's Influence on English Language and Literature*. C. Grentzebach, Chicago. Digital Library for Dutch Literature, http://www.dbnl.org/tekst/vrie035holl01_01/, accessed September 19, 2007.

Dinerstein, Joel

2006 Technology and Its Discontents: On the Verge of the Posthuman. *American Quarterly* 58(3): 569–595.

Dinsdale, Evelyn M.

1965 Spatial Patterns of Technological Change: The Lumber Industry of Northern New York. *Economic Geography* 41: 258–265.

Dinsmore, Rebecca E.

1985 Archaeological Perspectives of the Lumber Industry in Northern Lower Michigan, 1865–1920. MA thesis, Department of Anthropology, Western Michigan University, Kalamazoo.

Dixon, Kelly J., and Carrie Smith

2017 Rock Hearths and Rural Wood Camps in Jīn Shān/Gām Saan 金山: National Register of Historic Places Evaluations of Nineteenth-Century Chinese Logging Operations at Heavenly Ski Resort in the Lake Tahoe Basin. In *Historical Archaeology of the American West*, edited by Margaret Purser and Mark Warner, pp. 138–173. University of Nebraska Press, Lincoln.

Donegan, Connor M.

2013 Incarceration and State Terror: Racial Capitalism in the American South, 1865–1945. MA thesis, Department of Geography, University of British Columbia, Vancouver.

Douglass, Robert G.

2000 The Chinese Bunkhouse in Miller Gulch: Preliminary Results from the Excavation of an Overseas Chinese Site at the Sonoma Coast Sawmill. *Proceedings of the Society for California Archaeology* 13: 126–135. Chico.

2002 The Sawmill in Miller Gulch: History and Archaeology on the Redwood Coast. MA thesis, Cultural Resources Management Program, Department of Anthropology, Sonoma State University, Rohnert Park.

Drake, Eric C.

2003 *Archaeological Evaluation of the Moses Camp: An Early Twentieth-Century Native American Logging Camp in Michigan's Upper Peninsula.* Heritage Resource Program Report No. 12, USDA Forest Service, Hiawatha National Forest, Escanaba, Michigan.

2018 Working to Stay Together in "Forsaken Out of the Way Places:" Examining Anishinaabe Logging Camps as Sites of Social Refuge on the Industrial Frontier of Michigan's Upper Peninsula. Paper presented at the Annual Meeting of the Society for Historical Archaeology, New Orleans, Louisiana.

Drake, Eric C., and Melissa Drake

2007 Logging, Labor, and Landscapes: Transformations in Labor Relations and the Spatial Organization of Late Nineteenth- and Early Twentieth-Century Logging Camps in the Upper Great Lakes. Paper presented at the Annual Meeting of the Society of Historical Archaeology, Williamsburg, Virginia.

Drake, Eric, John Franzen, and Melissa Drake

2006 Working at Home and Living at Work: Negotiating Tensions of Work, Leisure, and Place in Late Nineteenth- and Early Twentieth-Century Logging Camps. Paper presented at the Annual Meeting of the Society for American Archaeology, San Juan, Puerto Rico.

Drury, John

1966 *Rare and Well Done: Some Historical Notes on Meats and Meatmen.* Quadrangle Books, Chicago.

Dulitz, David

1998 CAL FIRE Archaeology Program: Enterprise Mill Historic Site, CA-TUL-814H Mountain Home State Forest, Tulare County, California. Electronic document, http://calfire.ca.gov/resource_mgt/archaeology-enterprise_mill, accessed October 27, 2016.

Dunham, Sean B., and Mark C. Branstner

1995 1994 Phase II Cultural Resource Evaluations: Hiawatha National Forest. Great Lakes Archaeological Research Associates, Williamston, Mich. Submitted to USDA Forest Service, Escanaba, Michigan, Contract 53-54BO-4-00920.

Dunham, Sean B., and John G. Franzen

1997 Bottles and Berms: Test Excavations at Four Pine Era Lumber Camps in Michigan's Upper Peninsula. *Michigan Archaeologist* 43(2–3): 127–152.

Dunn, Oscar

1880 Glossaire Franco-Canadien et vocabulaire de locutions vicieuses usitées au Canada enregistré suivant la loi, à Ottawa, au bureau du ministre de l'agriculture. Project Gutenberg e-book, http://www.gutenberg.org/catalog/world/readfile?fk_files=88848, accessed September 19, 2007.

Durocher, Matthew

2018 Music in the Northern Woods: An Archaeological Exploration of Musical Instrument Remains. MA thesis, Industrial Archaeology Program, Michigan Technological University, Houghton.

Duster, Troy

1981 Commentary on Alcohol and Aggression in Subcultures. In *Alcohol and Disinhibition: The Nature and Meaning of the Link,* edited by Robin Room and Gary Collins. U.S. Department of Health and Human Services, Washington, D.C.

Dye, Rex

1975 *Lumber Camp Life in Michigan*. Exposition Press, Hicksville, New York.

Edelsward, Lisa M.

2001 *Sauna as Symbol: Society and Culture in Finland*. Peter Lang, New York.

Edgeworth, Matt

2018a Review of *Climate without Nature: A Critical Anthropology of the Anthropocene* by Andrew Bauer and Mona Bhan. *American Antiquity* 83(4): 758–759.

2018b More than Just a Record: Active Ecological Effects of Archaeological Strata. In *Historical Archaeology and Environment*, edited by Marcos A. Torres de Souza and Diogo M. Costa, pp. 19–40. Springer, Cham, Switzerland.

Edgeworth, Matt, Daniel D. Richter, Colin Neil Waters, Peter Haff, Cath Neal, and Simon James Price

2015 Diachronous Beginnings of the Anthropocene: The Lower Bounding Surface of Anthropogenic Deposits. *Anthropocene Review* 2(1): 1–26.

Edmonds, Michael

2009 *Out of the Northwoods: The Many Lives of Paul Bunyan*. Wisconsin Historical Society Press, Madison.

Elliott, Daniel R.

1990 Historical Archaeology at the Tate Creek Logging Camp (CA-SS-1535-H), McCloud River Lumber Company, Siskiyou County, California. USDA Forest Service, Shasta-Trinity National Forests, Redding, Calif. Available from California Historical Resources Information System, State Historic Preservation Office, Sacramento.

Elliott, Michael L.

1992 Railroad Logging Era Resources of the Canon de San Diego Land Grant in North-Central New Mexico. National Register of Historic Places Multiple Property Documentation Form NM 64500426. U.S. Department of Interior, National Park Service, Washington, D.C.

Engberg, George B.

1948 Who Were the Lumberjacks? *Michigan History* 32: 238–246.

Engels, Friedrich

1958 *The Condition of the Working Class in England*. Translated and edited by William Otto Henderson and William Henry Chaloner. Blackwell, Oxford, UK.

Ennals, Peter M., and Deryck W. Holdsworth

1998 *Homeplace: The Making of the Canadian Dwelling over Three Centuries*. University of Toronto Press, Buffalo, New York.

Escanaba Tribune

1870 Lumbering in Delta County. 11 June and 31 December. Newspapers on microfilm, Escanaba Public Library, Escanaba, Michigan.

Feinman, Gary M.

1997 Thoughts on Combining the Archaeological and Historical Records. *Journal of Archaeological Method and Theory* 4(3/4): 367.

Fenenga, Franklin

1947 Artifacts from Excavation of Sutter's Sawmill. *California Historical Society Quarterly* 26(2): 160–162.

Ferone, Jill G., Troy J. Ferone, and Mark A. Hill

1997 Logging Landscapes of the Late Nineteenth Century: A Case Study from Michigan's Western Upper Peninsula. *Michigan Archaeologist* 43(2/3): 87–102.

Fickle, James E.

1970 Early Lumber Trade Associations and the Lone Star State. *East Texas Historical Journal* 8(2): 148–162.

Fitzmaurice, John W.

1889 *The Shanty Boy*. Democrat Steam Printing, Cheboygan, Michigan.

Forney, Sandra Jo

1985 Importance of Sites Related to the Naval Stores Industry in Florida. *Florida Anthropologist* 38: 275–281.

Foster, David R., Benjamin Baiser, Audrey B. Plotkin, Anthony A. D'Amato, Aaron M. Ellison, David Orwig, Wyatt Oswald, Jonathan Thompson, and Stephen Long

2014 *Hemlock: A Forest Giant on the Edge*. Yale University Press, New Haven, Connecticut.

Foster, John B.

2013 Marx and the Rift in the Universal Metabolism of Nature. *Monthly Review* 65(7): 1–19.

Four L Bulletin

1922 M. Seller and Company Advertisement. *Four L Bulletin*, May, 4(5): 22. Loyal Legion of Loggers and Lumbermen, Portland, Oregon.

Fox, Georgia L.

2015 *The Archaeology of Smoking and Tobacco*. University Press of Florida, Gainesville.

Fracchia, Adam, Michael Roller, and Erika M. Sievert

2014 Labor Archeology of the Industrial Era: Identifying and Evaluating Nationally Significant Archeological Sites of Labor in the Industrial Era in the United States. A National Historic Landmarks Theme Study. U.S. Department of the Interior, National Park Service, National Historic Landmarks Program, Washington, D.C.

Franzen, John G.

1984 Intrasite Settlement Pattern at Nineteenth and Twentieth-Century Logging Camps in Michigan's Upper Peninsula. Paper presented at the 17th Annual Meeting of the Society for Historical Archaeology, Williamsburg, Virginia.

1992 Northern Michigan Logging Camps: Material Culture and Worker Adaptation on the Industrial Frontier. *Historical Archaeology* 26(2): 74–98.

1995 Comfort for Man or Beast: Alcohol and Medicine Use in Northern Michigan Logging Camps, ca. 1880–1940. *Wisconsin Archaeologist* 76(1–2): 1–45.

1998 *Archaeological Test Excavation, Monitoring, and Surface Collection, Hiawatha National Forest*. Heritage Resource Program Report No. 10, USDA Forest Service, Hiawatha National Forest, Escanaba, Michigan.

1999 The Archaeology of the Lumber Industry in Northern Michigan. In *Retrieving Michigan's Buried Past: Prehistoric and Historic Archaeology in the Great Lakes State*, edited by John R. Halsey, pp. 338–346. Cranbrook Institute of Science, Bloomfield Hills, Michigan.

Franzen, John G., and Eric C. Drake

2010 *Domestic Life on a Nineteenth-Century Industrial Frontier: Archaeological Data Recovery at the First Nahma Sawmill, 20DE104, Hiawatha National Forest, Michigan*. Heritage Resource Program Monograph No. 3, USDA Forest Service, Hiawatha National Forest, Escanaba, Michigan.

Franzen, John G., and Eric C. Drake, with Terrance Martin

2013 The Camboose Shanty in Northern Michigan: Archaeological Evaluation of Two Nineteenth-Century Lumber Camp Sites in the Hiawatha National Forest. USDA Forest Service. Manuscript on file at supervisor's office, Hiawatha National Forest, Gladstone, Michigan.

Fraser, Joshua
1883 *Shanty, Forest and River Life in the Backwoods of Canada*. J. Lovell and Son, Montreal.

Frye, Lori A., Ronald C. Carlisle, J. Steven Kite, Paula A. Zitzler, and Eric Davis
1995 Archaeological Assessment and Data Recovery of the Gallatin Sawmill at 36FA428, the Eberhart Grist Mill, Dam, and Gallatin Sawmill. Woolpert Consultants and Archaeological Services Consultants. Submitted to U.S. Army Corps of Engineers, Pittsburgh District.

Frye, Susan V., and Dennis E. Frye
1989 *Maryland Heights Historical and Archeological Resources Study*. Occasional Report No. 2, Regional Archeology Program, National Capitol Region. National Park Service, Washington, D.C.

Galloway, George B.
1931 Condition of the Lumber Industry. Editorial Research Reports, Vol. 1, CQ Press, Washington, D.C. Electronic document, http://library.cqpress.com/cqresearcher/cqresrre1931031200, accessed January 30, 2017.

Gan, Elaine, Anna Tsing, Heather Swanson, and Nils Bubandt
2017 Introduction: Haunted Landscapes of the Anthropocene. In *Arts of Living on a Damaged Planet: Ghosts and Monsters of the Anthropocene*, edited by Anna L. Tsing, Heather A. Swanson, Elaine Gan, and Nils Bubandt, pp. 1–14. University of Minnesota Press, Minneapolis.

Ganter, Florian
2011 Kanto: Instant Outdoor Sauna. MS thesis, Department of Spatial Design, Aalto University, Espoo, Finland.

Gassaway, Linn, and Rachel D. Kline
2011 Determination of Eligibility and Historic Properties Management Plan for Millwood, Hume Lake Ranger District, Sequoia National Forest. USDA Forest Service, Sequoia National Forest, Kernville, California.

Gibbons, William H.
1918 *Logging in the Douglas Fir Region*. USDA Bulletin 711. Government Printing Office, Washington, D.C.

Gilbert/Commonwealth Inc.
1985 1984 Cultural Resource Survey and Test Excavation, Hiawatha National Forest. Gilbert/Commonwealth Inc., Jackson, Mich. Submitted to USDA Forest Service, Hiawatha National Forest, Escanaba, Michigan, Contract No. 53-54-30-4-0096.
1988 1987 Cultural Resource Survey, Hiawatha National Forest. Gilbert/Commonwealth Inc., Jackson, Mich. Submitted to USDA Forest Service, Hiawatha National Forest, Escanaba, Michigan, Contract No. 53-54-30BO-7-00074.

Glover, Vernon J.
1984 *Logging Railroads of the Lincoln National Forest, New Mexico*. USDA Forest Service, Southwestern Region, Albuquerque, New Mexico.

González-Ruibal, Alfredo
2016a Archaeology and the Time of Modernity. *Historical Archaeology* 50(3): 144–164.
2016b *Reclaiming Archaeology: Beyond the Tropes of Modernity*. Routledge, London.
2018 Beyond the Anthropocene: Defining the Age of Destruction. *Norwegian Archaeological Review* 51(1–2): 10–21.
2019 *An Archaeology of the Contemporary Era*. Routledge, New York.

González-Tennant, Edward
2010 Community Centered Praxis in Conflict Archaeology: Creating an Archaeology of

Redress with the 1923 Race Riot in Rosewood, Florida. *SAA Archaeological Record* 10(4): 46–49.

Goodman, Jordan

2005 *Tobacco in History: The Cultures of Dependence*. Routledge, London and New York.

Greeley, Horace, Leon Case, and Edward Howland

1872 Files and Their Manufacture. In *The Great Industries of the United States: Being an Historical Summary of the Origin, Growth, and Perfection of the Chief Industrial Arts of This Country*, pp. 445–455. J. R. Burr and Hyde, Hartford, Connecticut.

Greeley, William B.

1917 *Some Public and Economic Aspects of the Lumber Industry.* Studies of the Lumber Industry, Part 1. USDA Office of the Secretary, Report 114. Washington, D.C.

1951 *Forests and Men*. Doubleday, Garden City, New Jersey.

Green, James R.

1973 The Brotherhood of Timber Workers 1910–1913: A Radical Response to Industrial Capitalism in the Southern U.S.A. *Past and Present* 60: 161–200.

Gregory, Ronald L.

2001 *Life in Railroad Logging Camps of the Shevlin-Hixon Company, 1916–1950*. Anthropology Northwest No. 12. Department of Anthropology, Oregon State University, Corvallis.

Grinnan, Joseph J.

2013 Molino Mills: The Maritime Cultural Landscape of a Reconstruction Era Sawmill in Molino, Florida. MA thesis, Department of Anthropology, University of West Florida, Pensacola.

HABS/HAER (Historic American Buildings Survey and Historic American Engineering Record)

1936 Logging Camp, St. Louis County, Minn. Call No. HABS MINN,69-ELY.V,1-. Library of Congress Prints and Photographs Division, Washington, D.C.

1937 Charcoal Pits, Ocean County, N.J. Call No. HABS NJ,15-LAK.V,1-. Library of Congress Prints and Photographs Division, Washington, D.C.

1980 Round Lake Logging Dam, Price County, Wisc. Call No. HAER WIS,50-PAFA.V,1-. Library of Congress Prints and Photographs Division, Washington, D.C.

1984 Nichols Saw Mill, Bow Mills, Merrimack County, N.H. Call No. HABS NH,7-BOWMIL.V,1-. Library of Congress Prints and Photographs Division, Washington, D.C.

1994 Crowell Lumber Mill, Rapides Parish, La. Call No. HABS LA,40-LONG,1-. Library of Congress Prints and Photographs Division, Washington, D.C.

1997 Hull-Oakes Lumber Company, 23837 Dawson Road, Monroe, Benton County, Ore. Call No. HAER ORE,2-MONR,1-. Library of Congress Prints and Photographs Division, Washington, D.C.

2012 Fryingpan Charcoal Kilns, Elk Mountain Drive, Arbaney Park, Basalt, Eagle County, Colo. Call No. HALS CO-5. Library of Congress Prints and Photographs Division, Washington, D.C.

Hahn, Roger

2015 Roosevelt Sykes. In *Encyclopedia of Louisiana*, edited by David Johnson. Louisiana Endowment for the Humanities. Electronic document, http://www.knowlouisiana.org/entry/roosevelt-sykes, accessed November 18, 2018.

Hahn, Thurston H. G., Joanne Ryan, Sara A. Hahn, Jerame J. Cramer, Douglas Wells, and Carey Coxe

2005 Sawmills and Cordwood: Life in Natchez-Under-the-Hill during the Nineteenth and Early Twentieth Centuries. Coastal Environments, Inc. (CEI) Archaeological Reports, Baton Rouge, La. Submitted to the U.S. Army Corps of Engineers, Vicksburg District.

Hahn, Thurston H. G., and Cherie A. Schwab

1998 Donner, Louisiana: Historical and Archaeological Investigations of an Early Twentieth-Century Sawmill Community. Coastal Environments, Inc. (CEI) Archaeological Reports, Baton Rouge, La. Submitted to Louisiana Department of Transportation, Baton Rouge. Available from Louisiana Department of Culture, Recreation and Tourism, Division of Archaeology, Baton Rouge.

Halsey, John R., Eric McDonald, and Rose L. Moore

1997 The East Branch Big Creek Logging Dam and Sluiceway (20 OD 25) Oscoda County. *Michigan Archaeologist* 43(2–3): 115–126.

Hammond, Lorne F.

1994 Capital, Labour and Lumber in A.R.M. Lower's Woodyard: James MacLaren and the Changing Forest Economy, 1850–1906. PhD dissertation, Department of History, University of Ottawa, Ontario.

HARD Work Camps Team and Caltrans Staff

2013 Historical Context and Archaeological Research Design for Work Camp Properties in California. Available from Cultural Studies Office, Division of Environmental Analysis, California Department of Transportation, Sacramento.

Hardesty, Donald L.

1999 Historical Archaeology in the Next Millenium: A Forum. *Historical Archaeology* 33(2): 51–58.

2010 *Mining Archaeology in the American West: A View from the Silver State*. University of Nebraska Press and the Society for Historical Archaeology, Lincoln.

Harding, Bertha

1982 Transcript of taped oral history interview conducted by Theodore J. Karamanski at Manistique, Mich. On file, Mid-American Research Center, Loyola University, Chicago, Illinois, and Hiawatha National Forest, Gladstone, Michigan.

Hardwick, Nathaniel A.

2008 The Underhill Camp: Exploring the Life History of an Early Twentieth-Century Logging Site. MA thesis, Department of Anthropology, Illinois State University, Bloomington.

Harper's New Monthly Magazine

1868 The Minnesota Pineries. March, 409–423. New York, New York.

Hartse, Caroline M.

2017 Yama and Beyond: Construction and Negotiation of Identity at a Late Nineteenth- to Early Twentieth-Century Japanese-American Community. *Archaeology in Washington* 17: 16–29.

Hartt, Rollin L.

1900 Notes on a Michigan Lumber Town. *Atlantic Monthly* 85: 507.

Hatlestad, Kailin

2016 The Bitterroot Socio-Natural Model: Applying Bunkhouse Creek Archaeological Project Data to Test Resilience. MA thesis, Department of Anthropology, University of Montana, Missoula.

Haynes, John E.

1971 Revolt of the Timber Beasts: The IWW Lumber Strike in Minnesota. *Minnesota History* 42(5): 162–174.

Haywood, William D.

1983 [ca. 1929] *Bill Haywood's Book: The Autobiography of William D. Haywood.* Greenwood Press, Westport, Connecticut.

Healey, Martin, and S. Dwight Kirkland

2015 A Historical Context of the Turpentine (Naval Stores) Industry in the Atlantic and Gulf Coastal Plains of Georgia, South Carolina, and Florida. Southeastern Horizons, Inc., Douglas, Georgia. Report Submitted to U.S. Army Corps of Engineers, Savannah District. Available from Department of Defense Cultural Resources Program Information Exchange (DENIX).

Heizer, Robert F.

1947 Archaeological Investigation of Sutter Sawmill Site in 1947. *California Historical Society Quarterly* 26(2): 134–159.

Herskovitz, Robert M.

1978 *Fort Bowie Material Culture.* University of Arizona Press, Tucson.

Hickman, Nollie W.

2009 *Mississippi Harvest: Lumbering in the Longleaf Pine Belt, 1840–1915.* University Press of Mississippi, Jackson.

Hills, Timothy J., Judith S. Chapman, and Douglas C. Wilson

1996 Weyerhaeuser Camp 2 (OR-KL-46): The Archaeology and Socioeconomic History of a Depression-Era Railroad Logging Camp in Southern Oregon. Archaeological Investigations Northwest, Inc., Portland, Ore. Submitted to Pacific Gas Transmission Co., San Francisco, California.

Hindle, Brooke

1975 *America's Wooden Age: Aspects of Its Early Technology.* Sleepy Hollow Restorations, Tarrytown, New York.

Hirsch, Florian, T. Raab, William Ouimet, David Dethier, Anna Schneider, and Alexandra Rabb

2017 Soils on Historic Charcoal Hearths: Terminology and Chemical Properties. *Soil Science Society of America Journal* 81: 1427–1435.

Holbrook, Stewart H.

1936 The Lumberjacks Go Sissy. *American Mercury* 39(154): 193–198.

1943 *Holy Old Mackinaw; A Natural History of the American Lumberjack.* Macmillan, New York.

1948 *Northwest Harvest.* Macmillan, New York.

2016 *Holy Old Mackinaw; A Natural History of the American Lumberjack.* North West Corner Books, Seattle, Washington.

Holden, James

1916 Early Camp Life Reminiscences Told by Holden. *Eau Claire Telegram* 10 November: 2. Wisconsin Historical Society, Wisconsin Local History and Biography Articles, https://www.wisconsinhistory.org/records/newspaper/BA5794, accessed January 16, 2016.

Hollenbeck, Barbara

1983 CB and M Logging Camp, Olympic National Forest, Washington. Manuscript on file, Washington State Historic Preservation Office, Olympia.

Honerkamp, Nicholas

1988 Preface to Articles from Plenary Session: Questions That Count in Historical Archaeology, 1987 Meeting of the Society for Historical Archaeology, Savannah, Georgia. *Historical Archaeology* 22(1): 5–6.

Horn, Jonathan C.

1987 Bingham's Camp: Historical Archaeology of an 1890s Eastern Oregon Logging Camp. MA thesis, Department of Anthropology, University of Idaho, Moscow.

Hornborg, Alf

2017 Dithering While the Planet Burns: Anthropologists' Approaches to the Anthropocene. *Reviews in Anthropology* 46(2): 61–77.

Horton, David

1943 The Functions of Alcohol in Primitive Societies: A Cross-Cultural Study. *Quarterly Journal of Studies on Alcohol* 4: 199–320.

Hotchkiss, George W.

1894 *Industrial Chicago, the Lumber Interests*, Vol. 6. Goodspeed Publishing, Chicago.

Howd, Cloice R.

1924 Industrial Relations in the West Coast Lumber Industry. Bulletin of the United States Bureau of Labor Statistics no. 349. Government Printing Office, Washington, D.C.

Howe, Aaron

2015 "Men of Good Timber": An Archaeological Investigation of Labor in Michigan's Upper Peninsula. MA thesis, Department of Anthropology, Western Michigan University, Kalamazoo.

Howe, Edward T.

2018 The Rise and Fall of the Albany Lumber District. Hudson River Valley Institute, Poughkeepsie, New York. Electronic document, http://www.hudsonrivervalley.org/library/pdfs/articles_books_essays/albany_lumber_district_edward_t_howe.pdf, accessed March 12, 2018.

Huhta, Aleksi

2014 Debating Visibility: Race and Visibility in the Finnish-American Press in 1908. *Nordic Journal of Migration Research* 4(4): 168–175.

IWW (Industrial Workers of the World)

1922 *The Lumber Industry and Its Workers*. 3rd ed. IWW, Chicago. Available through Hathi Trust Digital Library, https://catalog.hathitrust.org/Record/102288333, accessed May 22, 2018.

Irwin, Will

1908 The American Saloon. *Collier's Weekly* 16 May: 10.

Isaacs, Paul W.

1989 History and Evaluation of the Yosemite Lumber and Yosemite Sugar Pine Lumber Company with a Framework for Evaluation and Management of the Historic Archaeological Properties of the Logging Railroad System. USDA Forest Service, Stanislaus National Forest, Sonora, California.

Jager, Ronald

1999 Tool and Symbol: The Success of the Double-Bitted Axe in North America. *Technology and Culture* 40(4): 833–860.

Jensen, Vernon H.

1945 *Lumber and Labor.* Farrar and Rinehart, New York.

Johnson, Aili

1951 Lore of the Finnish-American Sauna. *Midwest Folklore* 1(1): 33–39.

Johnson, Katherine M., Robert B. Ouimet, and Z. Raslan

2015 Geospatial and LiDAR-Based Analysis of Eighteenth- to Early Twentieth-Century Timber Harvesting and Charcoal Production in Southern New England. *GSA Abstracts with Programs* 47(3): 65.

Jones, William P.

2005 *The Tribe of Black Ulysses: African American Lumber Workers in the Jim Crow South.* University of Illinois Press, Urbana.

Karamanski, Theodore J.

1989 *Deep Woods Frontier: A History of Logging in Northern Michigan.* Wayne State University Press, Detroit, Michigan.

2005 Lumber. *Electronic Encyclopaedia of Chicago.* Chicago Historical Society, http://www.encyclopedia.chicagohistory.org/, accessed June 19, 2017.

Karamanski, Theodore J., Gerald Morin, and David J. Keene

1984 History and Cultural Resources: Logging, Mining, and Pioneer Agriculture on the Ottawa National Forest. Mid-American Research Center. Submitted to USDA Forest Service, Eastern Region, Milwaukee.

Karamanski, Theodore J., John Vogel, Gerald Morin, and David J. Keene

1983 Historical Records Study of Logging Industry and Pioneer-Homesteading Cultural Resources on the Hiawatha National Forest. Mid-American Research Center. Submitted to USDA Forest Service, Eastern Region, Milwaukee.

Kauffman, Henry J.

1972 *American Axes: A Survey of Their Development and Their Makers.* Greene Press, Brattleboro, Vermont.

Kaups, Matti

1976a A Finnish Savusauna in Minnesota. *Minnesota History* 45: 11–20.

1976b From Savusaunas to Contemporary Saunas: A Century of Tradition in Minnesota, Michigan, and Wisconsin. In *Sauna Studies: Papers Read at the 6th International Sauna Congress in Helsinki on August 15–17, 1974,* edited by Harold Tier, Yrjö Collan, and Pirkko Valatakari, pp. 34–56. Finnish Sauna Society, Helsinki.

Kelly, Robert

1998 Native Americans and Archaeology: A Vital Partnership. *SAA* (Society for American Archaeology) *Bulletin* 16: 4.

Kero, Reino

1973 *The Roots of Finnish-American Left Wing Radicalism.* Publications of the Institute of General History No. 5. University of Turku, Finland. http://www.genealogia.fi/emi/art/article195e.htm, accessed August 11, 2018.

Kilar, Jeremy W.

1990 *Michigan's Lumbertowns: Lumbermen and Laborers in Saginaw, Bay City, and Muskegon, 1870–1905.* Wayne State University Press, Detroit, Michigan.

Kloss, Julie A.

2002 Defining a Historic Cultural Landscape: The Choate Branch Logging Landscape, Ottawa National Forest, Michigan. MS thesis, Industrial Archaeology Program, Michigan Technological University, Houghton.

Knight, George C.

1981 *Testing Archaeological Inference at an Historical Logging Site in Montana.* Cultural Resources Report No. 1, Idaho Panhandle National Forests, Coeur d'Alene.

Lacy, David M., and Sheila Charles

2000 "Relics and Ruins" at Aldrichville. *Journal of Vermont Archaeology* 3: 76–85.

Lankton, Larry D.
1997 *Beyond the Boundaries: Life and Landscape at the Lake Superior Copper Mines, 1840–1875.* Oxford University Press, New York.
Larson, Agnes M.
1949 *The White Pine Industry in Minnesota: A History.* University of Minnesota Press, Minneapolis.
Lee, David
2006 *Lumber Kings and Shantymen: Logging, Lumber and Timber in the Ottawa Valley.* James Lorimer, Toronto.
Lee, Jane M.
2008 Fidelity and Industry: The Archaeology of a Late Nineteenth-Century Chinese Woodcutter Camp in Dog Valley, California. MA thesis, Department of Anthropology, University of Nevada, Reno. UMI, Ann Arbor, Michigan.
Lee, Russell
1937 Photographs of Logging Camp Near Effie, Minnesota. Call No. LC-USF33. Farm Security Administration,Office of War Information Photograph Collection. Library of Congress Prints and Photographs Division, Washington, D.C.
Lees, William B.
1999 Comments on "Historical Archaeology in the Next Millennium: A Forum." *Historical Archaeology* 33(2): 63–65.
Le Guin, Ursula K.
1972 *The Word for World Is Forest.* 2nd ed. Hainish Cycle. Tor Books, New York, New York.
Leone, Mark P.
1999 Setting Some Terms for Historical Archaeologies of Capitalism. In *Historical Archaeologies of Capitalism*, edited by Mark P. Leone and Parker B. Potter, pp. 3–20. Kluwer Academic, New York.
2010 *Critical Historical Archaeology.* Left Coast Press, Walnut Creek, California.
Leone, Mark P., and Parker B. Potter
1999 *Historical Archaeologies of Capitalism.* Kluwer Academic, New York.
Lewis, Jamie
2012 McNary, Arizona: A Town on the Move. *Peeling Back the Bark* (Forest History Society blog), May 7, 2012. https://foresthistory.org/blog/, accessed January 20, 2017.
Li, Yuguo, Gabriel M. Leung, and Julian Wei-Tze Tang
2007 Role of Ventilation in Airborne Transmission of Infectious Agents in the Built Environment—A Multidisciplinary Systematic Review. *Indoor Air* 17(1): 2–18.
Lidskog, Rolf, and Claire Waterton
2016 Anthropocene—A Cautious Welcome from Environmental Sociology? *Environmental Sociology* 2(4): 395–406. DOI: 10.1080/23251042.2016.1210841.
Lillard, Richard G.
1947 *The Great Forest.* A. A. Knopf, New York.
Lins, Laura, and Heather Johnson
2019 What Happened That Day in Everett. Everett Massacre of 1916 Collection, University of Washington Library, Seattle. Electronic document, https://content.lib.washington.edu/pnwlaborweb, accessed August 22, 2018.
Lipe, William D.
2009 Archaeological Values and Resource Management. In *Archaeology and Cultural Resource Management: Visions for the Future*, edited by Lynne Sebastian and William D. Lipe, pp. 41–63. School for Advanced Research Press, Santa Fe, New Mexico.

Little, Barbara J.
2007 *Historical Archaeology: Why the Past Matters.* Left Coast Press, Walnut Creek, California.
Lockard, Charles R.
1959 *What's Known about Managing Eastern White Pine.* Station Paper NE-121. USDA Forest Service. Northeastern Forest Experiment Station, Upper Darby, Pennsylvania.
Lockwood, Yvonne R.
1977 The Sauna: An Expression of Finnish-American Identity. *Western Folklore: Studies in Folklore and Ethnicity* 36(1): 71–84.
Louisiana Division of Archaeology
2015 Bailey's Dam. Louisiana Department of Culture, Recreation and Tourism. Electronic document, www.crt.state.la.us/cultural-development/archaeology/discover-archaeologybaileysdam, accessed March 25, 2016.
Lower, Arthur R. M.
1968 *The North American Assault on the Canadian Forest: A History of the Lumber Trade Between Canada and the United States.* Greenwood Press, New York.
Lucia, Ellis
1981 A Lesson from Nature: Joe Cox and His Revolutionary Saw Chain. *Forest and Conservation History* 25(3): 158–165.
Lustick, Robert
1995 Transcript of interview conducted by Anthony Godfrey. U.S. West Research, LaCrosse, Wisc. Submitted to USDA Forest Service, Hiawatha National Forest, Escanaba, Michigan.
Luyssaert, Sebastiaan, Ernst D. Schulze, Annett Börner, Alexander Knohl, Dominik Hessenmöller, Beverly E. Law, Philippe Ciais, and John Grace
2008 Old-Growth Forests as Global Carbon Sinks. *Nature* 455(7210): 213–215. https://doi.org/10.1038/nature07276.
MacCleery, Douglas W.
2011 *American Forests: A History of Resiliency and Recovery.* USDA Forest Service and Forest History Society, Durham, North Carolina.
Mack, Cheryl
2005 Hook Tenders and Rigging Rustlers: Data Recovery Excavations at Wind River Lumber Company's Camp 3, Trout Creek Archaeological Site (45SA222), Gifford Pinchot National Forest. USDA Forest Service, Gifford Pinchot National Forest Heritage Program, Trout Lake, Washington.
MacKay, Donald
1978 *The Lumberjacks.* McGraw-Hill Ryerson, Toronto.
Macnamara, Charles
1959 The Camboose Shanty. *Ontario History* 51: 73–78.
Maine Historic Preservation Commission
2017 Historical Archaeology. Maine Historic Preservation Commission. Electronic document, http://www.maine.gov/mhpc/archaeology/historic_archaeology.html, accessed June 14, 2017.
Malm, Andreas
2018 *The Progress of This Storm: On Society and Nature in a Warming World.* Verso, London.

Malm, Andreas, and Alf Hornborg

2014 The Geology of Mankind? A Critique of the Anthropocene Narrative. *Anthropocene Review* 1(1): 62–69.

Maniery, Mary L.

1991 Logging Chute Systems in Northeastern California: A Case Study on Plumas National Forest. *Proceedings of the Society for California Archaeology* 4: 151–158.

2002 Health, Sanitation, and Diet in a Twentieth-Century Dam Construction Camp: A View from Butt Valley, California. *Historical Archaeology* 36(3): 69–84.

Maniery, Mary L., and Cindy L. Baker

1997 National Register of Historic Places Evaluation of the Red River, Fruit Growers, and Lassen Lumber and Box Railroad Logging Systems, Lassen National Forest, California. PAR Environmental Services, Sacramento, Calif. Submitted to USDA Forest Service, Lassen National Forest, Eagle Lake Ranger District, Susanville, California.

Marble, Webster L.

1896–1897 Timber Cruise Maps and Reports of Examination. Copies on file, Hiawatha National Forest, Gladstone, Michigan.

Marcot, Roy M.

1983 *Spencer Repeating Firearms*. Northwood Heritage Press, Irvine, California.

Marsh, Pearl A.

2015 A Black Logger's Journey: Jackson Parish, Louisiana, to Wallowa County, Oregon. *Oregon Historical Quarterly* 116(4): 500–521.

Marshall Wells Hardware Company

1912 Catalog. Marshall Wells Hardware Company, Duluth, Minn. Photocopy on file, Hiawatha National Forest, Gladstone, Michigan.

Martin, Patrick E.

1985 *The Mill Creek Site and Pattern Recognition in Historical Archaeology*. Mackinac Island State Park Commission, Archaeological Completion Report Series No. 10. Mackinac Island, Michigan.

2009 Industrial Archaeology. In *International Handbook of Historical Archaeology*, edited by Teresa Majewski and Daniel Gaimster, pp. 285–297. Springer, New York.

Marx, Karl

1910 *Capital: A Critique of Political Economy*. Vol. 2, *The Process of Circulation of Capital*, edited by Frederick Engels, translated from the 2nd German ed. by Ernest Untermann. Charles H. Kerr, Chicago.

1991 *Capital: A Critique of Political Economy*, Vol. 3. Translated by David Fernbach. Penguin Classics. Penguin Limited, London.

Massey, Doreen

1995 Places and Their Pasts. *History Workshop Journal* 39: 182–192.

Maybee, Rolland H.

1960 *Michigan's White Pine Era, 1840–1900*. Michigan Historical Commission, Lansing.

McClary, Daryl C.

2014 Longview—Thumbnail History. Washington Department of Archaeology and Historic Preservation, HistoryLink Essay 8560. Electronic document, https://www.historylink.org/File/8560, accessed June 19, 2017.

McDavid, Carol, Rachel Feit, Kenneth L. Brown, Fred L. McGhee, and Jannie Scott

2013 African American Archaeology in Texas: A Planning Document. Community Archaeology Research Institute, Inc. Houston, Tex. Submitted to Texas Historical Commission, Austin.

McKee, Dave F.
2009 Historic Logging in the Sierra Madre Mountains of Southern Wyoming: Investigations of a Historic Logging Landscape. *Wyoming Archaeologist* 53(2): 13–36.

McKem, Jem
1921 From the Diary of a Lumberjack: Reminiscences of Camps and Mills in Days Gone By. *American Lumberman*. 19 November: 37, 47.

McQueen, Robert
1995 Archaeological Investigations: The Robinson/Herrling Sawmill, Old Wade House State Park, Greenbush, Wisconsin. MS thesis, Industrial Archaeology Program, Michigan Technological University, Houghton.

Mercer, Henry C.
1929 *Ancient Carpenters' Tools: Illustrated and Explained, Together with the Implements of the Lumberman, Joiner and Cabinet Maker in Use in the Eighteenth Century*. Bucks County Historical Society, Doylestown, Pennsylvania.

Merritt, Christopher W.
2015 Archie Creek Camp National Register of Historic Places Registration Form 20SM591. U.S. Department of Interior, National Park Service, Washington, D.C.

Merritt, Christopher W., and James E. Ayres
2014 Tie Cutting Industry of the North Slope of the Uinta Mountains (1867–1940s). National Register of Historic Places Multiple Property Documentation Form UT 64501215. U.S. Department of Interior, National Park Service, Washington, D.C.

Meskell, Lynn, and Robert W. Preucel
2007 *A Companion to Social Archaeology*. Blackwell, Oxford, UK.

Mills, Frederick C.
1992 Work in a Sierra Lumber Camp. In *In the Floating Army: F. C. Mills on Itinerant Life in California, 1914*, edited by Gregory R. Woirol, pp. 41–64. University of Illinois Press, Urbana.

Miner, Horace M.
1963 *St. Denis: A French-Canadian Parish*. University of Chicago Press, Chicago.

Mining Journal (Marquette, Michigan)
1869 Advertisements. 13 January and 12 May. Newspapers on microfilm, Peter White Public Library, Marquette, Michigan.

Minnesota State Archaeologist Office
2018 An Overview of Post-Contact Period Archaeology in Minnesota (1837–Present). Minnesota Department of Administration, St. Paul. Electronic document, https://shermanmn.gov/admin/archaeologist/the-public/mn-archaeology/post-contact-period/, accessed July 23, 2017.

Miss, Christian J., Lorelea Hudson, and Sharon Boswell
2000 Data Recovery Excavations and Documentation of Manley-Moore Lumber Company Logging Sites, Pierce County, Washington. Northwest Archaeological Associates, Inc., Seattle, Wash. Submitted to USDA Forest Service, Mt. Baker-Snoqualmie National Forest, Everett, Washington, Contract No. 53-04H 1-7-3382.

Mitchell, Stacy
1999 Union in the North Woods: The Timber Strikes of 1937. *Minnesota History* 56(5): 262–277.

Moffatt, Charles R., Mark E. Bruhy, Sean B. Dunham, and Kathryn C. Egan-Bruhy
2011 Historic Logging Industry Sites in the Chequamegon-Nicolet National Forest. Na-

tional Register of Historic Places Multiple Property Documentation Form 64501146. U.S. Department of Interior, National Park Service, Washington, D.C.

Morris, Rick, Monique E. Kimball, Thomas F. Messerli, and Harding Polk II

1994 *Across the Colorado Plateau: Anthropological Studies for the Transwestern Pipeline Expansion Project.* Vol. 19: *Hot Nights, San Francisco Whiskey, Baking Powder, and a View of the River: Life on the Southern Frontier.* Office of Contract Archaeology, University of New Mexico, Albuquerque. Submitted to Transwestern Pipeline Co., Houston, Texas.

Morton, Timothy

2016 *Dark Ecology for a Logic of Future Coexistence.* Columbia University Press, New York.

Mrozowski, Stephen A.

2006 Environments of History: Biological Dimensions of Historical Archaeology. In *Historical Archaeology*, edited by Martin Hall and Stephen W. Silliman, pp. 23–41. Blackwell, Oxford, UK.

2010 New and Forgotten Paradigms: The Environment and Economics in Historical Archaeology. *Historical Archaeology* 44(3): 117–127.

2018 The Archaeology of Climate Change: Is Unbridled Commodity Production Sustainable? In *Historical Archaeology and Environment*, edited by Marcos André Torres de Souza and Diogo Menezes Costa, pp. 41–61. Springer, Cham, Switzerland.

Muckle, Robert

2016 Archaeology of an Early Twentieth-Century Nikkei Camp in the Seymour Valley: A Photo Essay. *BC Studies* 192: 125–148.

Mueller, Jesse R.

1921 Feeding Problems in the Lumber Camps of the Northwest. *Journal of Home Economics* 13(6): 241–245.

Muir, John

1897 The American Forests. *Atlantic Monthly* 80: 145–157.

1916 *A Thousand-Mile Walk to the Gulf.* Houghton Mifflin, Boston.

1918 *Steep Trails: California, Utah, Nevada, Washington, Oregon, the Grand Canyon.* Houghton Mifflin, Boston.

Muir, John, and William Frederic Badè

1924 *The Life and Letters of John Muir.* Houghton Mifflin, Boston.

Myers, Natasha

2018 How to Grow Livable Worlds: Ten Not-So-Easy Steps. In *The World to Come*, edited by Kerry O. Smith, pp. 53–63. Harn Museum of Art, Gainesville, Florida.

Nelson, Robert E.

1999 *Directory of American Toolmakers.* Early American Industries Association, South Dartmouth, Massachusetts.

Newman, T. Stell

1970 A Dating Key for Post-Eighteenth-Century Bottles. *Historical Archaeology* 4: 70–75.

North Shore Stewardship Association

2016 Sugarloaf Cove History. North Shore Stewardship Association, Duluth, Minnesota. Electronic document, http://sugarloafnorthshore.org/explore-sugarloaf/sugarloaf-cove-history/ Sugarloaf, accessed October 29, 2016.

Oldfield, Frank, Anthony D. Barnosky, John Dearing, Marina Fischer-Kowalski, John McNeill, Will Steffen, and Jan Zalasiewicz

2013 The Anthropocene Review: Its Significance, Implications and the Rationale for a New Transdisciplinary Journal. *The Anthropocene Review* 1(1): 3–7.

Oleson, Charles W.

1891 Secret Nostrums and Systems of Medicine: A Book of Formulas. 3rd. ed. Oleson, Chicago. https://catalog.hathitrust.org/Record/100129390, accessed February 26, 2017.

Ontario Legislative Assembly

1902 *Smallpox Outbreaks in the Lumbering Districts of Ontario*. Sessional Papers, Vol. 34, Part 8, 5th Session, 9th Legislature. L. K. Cameron, Toronto.

O'Rourke, Daniel J.

1997 Rock Kilns: A Case Study of Michigan's Charcoal Industry. MS thesis, Industrial Archaeology Program, Michigan Technological University, Houghton.

Osborn, Chase S.

1919 *The Iron Hunter*. Macmillan, New York.

Overstreet, David F.

1982 *Identification and Evaluation of Logging Industry–Related Cultural Resources, Nicolet National Forest, Wisconsin*. Reports of Investigations No. 114. Great Lakes Archaeological Research Center, Waukesha, Wisconsin.

Overstreet, David F., Annette Nekola, and Andrew Ippolito

1983 *Identification and Evaluation of Logging Industry–Related Cultural Resources, Nicolet National Forest, Wisconsin—1983 Addendum*. Reports of Investigations No. 114. Great Lakes Archaeological Research Center, Milwaukee, Wisconsin.

Oxley, James M.

1895 *My Strange Rescue and Other Stories of Sport and Adventure in Canada*. Thomas Nelson and Sons, London.

Pacific Logging Congress

1917 *Ninth Annual Session of the Pacific Logging Congress Held on October 18th, 19th, and 20th, 1917, at Seattle, Washington*. Compiled and issued by the Timberman, Portland, Oregon. https://books.google.com/books?id=eo4qAQAAMAAJ, accessed November 19, 2018.

Pan, Yude, Richard A. Birdsey, Oliver L. Phillips, and Robert B. Jackson

2013 The Structure, Distribution, and Biomass of the World's Forests. *Annual Review of Ecology, Evolution, and Systematics* 44: 593–622.

Pappas, Efstathios

2004 Fictive Kin in the Mountains: The Paternalistic Metaphor and Households in a California Logging Camp. In *Household Chores and Household Choices: Theorizing the Domestic Sphere in Historical Archaeology*, edited by Kerri S. Barile and Jamie C. Brandon, pp. 176–193. University of Alabama Press, Tuscaloosa.

Parlin, John, Bernice Anderson, and James L. Carter

2011 *Harvesting the Wilderness: The Tyoga Lumber Company and Onota Township; A Microcosm of the Upper Peninsula of Michigan*. Grosbeak Trail Press and Global Printing, Ishpeming, Michigan.

Paskoff, Paul F.

1983 *Industrial Evolution: Organization: Structure and Growth of the Pennsylvania Iron Industry*. Studies in Industry and Society. Johns Hopkins University Press, Baltimore, Maryland.

Paullin, Pamela

2007 Boring to the Core: The Archaeology, History, and Dendrochronology of a Railroad Logging Camp, Ladee Flat, Clackamas County, Oregon. MA thesis, Interdisciplinary Studies, Oregon State University, Corvallis.

Pearson, Gregg S.

2016 The Democratization of Food: Tin Cans and the Growth of the American Food Processing Industry, 1810–1940. PhD dissertation, Department of History, Lehigh University, Bethlehem, Pennsylvania.

Peattie, Donald C., and Paul Landacre

2007 *A Natural History of North American Trees*. Houghton Mifflin, Boston.

Penn, Theodore Z., and Roger Parks

1975 Nichols–Colby Sawmill in Bow, New Hampshire. *IA: The Journal of the Society for Industrial Archeology* 1(1): 1–12.

Pennier, Henry

2006 *Call Me Hank: A Stó:lō Man's Reflections on Logging, Living, and Growing Old*. University of Toronto Press, Toronto.

Petersen, Keith

1987 *Company Town: Potlatch, Idaho, and the Potlatch Lumber Company*. Washington State University Press, Pullman.

Pike, Robert E.

1999 *Tall Trees, Tough Men*. W. W. Norton, New York.

Platt, Rutherford H.

1965 *The Great American Forest*. Prentice-Hall, Englewood Cliffs, New Jersey.

Pletka, Karyn L.

1993 Industrial Archaeology at the Robinson-Herring Sawmill Site, Greenbush, Wisconsin. *Michigan Archaeologist* 39(1): 1–35.

Praetzellis, Adrian, and Mary Praetzellis

1993 Life and Work at the Cole and Nelson Sawmill, Sierra County, California: Archaeological Data Recovery for the Granite Chief Land Exchange. Anthropological Studies Center, Sonoma State University, Rohnert Park, Calif. Submitted to USDA Forest Service, Tahoe National Forest, Nevada City, California.

Prescott, De Witt C.

1910 The Evolution of Modern Band Saw Mills for Sawing Logs. Prescott Company, Menominee, Michigan. Internet Archive, http://www.openlibrary.org/books/OL7058583M, accessed November 1, 2017.

Prouty, Andrew M.

1988 *More Deadly Than War!: Pacific Coast Logging, 1827–1981*. Garland, New York.

Quinlan, Maria

1975 *Lumbering in Michigan*. Michigan History Division, Michigan Department of State, Lansing.

Rajala, Richard

1989 Bill and the Boss: Labor, Labor Protest, Technological Change, and the Transformation of the West Coast Logging Camp, 1890–1930. *Journal of Forest History* 33: 168–179.

1993 The Forest as Factory: Technological Change and Worker Control in the West Coast Logging Industry, 1880–1930. *Labour/Le Travail* 32: 73–104.

1999 *Clearcutting the Pacific Rain Forest: Production, Science, and Regulation*. UBC Press, Vancouver.

Raskin, Karen, William Rich, and James Roscoe

2014 Archaeological Excavations at the Locus 7 Homesite in the Town Site of Falk and the Elk River Mill and Lumber Company, Headwaters Forest Reserve. Cultural Resource

Facility, Humboldt State University, Arcata, Calif. Submitted to U.S. Department of Interior, Bureau of Land Management, Humboldt County, California.

Reams, Robert, and Jerame J. Cramer
1998 A Passport-in-Time Excavation of a Piney Woods Logging and Turpentine Camp. Paper presented at 31st Annual Society for Historical Archaeology Conference, Atlanta, Georgia.

Rector, William G.
1953 *Log Transportation in the Lake States Lumber Industry, 1840–1918: The Movement of Logs and Its Relationship to Land Settlement, Waterway Development, Railroad Construction, Lumber Production, and Prices.* A. H. Clark, Glendale, California.

Reimann, Lewis Charles
1951 *Between the Iron and the Pine: A Biography of a Pioneer Family and a Pioneer Town.* Northwoods, Ann Arbor, Michigan.

Reinhardt, Hazel H.
1983 Social Adjustments to a Changing Environment. In *The Great Lakes Forest*, edited by Susan L. Flader, pp. 205–222. University of Minnesota Press, Minneapolis.

Reno, Ronald L.
1996 Fuel for the Frontier: Industrial Archaeology of Charcoal Production in the Eureka Mining District, Nevada, 1869–1891. PhD dissertation, Department of Anthropology, University of Nevada, Reno.

Rich, William, and James Roscoe
2009 Historical Archaeological Investigations at the Train Engine House in the Town Site of Falk and the Elk River Mill and Lumber Company, Headwaters Forest Reserve, Humboldt County, California. Submitted to U.S. Department of Interior, Bureau of Land Management, Arcata, California.

Richner, Jeffrey
1986 *An Archaeological Evaluation of the Trout Point Logging Camp.* Midwest Archaeological Center Occasional Studies in Anthropology No. 17. U.S. Department of Interior, National Park Service, Lincoln, Nebraska.

Rick, Torben C.
2017 Archaeology and the Future of Our Planet. In *Living in the Anthropocene: Earth in the Age of Humans*, edited by W. John Kress and Jeffrey K. Stine, pp. 74–77. Smithsonian Institution Press, Washington, D.C.

Rickaby, Franz
1926 *Ballads and Songs of the Shanty-Boy.* Harvard University Press, Cambridge, Massachusetts.

Riordan, Timothy B.
1980 Phase II Test Excavation of Two Historical Archaeological Sites along M-32, Montmorency County, Michigan. Resource Analysts Inc., Bloomington, Indiana. Submitted to Michigan Department of Transportation, Lansing.

Riordan, Timothy B., and David F. Barton
1982 Archaeological and Historical Phase II Investigations at the South Manistique Townsite (20ST72), Schoolcraft County, Michigan. Resource Analysts, Inc., Bloomington, Indiana. Submitted to Michigan Department of Transportation, Lansing.

Ritter, Luke
2015 Frederick Weyerhaeuser. In *Immigrant Entrepreneurship: German-American Business Biographies, 1720 to the Present.* Vol. 3, *From the End of the Gilded Age to the Progres-*

sive Era, 1893–1918, edited by Giles R. Hoyt. German Historical Institute, Washington, D.C.

Rock, James
1984 Cans in the Countryside. *Historical Archaeology* 18(2): 97–111.
1986 Railroad Logging, a Capital Resource. *Journal of New World Archaeology* 6(4): 57–68.

Rogozinski, Jan
1990 *Smokeless Tobacco in the Western World: 1550–1950.* Praeger, New York.

Rominger, Carl L.
1881 *Geologic Survey of Michigan.* Vol. 4, *Upper Peninsula, 1878–1880.* Legislature of Michigan, Board of Geologic Survey. Julies Bien, New York.

Rosholt, Malcolm
1980 *Wisconsin Logging Book 1839–1939.* Rosholt House, Rosholt, Wisconsin.

Rostow, Walter W.
1962 *The Stages of Economic Growth: A Non-Communist Manifesto.* Cambridge University Press, Cambridge, UK.

Rutkow, Eric
2012 *American Canopy: Trees, Forests, and the Making of a Nation.* Scribner, New York.

Ryan, James C.
1973 *Early Loggers in Minnesota,* Vol. 1. Minnesota Timber Producers Association, Duluth.
1976 *Early Loggers in Minnesota,* Vol. 2. Minnesota Timber Producers Association, Duluth.
1980 *Early Loggers in Minnesota,* Vol. 3. Minnesota Timber Producers Association, Duluth.

Sams, James, Harry M. Edenborn, and Paul T. Fagley
2012 LiDAR Footprint of Historic Charcoal Hearths at Greenwood Furnace, Huntington County, Pennsylvania. *Geological Society of America Abstracts* 44(5): 74.

Sandor, Shana, and Chelsea Rose
2017 Jim Rock Historic Can Collection: Southern Oregon University's Digital Collection Celebrating Jim Rock's Contributions to Tin Can Archaeology. *Oregon Historical Quarterly* 118(1): 140–150.

Santana, Carlos
2018 Waiting for the Anthropocene. *British Journal for the Philosophy of Science,* https://doi.org/10.1093/bjps/axy022, accessed January 3, 2019.

Saunt, Claudio
2015 *West of the Revolution: An Uncommon History of 1776.* W. W. Norton, New York.

Sawyer, Alvin L.
1911 *A History of the Northern Peninsula of Michigan.* Lewis Publishing, Chicago.

Sawyer, William A.
1988 A History and Evaluation of the Mono Mills Railroad Logging District, Inyo National Forest, California, Report No. MN-01008. Archaeological Advisory Group, Newport Beach, Calif. Submitted to USDA Forest Service, Bishop, California. Available from California Historical Resources Information System, State Historic Preservation Office, Sacramento.

Schroeder, Joe J. (editor)
1971 *1908 Sears Roebuck Catalog.* Reprint of 1908 ed. DBI Books, Northfield, Illinois.

Schuyler, Robert L.
1999 Comments on "Historical Archaeology in the Next Millennium: A Forum." *Historical Archaeology* 33(2): 66–70.

Shackle, Paul A.
2004 Labor's Heritage: Remembering the American Industrial Landscape. *Historical Archaeology* 38(4): 44–58.
2009 *Archaeology of American Labor and Working-Class Life*. University Press of Florida, Gainesville.
Shackel, Paul A., and Matthew Palus
2010 Industry, Entrepreneurship, and Patronage: Lewis Wernwag and the Development of Virginius Island. *Historical Archaeology* 44(2): 97–112.
Sharrah, David M., and George S. Bause
2017 Perry Davis' Pain Killer: America's First Nationally Advertised Drug for Analgesia? *Journal of Anesthesia History* 3(3): 112–113.
Sherman, Elaine
1999 Early Twentieth-Century Logging Industry Historic Resources on the National Forests and Grasslands in Texas. National Register of Historic Places Multiple Property Documentation Form TX 64500633. U.S. Department of Interior, National Park Service, Washington, D.C.
Sherwood, H. B.
1872 Lumbering in Canada. *Appleton's Journal* 8(191): 573–574.
Shofner, Jerrell H.
1981 Forced Labor in the Florida Forests 1880–1950. *Journal of Forest History* 25(1): 14–25.
Shong, Michael, and Christian J. Miss
2009 Archaeological Testing of 45-SK-256, Camp 6 of the Hamilton Logging Company, Skagit County, Washington. Northwest Archaeological Associates, Inc., Seattle, Washington. Submitted to Centennial Resources, LLC. Available from Washington Department of Archaeology and Historic Preservation, Olympia.
Shoup, Laurence H., and Suzanne Baker
1981 Speed, Power, Production, and Profit: Railroad Logging in the Goosenest District, Klamath National Forest, 1900–1956. USDA Forest Service, Klamath National Forest, Yreka, California. Available from California Historical Resources Information System, State Historic Preservation Office, Sacramento.
Similä, Gusti
1938 *Yli kymmenen vuotta Korpiinissa oli jo asuttu* [Over ten years we have lived in Corbin]. Disc audio recording AFS 2393A1. Alan Lomax Collection of Michigan and Wisconsin Recordings. Library of Congress, American Folklife Center, Washington, D.C.
Sims, Cort
1983 *The Log Chutes of North Idaho*. Cultural Resources Report No. 8, USDA Forest Service Northern Region, Missoula, Montana.
1998 Flumes and Fluming in Northern Idaho. Manuscript on file, USDA Forest Service, Idaho Panhandle National Forests, Coeur d'Alene.
Skibo, James M., and Michael B. Schiffer
2008 *People and Things: A Behavioral Archaeological Perspective*. Springer, New York.
Slater, John T.
2013 Tonawanda Harbor: The Lumber Capital of the World. *Western New York Heritage* 16(1): 7–10.
Sloane, Eric
1965 *A Reverence for Wood*. Ballantine Books, New York.

Smith, Dottie

1992 The Historic Blue Ridge Flume of Shasta and Tehama Counties, California. In *Gold and Lumber: Two Papers on Northern California History and Archaeology*, edited by Eric W. Ritter. U.S. Department of Interior, Bureau of Land Management, Redding, California.

Smith, Duane A.

2001 A Social History of McPhee, Colorado's Largest Lumber Town. In *Forests Under Fire: A Century of Ecosystem Mismanagement in the Southwest*, edited by Christopher J. Huggard and Arthur R. Gomez, pp. 41–66. University of Arizona Press, Tucson.

Smith, Frederick H.

2008 *The Archaeology of Alcohol and Drinking*. University Press of Florida, Gainesville.

Snyder, Gary

1990 *The Practice of the Wild: Essays*. North Point Press, New York.

Society of American Foresters

1919 Forest Devastation: A National Danger and a Plan to Meet It. Report of the Committee for the Application of Forestry, Society of American Foresters. *Journal of Forestry* 17(8): 911–945.

Solli, Brit, Mats Burström, Ewa Domanska, Matt Edgeworth, Alfredo González-Ruibal, Cornelius Holtorf, Gavin Lucas, Terje Oestigaard, Laurajane Smith, and Christopher Witmore

2011 Some Reflections on Heritage and Archaeology in the Anthropocene. *Norwegian Archaeological Review* 44(1): 40–88.

Solury, Theresa E.

2004 "Everlasting Remembrance": The Archaeology of Nineteenth-Century Chinese Labor in the Western Lumber Industry. MA thesis, Department of Anthropology, University of Nevada, Reno.

Sorensen, Nicole E.

2005 Where There's Smoke, There's Fire: A Historical Archaeological Investigation of the Peshtigo Fire's Impact at the Williamsonville Site (47DR241), Door County, Wisconsin. MA thesis, Department of Anthropology, University of Wisconsin, Milwaukee.

South, Stanley

1977 *Method and Theory in Historical Archaeology*. Academic Press, New York.

1978 Pattern Recognition in Historical Archaeology. *American Antiquity* 43: 223–230.

Southerlin, Bobby

2008 Toward Development of an Archaeological and Historic Context for South Carolina's Sawmill, Timber, and Lumber Industry. *South Carolina Antiquities* 40: 48–88.

2013 A Survey of Tar and Pitch Production Sites in the Francis Marion National Forest. Paper presented at the 2013 Archaeological Society of South Carolina Conference, Columbia, South Carolina. http://archcon.org/wp-content/uploads/2013/05/Tar-and-Pitch-Production-Sites-Paper.pdf, accessed March 5, 2019.

Sprague, Roderick

1981 A Functional Classification for Artifacts from Nineteenth- and Twentieth-Century Historical Sites. *North American Archaeologist* 2(3): 251–261.

Springer, Anna-Sophie, and Etienne Turpin

2017 *The Word for World Is Still Forest*. K. Verlag and Haus der Kulturen der Welt, Berlin, Germany.

Springer, John S.

1851 *Forest Life and Forest Trees: Comprising Winter Camp Life among the Loggers, and*

Wild-Wood Adventure, with Descriptions of Lumbering Operations on the Various Rivers of Maine and New Brunswick. Harper and Brothers, New York.

State Library and Archives of Florida

192- Wilson Cypress Company houseboats for logging crews. Photoprint, Image No. RC11909. Reference Collection, Florida Memory Project. https://www.floridamemory.com/items/show/34365, accessed December 30, 2019.

Steer, Henry. B.

1948 *Lumber Production in the United States, 1799–1946.* USDA Miscellaneous Publication No. 669. Washington, D.C.

Stein, Pat H.

1993 Logging Railroad Resources of the Coconino and Kaibab National Forests. National Register of Historic Places Multiple Property Documentation Form AZ 64500041. U.S. Department of Interior, National Park Service, Washington, D.C.

2006 Logging Railroads of the Coconino and Kaibab National Forests: Supplemental Report to a National Register of Historic Places Multiple Property Nomination. USDA Forest Service, Southwestern Region, Coconino and Kaibab National Forests, Flagstaff, Arizona.

Stencel, Craig

2000 Life at a Logging Camp: A Case Study of Goodman Lumber Company Camp E. MS thesis, Industrial Archaeology Program, Michigan Technological University, Houghton.

Stephenson, Isaac

1915 *Recollections of a Long Life.* R. R. Donnelly and Sons, Chicago.

Stevenson, Shanna

1991 Weyerhaeuser South Bay Log Dump Rural Historic Landscape. National Register of Historic Places Documentation Form, Reference No. 91001441. U.S. Department of Interior, National Park Service, Washington, D.C.

Steyaert, Louis T., and Robert G. Knox

2008 Reconstructed Historical Land Cover and Biophysical Parameters for Studies of Land-Atmosphere Interactions within the Eastern United States. *Journal of Geophysical Research* 113. DOI: 10.1029/2006JD008277.

Stiles, Cynthia M.

1994a *Cultural Study Unit: The Historic Logging Industry in State Region 2 and Nicolet National Forest.* Report of Investigations No. 3. USDA Forest Service, Nicolet National Forest, Rhinelander, Wisconsin.

1994b Historic Logging Industry in State Region 2 and the Nicolet National Forest. National Register of Historic Places Multiple Property Documentation Form WI 64500774. U.S. Department of Interior, National Park Service, Washington, D.C.

St. Mary's Falls Ship Canal Company

1863 *Catalogue of 525,000 Acres of Pine Timber Lands Belonging to the Saint Mary's Falls Ship Canal Company, Arranged in Groups, As They Will Be Offered at . . . Detroit, On the 2nd. Day of September, 1863.* St. Mary's Falls Ship Canal Company, Detroit, Michigan. Internet Archive, https://archive.org/details/cu31924030121499/page/n15/mode/2up.

Strachan, Scotty, Franco Biondi, Susan G. Lindstrom, Robert McQueen, and Peter E. Wigand

2013 Application of Dendrochronology to Historical Charcoal-Production Sites in the Great Basin, United States. *Historical Archaeology* 47(4): 103–119.

Straka, Thomas J.

2014 Historic Charcoal Production in the U.S. and Forest Depletion: Development of Production Parameters. *Advances in Historical Studies* 3(2): 104–114.

Surface-Evans, Sarah

2017 Day of Archaeology at a Great Lakes Lumbering Camp. *Day of Archaeology* (blog), July 28, 2017. https://www.dayofarchaeology.com/tag/michigan/, accessed July 1, 2019.

Sykes, Roosevelt

2000 Devil's Island Gin Blues. In *Complete Recorded Works of Roosevelt Sykes in Chronological Order*. Vol. 3, *19 September 1931 to 11 December 1933*. Document Records, Ltd., Catalog No. DOCD 5118. Scotland, UK.

Taber, Thomas T., III

1995 *Williamsport Lumber Capital*. Paulhamus Litho, Montoursville, Pennsylvania.

Tamez, Sonia A., Dana E. Supernowicz, and James T. Rock

1988 On the Track of Railroad Logging History: A Contextual History for Railroad Logging in California. USDA Forest Service, Southwestern Region, San Francisco, California. Manuscript available from California Historical Resources Information System, State Historic Preservation Office, Sacramento.

Tatrow, Lenore

1982 The Van Winkle Lumber Camps. In *Our Heritage*, edited by Leona LaVallee, Pat Rasmussen, and William Manning, pp. 69–71. Garden Peninsula Historical Society, Garden, Michigan.

Taylor, Frederick W.

1911 *Principles of Scientific Management*. Harper and Brothers, New York.

Terrell, Michelle M.

2005 Intensive Literature Search and Phase I/II Archaeological Investigations for the St. Croix River Crossing Project, Washington County, Minnesota. Two Pines Resource Group, Shafer, Minn. Submitted to Minnesota Department of Transportation, St. Paul.

Thompson, George S.

1895 *Up to Date, or, The Life of a Lumberman*. Times Printing, Peterborough, Ontario.

Thoreau, Henry David

1862 Walking. *Atlantic Monthly* 9: 657–674.

1981 [1854] *Walden; or, Life in the Woods*. Easton Press, Norwalk, Connecticut.

1988 [1864] *The Maine Woods*. Penguin Books, New York.

Tonsfeldt, Ward A.

2013 The U.S. Army Spruce Production Division at Vancouver Barracks, Washington, 1917–1919. East Slope Cultural Services, Inc. Prepared for Ft. Vancouver National Historic Site, National Park Service, Vancouver, Washington, Contract No. PP11PX842-51.

Tonsfeldt, Ward, and Paul G. Claeyssens

2004 Central Oregon: Adaptation and Compromise in an Arid Landscape—Euro-Americans. Oregon Historical Society, Oregon History Project. Electronic document, https://oregonhistoryproject.org/narratives/central-oregon-adaptation-and-compromise-in-an-arid-landscape/, accessed December 2, 2018.

Tonsfeldt, Ward, and Dennis Gray

2008 Determination of Eligibility for the Winslow Lumber Company Logging Railroad, Little Pend Oreille National Wildlife Refuge, Stevens County, Washington. East Slope

Cultural Services, Inc., Bend, Oregon. Submitted to U.S. Fish and Wildlife Service, Portland, Oregon, Contract No. 101817M338.

Tourigny, Eric D.
2016 Upper Canada Foodways: An Analysis of Faunal Remains Recovered from Urban and Rural Domestic Sites in Toronto (York), AD 1794–1900. PhD dissertation, Archaeology and Ancient History, University of Leicester, Leicester, UK.

Towner, Robin H., and Nicolas V. Kessler
2016 Slash and Trash: Dendroarchaeological and Ecological Inferences from a Twentieth-Century Logging Camp in Western New Mexico. *International Journal of Historical Archaeology* 20: 249–263.

Trice, Gwen
2018 Maxville. *Oregon Encyclopedia.* Oregon Historical Society and Portland State University. Electronic document, https://oregonencyclopedia.org/articles/maxville/#.W9T38hopDmq, accessed March 23, 2018.

Tsing, Anna L.
2015 *The Mushroom at The End of the World: On the Possibility of Life in Capitalist Ruins.* Princeton University Press, Princeton, New Jersey.

Tsing, Anna L., Heather A. Swanson, Elaine Gan, and Nils Bubandt
2017 *Arts of Living on a Damaged Planet: Ghosts and Monsters of the Anthropocene.* University of Minnesota Press, Minneapolis.

Tugwell, Rexford G.
1920 The Casual of the Woods. *Survey* 44: 472–474. Internet Archive, https://archive.org/details/surveycharityorg44survrich/page/n5, accessed August 15, 2019.

United States Bureau of Census
1989 *Historical Statistics of the United States: Colonial Times to 1970.* Kraus International, Millwood, New York.
1960 *Historical Statistics of the United States, Colonial Times to 1957.* U.S. Department of Commerce, Bureau of the Census, Washington, D.C.

USDA (United States Department of Agriculture) Forest Service
1911 *National Forest Manual: Regulations of the Secretary of Agriculture and Instructions to Forest Officers.* Government Printing Office, Washington, D.C. https://archive.org/details/nationalforestm11servgoog, accessed January 26, 2018.
1965 *Silvics of Forest Trees of the United States.* Agriculture Handbook No. 271. USDA Forest Service, Washington, D.C.
1967 Abstract of Land Title Records, Case No. 1862, Warren P. Miller. File Designation 5420, Land Acquisition Records. Hiawatha National Forest, Gladstone, Michigan.
2017 Success Story: Courageous Archaeology. Hiawatha National Forest, Gladstone, Michigan. Electronic document, https://www.fs.usda.gov/detail/hiawatha/learning/history-culture/?cid=stelprdb5106493, accessed June 22, 2018.
2012 The Role of Splash Dams in Northern Idaho—Marble Creek Splash Dam Passage Project. Idaho Panhandle National Forest, Coeur d'Alene. Electronic document, https://www.fs.usda.gov/Internet/FSE_DOCUMENTS/stelprd3798862.pdf, accessed June 21, 2017.

United States Department of Interior, National Park Service
2002 Falk Historic District, Humboldt County, California. National Register of Historic Places Registration Form 04000067, U.S. Department of Interior, Bureau of Land Management, National Park Service, Washington, D.C.

United States Library of Congress
2017 Historic American Buildings Survey/Historic American Engineering Record/Historic American Landscapes Survey (HABS/HAER/HALS). Prints and Photographs Online Catalog, Washington, D.C. https://www.loc.gov/pictures/collection/hh/about.html, accessed May 20, 2017.
University of Wisconsin–Milwaukee
2012 Archaeology and History of the WIS 57 Transportation Corridor. Electronic document, https://www.hmdb.org/marker.asp?marker=80215, accessed March 23, 2018.
Upham, Mary C.
1892 The Lumber Camp Report of the Wisconsin Women's Christian Temperance Union for Winter 1891–92. Wisconsin State Archives, http://digital.library.wisc.edu/1711.dl/WI.LCRoWCTU, accessed February 19, 2011.
Usher, John P.
2016 Untranslating the Anthropocene. *Diacritics* 44(3): 56–77.
Valentino, Alicia B., and Jamie C. Brandon
2005 Van Winkle's Mill Update: 2005 Excavations at the Blacksmith Shop. *African Diaspora Archaeology Newsletter* 8(4): article 11. http://www.diaspora.illinois.edu/news0905/news0905-3e.html.
Van Ravenswaay, Charles
1970 America's Age of Wood. *Proceedings of the American Antiquarian Society* 80(1): 49–66.
Vaughan, Trudy
1990 West Side Lumber Company Historical Archaeological Investigations and Evaluation Project, Stanislaus National Forest, Tuolumne County, California. Coyote and Fox Enterprises, Redding, Calif. Submitted to USDA Forest Service, Stanislaus National Forest, Sonora, California. Available from California Historical Resources Information System, State Historic Preservation Office, Sacramento.
Vestergaard, Christina S., and Felix Riede
2017 Modern Climate Change and Contemporary Environmental Archaeology? *Archaeological Review from Cambridge* 32(2): 10–24.
Vietze, Andrew
2018 *White Pine: American History and the Tree That Made a Nation.* Globe Pequot Press, Guilford, Connecticut.
Vogel, John N.
1980 Folk Technology: A History of the Round Lake Logging Dam. Raymond H. Merritt, River Falls, Wisconsin. Submitted to USDA Forest Service, Milwaukee, Wisconsin, Contract No. R9-02-80-6.
Von Schneidemesser, Luanne, Joan H. Hall, and Frederic G. Cassidy
2012 Bean Hole. *Dictionary of American Regional English.* Belknap Press of Harvard University Press. Cambridge, Massachusetts. https://dare.wisc.edu/words/quarterly-updates/quarterly-update-3/bean-hole.
Waisanen, Pamela J., and Norman B. Bliss
2002 Changes in Population and Agricultural Land in Conterminous United States Counties, 1790 to 1997. *Global Biogeochemical Cycles* 16(4). DOI: 10.1029/2001GB001843.
Walter, Robert C., and Dorothy J. Merritts
2008 Natural Streams and the Legacy of Water-Powered Mills. *Science* 319: 299–304.
Ward, Willis C.
1936 Reminiscences of Michigan's Logging Days. *Michigan History* 20: 301–312.

Weisgerber, Bernie
1999 *An Ax to Grind: A Practical Ax Manual.* USDA Forest Service, Technology and Development Program, Missoula, Montana.
Wells, Robert W.
1978 *Daylight in the Swamp!* Doubleday, New York.
Wettstaed, James R.
2003 Cutting It Back and Burning It Black: Archaeological Investigations of Charcoal Production in the Missouri Ozarks. *Journal of the Society for Industrial Archeology.* 29(2): 29–46.
Whelan, James Patrick, Jr., and Charles E. Pearson
1999 Archaeology of an Early Twentieth-Century Black Community: The Good Land Cypress Sawmill Company, Terrebonne Parish, Louisiana. Coastal Environments, Inc., Baton Rouge, La. Submitted to Louisiana Department of Transportation, Baton Rouge. Available from Louisiana Department of Culture, Recreation and Tourism, Division of Archaeology, Baton Rouge.
White, Lynn
1970 Introduction: The Reticences of the Middle Ages. In *Scientific Methods in Medieval Archaeology,* edited by Ranier Berger, pp. 3–14. University of California Press, Berkeley.
White, Paul J.
2017 *The Archaeology of American Mining.* University Press of Florida, Gainesville.
White, Richard
1992 *Land Use, Environment, and Social Change: The Shaping of Island County, Washington.* University of Washington Press, Seattle.
Whitney, Gordon G.
1994 *From Coastal Wilderness to Fruited Plain: A History of Environmental Change in Temperate North America, 1500 to the Present.* Cambridge University Press, Cambridge, UK.
Wilkie, Laurie A., and Kevin M. Bartoy
2000 Critical Archaeology Revisited. *Current Anthropology* 41(5): 747–777.
Williams, Gerald
2013 U.S. Army, Labor Unions, and World War I in the Pacific Northwest. Revised paper presented at the 106th Annual Meeting of the Pacific Coast Branch of the American Historical Association, Denver, Colorado.
2016 Spruce Production Division. Oregon Historical Society and Portland State University. Electronic document, https://oregonencyclopedia.org/articles/spruce_production_division/#.V8d4f5D3arU, accessed May, 11, 2018.
Williams, Michael
1982 Clearing the United States Forests: Pivotal Years 1810–1860. *Journal of Historical Geography* 27(2): 12–28.
1989 *Americans and Their Forests: A Historical Geography.* Cambridge University Press, Cambridge, UK.
Wilson, Jeremy S.
2005 Nineteenth-Century Lumber Surveys for Bangor, Maine: Implications for Pre-European Settlement Forest Characteristics in Northern and Eastern Maine. *Journal of Forestry* 103(5): 218–229.
Wisner, George B.
1995 *Hull-Oakes Lumber Company's Steam-Powered Sawmill: A Case Study in Industrial*

Archaeology. Anthropology Northwest No. 10. Department of Anthropology, Oregon State University, Corvallis.

Withrow, William H.

1889 *Our Own Country: Canada, Scenic and Descriptive: Being An Account of the Extent, Resources, Physical Aspect, Industries, Cities and Chief Towns of The Provinces*. W. Briggs, Toronto. Internet Archive, https://archive.org/details/cihm_16493, accessed November 17, 2017.

Wood, Casey A.

1905 Poisoning by Wood, or Methyl Alcohol. *New York Medical Journal and Philadelphia Medical Journal* 81(1): 5–11.

Woods, Charles D., and Edward R. Mansfield

1904 *Studies of the Food of Maine Lumbermen*. USDA, Office of Experiment Stations, Bulletin No. 149. Government Printing Office, Washington, D.C.

Woodward, John A.

1975 *Oxen, Axes, and China Teacups: Six Papers on the Pioneer Lumbering of Larch Mountain, Multnomah County, Oregon*. Mt. Hood Community College, Gresham, Oregon.

W.P.A. (Works Progress Administration)

1942 Michigan Log Marks. Michigan Agricultural Experiment Station, East Lansing.

Wurst, LouAnn

2016 MTU Archaeological Field School: Workers' Experience in the Northern Forests. Research design. Hiawatha National Forest. Ms. on file, Industrial Archaeology Program, Michigan Technological University, Houghton.

2017 Workers' Housing and Class Struggle in the Northern Forest. Paper Presented at the Society for Historical Archaeology, Fort Worth, Texas.

Wyatt, Barbara

1999 The Logging Era at Voyageurs National Park: Historic Contexts and Property Types. Institute for Environmental Studies, Department of Landscape Architecture, University of Wisconsin-Madison. Submitted to Midwest Support Office, National Park Service, Omaha, Nebraska.

Young, Amy L.

2004 The Beginning and Future of African-American Archaeology in Mississippi. *Historical Archaeology* 38(1): 66–78.

Zeier, Charles D.

1987 Historic Charcoal Production near Eureka, Nevada: An Archaeological Perspective. *Historical Archaeology* 21(1): 81–101.

Ziel, Deborah

2013 Which Way to the Jook Joint?: Historical Archaeology of a Polk County, Florida Turpentine Camp. MA thesis, Department of Anthropology, University of Central Florida, Orlando.

Index

John G. Franzen worked as an archaeologist with the USDA Forest Service in northern Michigan from 1980 to 2013. At the time of his retirement he served as the Heritage Resource Program Leader for the Hiawatha National Forest.

THE AMERICAN EXPERIENCE IN ARCHAEOLOGICAL PERSPECTIVE

Edited by Michael S. Nassaney

The Archaeology of Collective Action, by Dean J. Saitta (2007)
The Archaeology of Institutional Confinement, by Eleanor Conlin Casella (2007)
The Archaeology of Race and Racialization in Historic America, by Charles E. Orser Jr. (2007)
The Archaeology of North American Farmsteads, by Mark D. Groover (2008)
The Archaeology of Alcohol and Drinking, by Frederick H. Smith (2008)
The Archaeology of American Labor and Working-Class Life, by Paul A. Shackel (2009; first paperback edition, 2011)
The Archaeology of Clothing and Bodily Adornment in Colonial America, by Diana DiPaolo Loren (2010; first paperback edition, 2011)
The Archaeology of American Capitalism, by Christopher N. Matthews (2010; first paperback edition, 2012)
The Archaeology of Forts and Battlefields, by David R. Starbuck (2011; first paperback edition, 2012)
The Archaeology of Consumer Culture, by Paul R. Mullins (2011; first paperback edition, 2012)
The Archaeology of Antislavery Resistance, by Terrance M. Weik (2012; first paperback edition, 2013)
The Archaeology of Citizenship, by Stacey Lynn Camp (2013; first paperback edition, 2019)
The Archaeology of American Cities, by Nan A. Rothschild and Diana diZerega Wall (2014; first paperback edition, 2015)
The Archaeology of American Cemeteries and Gravemarkers, by Sherene Baugher and Richard F. Veit (2014; first paperback edition, 2015)
The Archaeology of Smoking and Tobacco, by Georgia L. Fox (2015; first paperback edition, 2016)
The Archaeology of Gender in Historic America, by Deborah L. Rotman (2015; first paperback edition, 2018)
The Archaeology of the North American Fur Trade, by Michael S. Nassaney (2015; first paperback edition, 2017)
The Archaeology of the Cold War, by Todd A. Hanson (2016; first paperback edition, 2019)
The Archaeology of American Mining, by Paul J. White (2017; first paperback edition, 2020)
The Archaeology of Utopian and Intentional Communities, by Stacy C. Kozakavich (2017)
The Archaeology of American Childhood and Adolescence, by Jane Eva Baxter (2019)
The Archaeology of Northern Slavery and Freedom, by James A. Delle (2019)
The Archaeology of Prostitution and Clandestine Pursuits, by Rebecca Yamin and Donna J. Seifert (2019)
The Archaeology of Southeastern Native American Landscapes of the Colonial Era, by Charles R. Cobb (2019)
The Archaeology of the Logging Industry, by John G. Franzen (2020)